DAVID BOULTON

Objection Overruled

MACGIBBON & KEE

FIRST PUBLISHED 1967 BY MACGIBBON & KEE LTD
COPYRIGHT © DAVID BOULTON 1967
PRINTED IN GREAT BRITAIN BY
THE GARDEN CITY PRESS LTD
LONDON AND LETCHWORTH

CONTENTS

ILLUSTRATIONS

Acknowledgements are due to the Peace Pledge Union for permission to
reproduce the photographs listed above, with the exception of the two of the
N-CF National Convention and Committee, which are reproduced with the
kind permission of Aylmer Rose, and that of Clifford Allen, by permission of
Lady Allen.

INTRODUCTION

'We are told that international Socialism is dead, that all our hopes and ideals are wrecked by the fire and pestilence of European war. It is not true. Out of the darkness and the depth we hail our working-class comrades of every land. Across the roar of guns we send sympathy and greeting to the German Socialists . . . They are no enemies of ours, but faithful friends.'—*Manifesto of the National Administrative Council of the Independent Labour Party*, 13 August 1914.

'Look! Christ in khaki, out in France, thrusting his bayonet into the body of a German workman. See! The Son of God with a machine gun, ambushing a column of German infantry, catching them unawares in a lane and mowing them down in their helplessness. Hark! The Man of Sorrows in a cavalry charge, cutting, hacking, thrusting, crushing, cheering. No! No! That picture is an impossible one, *and we all know it*. That settles the matter for me. I cannot uphold the war.'—DR ALFRED SALTER, *Labour Leader*: 24 September 1914.

'All forms of militarism belong to the past. It comes down to us as a relic of the days when kings and nobles ruled as well as reigned, and when the workers were voteless, voiceless serfs. Militarism and Democracy cannot be blended. The workers of the world have nothing to fight each other about . . . They have no country. Patriotism is for them a term of no meaning.'—KEIR HARDIE: Foreword to ILP pamphlet, *A Case Against Conscription*, April 1913.

'I wish the Government had not put in this clause about conscientious objectors. I don't agree with it myself. Application refused.'—CHAIRMAN, Wirral Tribunal, April 1916.

'From the Guardroom,
Drill Hall, Cardiff.
Dear Comrade,
Hope to smuggle you just a word. Escorted to roller rink, Cardiff, on

9

Monday evening. No supper, no beds. Slept on floor. Tuesday morning, no breakfast. Taken before Major and asked to sign rations form. Refused. Asked to see doctor and sign papers. Refused. Threat by Major of death penalty, or anything less court martial should determine. All orders disobeyed. Still no food. After 24 hours fast asked again to sign rations form or send out for food. Refused to do either. Victory at last! . . . Salmon for breakfast!!! Wild excitement. Flag flying cheerfully. Concerts on guardroom floor a speciality. Soldiers learning the *Red Flag*. Whatever lies before us we can face it. On behalf of the Guardroom Branch, No-Conscription Fellowship, Fraternally yours . . .'
—Letter to No-Conscription Fellowship national office, May 1916.

'I shall only consider the best means of making the path of that class a very hard one.'—DAVID LLOYD GEORGE, Secretary of State for War, 26 July 1916.

'My dear ones,
This [a cigarette packet] is the best stuff I can find to write what may be my last letter. Everything has been taken off me and I should not have this pencil but for chance.

I was bullied horribly when I was tried and sentenced to 28 days detention in solitary confinement—to be given raw rations and to cook for myself. This does not sound bad, but I have found the confinement was in a pit which started at the surface at three feet by two, and tapered off to two feet six inches by fifteen inches. Water was struck, but they continued until it was 10 feet deep. The bottom is full of water, and I have to stand on two strips of wood all day long just above the water line. There is no room to walk about, and sitting is impossible. The sun beats down and through the long day there are only the walls of clay to look at. Already I am half mad ∴ . . I feel sentenced to death, knowing that within a few days I shall be in France and shot. The fact that men are being sent to France at all is proof positive to me that the military authorities have captured the machine, and are able to do as they like with us. What have our friends been doing?'—Letter to his mother and sister from JAMES BRIGHTMORE, July 1917.

'This meeting desires to express its gratitude to the editor of the *Western Morning News* for the strong protest that is being made through the medium of his paper against the ridiculously lenient treatment that is accorded at Princetown Prison to so-called conscientious objectors; and guarantees its heartiest support in any steps that may be taken with a view to the introduction and enforcement of stricter methods of dealing with COs generally.'—Resolution passed at a meeting of Dartmoor district clergy, April 1917.

Ernest England, a young Quaker, was called up in 1917 despite having previously been rejected as medically unfit. Taken ill on his first night in Wormwood Scrubs, where he was sent to serve a sentence of two years hard labour, he was refused a chamber pot by the duty warder. After considerable suffering, England made use of the floor. The warder then proceeded to bury his face in his excrement. England was seriously ill for several weeks. Eventually he was transferred to Dartmoor where, despite his weakened condition, he was put on snow-shovelling work on a daily after-work diet of one slice of bread and margarine and a cup of tea. Three months after the Armistice he was continuing to work at Dartmoor, now in a desperately emaciated condition. He died on 6 March 1919.

★   ★   ★

This is the story of 16,000 men who refused to fight for Britain in the First World War. some refused because they held passionately the Socialist faith expressed in the ILP manifesto of August 1914, some because they held equally passionately the uncompromising Christian faith expressed by Dr Salter. Many held both faiths, believing the one to be the expression of the other. Some objected only to combatant service. Some objected to any kind of military service. Some even refused to undertake civil 'work of national importance', believing that this meant work useful for the prosecution of the war. Some, particularly among those who objected only to playing a combatant role, had their objection recognised. Many did not. Some had a quiet war. Others were brutally and systematically tortured. At least a hundred went through experiences no less harrowing than those of James Brightmore. Thirty-four heard themselves sentenced to death. Seventy-three died, like Ernest England, either in prison or as a direct result of their incarceration. Another thirty-one were driven mad.

This is their story. Wherever possible I have let them tell it in their own words, for their letters and diaries were more graphic than I could hope to be.

Unlike Kitchener's New Model Army, the army of conscientious objectors was not a sudden product of the climactic events of July and August 1914. Anti-militarism, pacifism and opposition to conscription had deep roots in the socialist and Nonconformist traditions. Roughly three-quarters of World War One COs were socialist objectors who refused to fight for capitalism. Only a minority were out-and-out pacifists whose objection was to violence itself, irrespective of the justice of its cause. The majority were standard-bearers of an international socialism which they held to be valid despite the war. As socialists they had tried to prevent the war. They had failed. So they agitated for a negotiated peace and against conscription. Again they failed. Conscription came, but they refused to be conscripted and took the consequences.

That is their story in outline. We look first at the political tradition which produced their objection; then at the events which led to conscription; then at their resistance.

OBJECTION OVERRULED

Chapter I

International Socialism and War

THE PRE-WAR socialists were not pacifists. The notion of absolute rejection of all war and violence, whatever the occasion and in however righteous a cause, remained through the nineteenth century a religious rather than a political tenet. Christian pacifism, like Buddhist non-violence, was essentially personal rather than political. From time to time it irritated the civil authorities, but never threatened their power. Its politics were the politics of the City of God, and not of this world.

The anti-war sentiment of the rising working-class movement was a product of enlightened self-interest rather than religious revelation. The ruling classes made wars, the working classes fought them. Thus the first affirmation of international socialism, Karl Marx's *Communist Manifesto*, emphasised in 1847 the unity, across national frontiers, of the 'workers of the world', substituting for the notion of nation against nation that of international working class against international ruling class and bourgeoisie. National war was irrelevant, class war superseded it. In his inaugural address at the founding of the International Working Men's Association in London on 28 September 1864, Marx urged the 'First International' to concern itself with foreign as well as domestic affairs, and to oppose all policies of conquest. Working-class standards, he urged, could be raised only in the absence of war, by class struggle at home rather than by 'expeditions to shoot working men abroad' at the arbitrary behest of capitalist Governments.

In response to overtures from the pacifist-supported League of Peace and Freedom in 1867 the International defined its attitude in more specific terms. War, it declared, 'weighs chiefly on the working class, in that it not only deprives it of the means of existence, but also constrains it to shed the workers' blood; armed peace paralyses the powers of production, demands of labour only useless tasks, and

15

intimidates production by putting it under the blow of the threats of war; peace, first condition of well-being, needs in its turn to be consolidated by a new order of things that will no longer know in society two classes, the one of which is exploited by the other.' With calculated deviousness, the International made its affiliation to the League conditional on the latter's acceptance of revolutionary socialism, which the broadly based League predictably declined. Marx congratulated himself on keeping the International free from the corrupting influences of 'impotent bourgeois ideologues', but his self-congratulation was premature. Fearful of being isolated from the working-class movement, the anarchist wing of the League, led by Michael Bakunin, disaffiliated and joined the International, thus beginning a bitter struggle between collectivists and anarchists which was soon to kill the First International stone dead.

The anarchists scored their first triumph at the Brussels Congress of 1868. Under Marx's leadership, the International had made all the right anti-war noises but had never formulated a strategy of working-class action to prevent war. Bakunin and his followers did have such a strategy: the international general strike. Despite Marx's scornful opposition, the Congress passed a resolution inviting 'all the sections of the Association, in their respective countries, and also all working-class societies, and all workers' groups of whatever kind, to take the most vigorous action to prevent a war between the peoples, which today could not be considered anything else than a civil war, seeing that, since it would be waged between the producers, it would only be a struggle between brothers and citizens; the Congress urges the workers to cease work should war break out in their respective countries'.

This resolution put the anarchists one up in the turbulent internal politics of the International but it meant little or nothing to the national labour movements, which were for the most part only dimly aware of the International's ideological disputes and much more concerned with their own domestic struggle. 1868 was, after all, the year of the Reform Act in Britain which for the first time gave the vote to working men in the boroughs. The first Socialist deputies had been elected to the North German Parliament. In such circumstances talk of a general strike against war was bound to fall on stony ground.

Indeed, when Bismarck engineered war with Napoleon III in

1870, the German and French labour movements made not the slightest effort to organise strike action. The five socialist deputies in the North German Parliament voted for the war credits (though the two representatives of the rival Social-Democratic Party, Wilhelm Liebknecht and August Bebel, abstained). Leaders of the French working-class movement supported their domestic enemy, the Emperor, against the external enemy, Germany. The International at first declared for Germany, and only condemned the war when Bismarck made plain his intention of annexing Alsace-Lorraine. Mass meetings against annexation were organised in France, Germany, England, Austria, Italy and the United States. But there was no strike action.

The war, the rise and fall of the Paris Commune and the continuing feud between anarchists and Marxists killed off the International Working Men's Association in the early 'seventies, though the patient lingered on in a comatose state until 1876. 'Let us give our fellow-workers a little time to strengthen their national affairs and they will surely soon be in a position to remove the barriers between themselves and working-men of other parts of the world', ran its final statement. Thirteen years later, in 1899, the Second International was founded in Paris, and a new chapter opened in the story of socialist action against war.

Deteriorating international relations determined that the war question occupied a much more vital and central place in the deliberations of the new International than it had in the old. The old had tried to grapple with the problem of localised national rivalries. By the time the Second International was formed the European powers were already building the complex alliance systems which, backed by an arms race of unprecedented ferocity, indicated only too clearly that a new war would be a world war. Germany, Austria and Italy had established the Triple Alliance in 1882, and in 1894 came the first moves which were to lead to the Triple Entente between Britain, France and Russia.

At its 1891 Congress in Brussels the International discussed the rising dangers of a European war and called on labour organisations to 'protest vigorously'. In 1893, at Zürich, Congress urged the workers to fight for a reversal of the arms race and for general disarmament, while Labour and Socialist deputies were urged to vote against war credits. In 1896, in London, Congress demanded the abolition of standing armies, the establishment of machinery for international arbitration and popular referenda before declaration of war, and the arming of the people as a substitute for regular armies.

All three Congresses debated and rejected proposals for a general strike against war, advanced from the anarchist and syndicalist wings of the International and supported by some of the reformists. The proposals were opposed by the German Socialists, who dominated the International, and by the orthodox Marxists. George Plekhanov of the Russian Social Democrats put their case in a nutshell at the Zürich Congress in 1893: 'A general strike is impossible within present-day society, for the proletariat does not possess the means to carry it out. On the other hand, were we in a position to carry out a general strike, the proletariat would already be in control of economic power and a general strike would be a sheer absurdity.'

In 1900 Congress in Paris reaffirmed its rejection of the general strike against war and passed a resolution, framed by Rosa Luxemburg, analysing the capitalist origins of war and urging that an anti-militarist programme be built on the socialist education of youth, Parliamentary Socialist opposition to war credits and massive anti-war demonstrations by the working classes during international crises. A rash of domestic strikes across Europe in 1902 and 1903 meant that the general strike theory was raised more forcefully at the 1903 Congress in Amsterdam; but again it was voted down, and anti-militarism this time took the form of pledges of solidarity and fraternity by the Russian and Japanese delegations, whose Governments were at war.

The Second International's position on war and the means of preventing it reached its fullest expression at the 1907 Congress at Stuttgart. The European situation had become highly explosive. The two triple alliances were locked in a spiralling arms race and the Algeciras Conference of 1906 had failed to reach any firm settlement between France and Germany on the Moroccan question. War seemed imminent.

Three contrasting viewpoints were debated at Stuttgart. The Germans argued, in brief, that Socialists should support a just war— for example, a war to liberate the Russian working class from Tsarist oppression. The French parliamentarian Socialists under Jean Jaurès argued that international socialism should invariably throw its weight against the aggressor party—the party firing the first shot. The French syndicalists, in contrast, wanted Congress to 'call on all comrades to answer any declaration of war, no matter from what side it is made, with the military strike and with insurrection'.

It is clear that such divergent viewpoints could not, in any satisfactory or significant sense, be accommodated within the terms of a single clear-cut resolution. But that is precisely what Congress attempted. A drafting sub-committee, in which Emil Vandervelde of Belgium, Jaurès of France, Rosa Luxemburg of Germany and (according to Marxist-Leninist legend) Vladimir Ilyitch Lenin of Russia had a hand, prepared a statement purporting to express the collective view of the International. Its introduction, in deference to the Germans, was a model of pragmatism, its middle paragraph condemned aggression in phrases borrowed direct from Jaurès' own oratory, and it came to a climax in a fine Marxist peroration which gave the revolutionaries all they wanted, and more:

> If a war threatens to break out, it is the duty of the working class and of its Parliamentary representatives in the country involved, supported by the consolidating activity of the International Socialist Bureau, to exert every effort to prevent the outbreak of war by means they consider most effective, which naturally vary according to the accentuation of the class struggle and of the general political situation.
>
> Should war break out none the less, it is their duty to intervene in favour of its speedy termination and to do all in their power to utilise the economic and political crisis caused by the war to rouse the peoples and thereby to hasten the abolition of capitalist class rule.

The resolution was carried with acclamation. This annoyed the French syndicalists, who openly questioned the good faith of the German Social Democrats in formally supporting it. The Germans and other reformists could claim that their real enthusiasm was for the non-committal preamble. To them, the final paragraph was a piece of revolutionary rhetoric, acceptable in the interests of socialist unity, but of little practical relevance.

The International reaffirmed the Stuttgart resolution in 1910, removing not a word but adding a call to Socialist parliamentary representatives to press for general disarmament and the abolition of secret diplomacy. Keir Hardie of Britain and Edouard Vaillant of France again advocated the general strike against war, 'especially in the industries which provide war supplies', but again the International would have none of it. The resolution was rejected by 119 votes to 58, but its promoters succeeded in pressing a recommendation that the subject be referred for further study to the International Socialist Bureau, which in turn referred it to the national sections. It was still being studied, as it had been in socialist circles for half a century, when war broke out in August 1914.

★   ★   ★

The Serbian assassin's shot that killed Austria's Archduke Ferdinand on 21 July put the world on an irreversible escalator to multiple war. 23 July: Austria delivers her war ultimatum to Serbia. 25 July: Austria declares war. 28 July: Austrian troops cross the Serbian frontier, and Russia declares immediate mobilisation in Serbia's defence. 1 August: Germany, bound by alliance with Austria, declares war on Russia. 3 August: France, bound by alliance with Russia, declares war on Germany. 4 August: Britain, bound by the entente with France, joins in. The Great War, the First World War, has begun.

On 25 July, the day of Austria's declaration against Serbia, the Austrian Socialist deputies (82 in a Parliament of 516) published an anti-war manifesto. The German Socialists held mass meetings against the war in Berlin. On 28 July the French and German sections of the International issued protests against the war, and the British Socialist Party—a small Marxist body outside the Labour Party—protested against the Austrian note and congratulated continental Socialists on their efforts to preserve peace. On 29 July the French General Confederation of Labour issued a manifesto against war.

An emergency meeting of the International Socialist Bureau was convened in Brussels on 29 July. It proved a contentious session. Representatives of each of the national sections pledged their Socialist movements, predictably enough, to march, demonstrate and lobby against war; but most were careful to indicate that, if the worst came to the worst, the call of national defence would not go unanswered. It was seven years since the International had accepted a paper commitment to answer war with social revolution, four since that commitment had been reaffirmed. But there was no talk of revolution at Brussels. The Bureau agreed to bring forward the International's next Congress from the end of August to 9 August (it was, in fact, cancelled altogether when war broke out) and published the following statement:

> In assembly of 29 July the International Socialist Bureau has heard declarations from representatives of all nations threatened by a world war, describing the political situation in their respective countries.
>
> With unanimous vote the Bureau considers it an obligation for the workers of all concerned nations not only to continue but even to strengthen their demonstrations against war in favour of peace and of a settlement of the Austro-Serbian conflict by arbitration.
>
> The German and French workers will bring to bear on their Governments the most vigorous pressure in order that Germany may secure in Austria a moderating action, and in order that France may obtain from Russia an undertaking that she will not engage in the conflict. On their side the workers of Great Britain and Italy shall sustain these efforts with all the power at their command.
>
> The Congress urgently convoked in Paris will be the vigorous expression of the peaceful will of the workers of the whole world.

The meeting was followed by a rally in the centre of Brussels. Nearly 6,000 Belgian Socialists listened as Vandervelde, Keir Hardie, Jaurès and Hugo Haase of Germany declared 'war on war' —the slogan inscribed on scores of banners. Speaker after speaker proclaimed the peaceful intentions of the workers of the world— but there was no call for revolution, general strike or insurrection. No one recalled or invoked the Stuttgart resolution. Instead there was an implicit assumption that working-class strength, merely by manifesting itself in mass demonstrations, would prevent war. This optimistic belief had become widespread in the immediate pre-war years. The old faith that working-class *action* would prevent war had gradually been displaced, as Socialist parties throughout Europe increased their Parliamentary strength and their share of political power, by an assumption that the mere *existence* of powerful Labour movements would suffice. The International had boasted in 1912 that 'the fear of the ruling class that a world war might be followed by a proletarian revolution has proved to be an essential guarantee of peace'. H. N. Brailsford, writing in 1914 only a few months prior to the war, had put a similar view:

Henceforward, every European Government which meditates war has to reckon with the certainty that it will be opposed, certainly morally, and perhaps physically, by a powerful and organised party at home. It may even have to pay at the polls for its adventure . . . But far more serious than the risk of disaster at the polls, is the danger that Socialist opposition within an army may sap the spirit which alone wins victories . . . In a German army in time of war one man in three would be a Socialist voter. Some of these at the best of times are only superficially under the influence of Socialism, and others would be carried away by the excitement of the national crisis. But it is hard to believe that if in a war of aggression this army were to be hurled against France today, German Socialists would show any ardour in shooting down French workmen . . . In no country with a conscript army in which Socialism deserves to be respected will a Government dare today to make an unnecessary war . . . The simple fact that the working class hated the idea of war, and the knowledge that it would fight half-heartedly, would in themselves suffice to keep the peace, at all events between nearly equal antagonists. In France and Germany, if not as yet in Austria and Italy, Socialism has already attained this degree of strength. It is even now perhaps the most formidable factor in the preservation of the peace of Europe, and its pressure is none the less real because Governments will never willingly admit that it has influenced them.[1]

This, rather than any widely held belief in a preventive general strike, was the great illusion of the Second International.

During that last fatal week of July 1914, the Socialist parties throughout Europe followed the International Socialist Bureau in delivering forthright condemnations of the impending war. The German Social Democrats on 25 July condemned Austria's ultimatum to Serbia as pressing demands 'more brutal than have ever been put to an independent State in the world's history', and demanded German neutrality. 'The ruling classes, who in time of peace gag you, despise you and exploit you, would misuse you as cannon-fodder. Everywhere must sound in the ears of those in power: "We will have no war! Down with war! Long live the international brotherhood of the people!" '

The French Socialist Party organised street meetings against the war, several of which were brutally broken up by the police. On

30 July the party published a manifesto blaming the crisis not only on 'the aggressive proceedings of Austro-Hungarian diplomacy' but also on 'the fundamental anarchy of our social system, the competition of capitalist groups, the colonial lusts, the intrigue and brutalities of imperialism'. The French Government was urged to exercise a moderating influence on its Russian ally, and the German Social-Democrats were commended for pressing their own Government to apply a moderating influence on Austria. 'Both (French and German Socialist movements) at their posts of action have the same work and the same end.'

Jean Jaurès, writing the following day in the party organ *l'Humanité*, urged that the danger now lay in 'the sudden impulse born of fear, acute uncertainty and prolonged anxiety'. Crowds could give way to mad panic and so could Governments. He clearly held the view that the German alliance bore most blame for the imminence of war, and he mentioned Russia's partial mobilisation as a stabilising rather than a provocative factor, along with the French Government's action in 'taking all necessary precautions compatible with the maintenance of peace'. Jaurès, despite his pacifist reputation, was already groping for the justifications that would soon be made for the war by virtually the entire French Socialist movement. The article was his last. Later the same day he was shot dead by French pro-war patriots while sitting in a Paris street café.

Manifestoes, marches and demonstrations failed to have the slightest impact on Governments which were by now caught up in a vortex from which there was no escape. Europe was engulfed in war fever. Within a matter of hours the Socialist parties found themselves discussing war not as an imminent danger to be averted by slogans and exhortations, but as an iron fact. International brotherhood suddenly counted for little compared with the primitive tribal instincts of national preservation. The streets that had been filled, on the first weekend of August, with men and women shouting 'Down with war!' were filled again on the second weekend with men and women lusting for the blood of the national enemy. Perhaps they were the same men and women.

The Socialist parties were faced with the grim choice of continuing their opposition to the war, thereby being branded as traitors, or tearing up their peace manifestoes and effecting a smart about-turn with as good a face as possible. As we have seen, there was never any real doubt as to which way they would go. All could claim to have adhered faithfully to the first part of their Stuttgart commitment, 'to exert every effort to prevent the outbreak of war by means they consider most effective'. All had to acknowledge these efforts as failures. Their remaining commitment, on paper, was to a revolutionary tactic that had been relegated to history by the advances made along the gradualist Parliamentary road to Socialism.

On 2 August the Kaiser announced that, in the interests of 'national unity' in face of the Russian threat, opposition parties in Germany were 'pardoned'. Trade union leaders met and agreed for the duration of the war a 'social peace' with the employers—no strikes, no militant industrial action, a truce in the class war. On 3 August the party's Parliamentary representatives met to determine their line of action. Karl Liebknecht later wrote of that meeting that 'the issues involved gave rise to diametrically opposite views within our Parliamentary Party, and these opposing views found expression with a violence hitherto unknown in our deliberations'. The majority, including the trade union deputies, argued that having failed to prevent war, the Socialists had no alternative but to support Germany against reactionary Russia and to vote for the war credits to be proposed by the Government the following day. A minority, including the party leader Hugo Haase, Rosa Luxemburg and Karl Liebknecht, urged that the party oppose the war credits and withhold support for the war. The party meeting divided seventy-eight to fourteen. The minority accepted party discipline and on 4 August there was unanimous support from the Socialists for the war credits. Haase told the Reichstag:

The present calamity is the result of a universal regime of Imperialist policy. The Social-Democratic Party, which has fought that policy at every point, refuses to accept any responsibility for it. But the Socialist opposition has failed. Before us stands the iron fact of war. We are threatened with the horrors of a hostile invasion. We have not to decide today for or against war, but the question of supplies for the defence of our country. For our people and for the future of their liberty much, if not all, is at stake with the victory of Russian despotism, which has stained itself with the blood of the best of its own people. This danger must be warded off for the sake of our civilisation and the independence of our country. We prove now what we have always said, that in the hour of danger we shall not desert our Fatherland.

The Reichstag had been kept in ignorance of the German army's violation of Belgium's neutrality, which was not announced until after the vote for war credits had been taken. When the facts were known the German Government was denounced by Liebknecht, who henceforward led a small minority of Socialists in opposition to the war. But it is unlikely that knowledge of the invasion of Belgium would have altered the majority decision to support the war credits. To German Socialists the war against Russia was a war of self-defence. Since France was allied to Russia they would reluctantly have to fight France too. Since Britain was allied to France they would fight their war of national defence against the whole Triple Entente. And if an effective strike against France involved the violation of Belgium neutrality, that was infinitely regrettable but grimly necessary—an inevitable by-product of the war they had done their best to prevent breaking out in the first place. This remained the majority view of German Social-Democrats throughout the war.

In France the war was supported as a defensive struggle for national survival, even by the militant anti-patriots on the syndicalist wing of the Labour movement. The Socialist party, 'after due deliberation and mature thought', authorised Jules Guèsde, Marcel Sembat and Edouard Vaillant to enter the Government as the German invasion began. The Parliamentary group of the party defended its participation in a capitalist Government thus: 'It is the future of the nation, the life of France, which are in the balance today. The party, therefore, has not hesitated . . . Spontaneously, without awaiting any other demonstration of the popular will, the Head of State has appealed to our party. Our party has replied, "We are ready!"'

Belgian Socialists followed a similar path. Vandervelde, leader of the party and chairman of the International Socialist Bureau, joined the Belgian War Cabinet. Only in Russia was there a sustained attempt by Socialist leaders to use the war as a lever for revolution. The Social Democrats in the Duma abstained in the vote for war credits, the Mensheviks declared themselves 'the irreconcilable enemies of the Russian Government', and the Bolsheviks declared it to be their intention 'to utilise the difficult position in which the Government is now placed in the interests of Russian liberty'. Ironically, however, and contrary to Marxist-Leninst mythology, the Russian revolution was delayed, not precipitated, by the outbreak of war. Revolution was imminent in July 1914. In Petrograd, 120,000 workers were on strike and the streets were barricaded against the Tsar's troops. But despite the Socialist leaders' appeals to the strikers to use the war for pressing their revolutionary demands, the strike collapsed as war fever hit the city and temporarily substituted old-fashioned patriotism for revolutionary ardour.

★ ★ ★

Although Keir Hardie was an enthusiast for the preventive general strike, the British Labour movement was the least revolutionary of all the major continental Socialist parties. Indeed, the Labour Party was the sore thumb of the International, being socialist neither in ideology nor temper. Its admission to the International had only been procured by a bending of the rules, which made a confession of socialist ideology the entry-ticket and defined the ideology in terms of willingness to engage in the class war. The Labour Party, as conscious heir-apparent to the Liberal tradition, was not prepared to make any such electorally damaging commitment, and was only admitted to the International when Kautsky and Lenin argued that, by setting itself in opposition to the two bourgeois parties, British Labour was willy-nilly engaging in class warfare whether it liked it or not.

The Labour Party was a coalition of socialist societies and non-socialist, Liberal-oriented trade unions. In the period of working-class consolidation which followed the enfranchisement of workmen in the boroughs in 1868 and the foundation of the Trades Union Congress the same year, Keir Hardie had founded his Scottish Labour Party in 1888, which became the Independent Labour Party in 1893, pledged to work for the return of Labour candidates independent of Liberal support or entanglements. The ILP, like the Marxist Social Democratic Federation and the Fabian Society, formed a decade earlier, was militantly socialist in its demands for the public ownership of industry. It was, indeed, less a political party than a moral crusade for a common-ownership kingdom of

God on earth. In the hard climate of the 1890s the crusade failed to prosper. Twenty-eight ILP candidates fought the 1895 general election, and twenty-eight failed—including Keir Hardie, who lost the seat he had earlier won at West Ham.

Hardie and his colleagues in the leadership of the ILP became convinced that their cause would have political impact only if they succeeded in harnessing the small socialist organisations to the growing mass strength of the trade unions. At the same time, the TUC was becoming disenchanted with the Liberal Party's patent lack of interest in fielding any more than a token number of working-class Liberal–Labour candidates, and consequently more disposed than it had been in the past to organise a party of its own. Moreover, while few of the major unions actually professed socialism, most had been conditioned by Fabian influences to be sympathetic to, or at least tolerant of, socialist rhetoric. The time was clearly ripe for alliance, and the 1899 Congress endorsed this view by 546 votes to 434. A joint committee of the TUC, ILP, SDF, and Fabian Society prepared an agenda for a conference in London on 27 February 1900, at which 129 delegates representing 568,127 members formally inaugurated the Labour Representation Committee, with J. Ramsay MacDonald as secretary.

The Committee, which changed its name to the Labour Party in 1906, was a very different body from most working-class parties on the continent. From the outset it turned down the proposal, put by the SDF delegates, that the party should be 'based upon the recognition of the class war' and should include as its principal objective 'the socialisation of the means of production, distribution and exchange'. It declared that 'as a Committee we have no hostility to other political parties', and proceeded to make what local pacts it could, openly or secretly, with the Liberal Party. The SDF withdrew from the coalition in disgust.

The embryonic Labour Party was organised not to inaugurate a new dawn of socialism but merely to look after working-class interests. The socialist minority, consisting of the ILP (which maintained its identity as a party within the party) and the Fabian Society were content to believe that a pragmatic organisation which sought to defend working-class interests would soon find itself forced to turn to socialist solutions. As MacDonald wrote in 1909 in his book *Socialism and Government*, the object of Socialists 'ought not to be to form a Socialist party, but a party that will journey towards Socialism'. The 'clamour for a Socialist party', he argued—and he meant a pure Socialist party divorced from non-Socialist trade unionism—'is a remnant of the revolutionary period, or a copying of methods proper to countries where parliamentary government is but a name. What is wanted here is a party which accepts the Socialist point of view and approaches the industrial problems of society with Socialist assumptions in mind . . . Socialism is to come through a Socialistic political party, and not through a Socialist one.'

Numerically the ILP-socialist wing of the Labour Party was small and could easily be swamped by the bloc votes of the trade union wing, which for a long time remained obstinately wedded to a Lib–Lab theory and strategy. But the minority had two advantages which gave it an influence beyond its numerical strength. First, the ILP was the only constituent body of the Labour Party organised with local branches on a basis of individual membership, so that the only way of joining the Labour Party as an individual member, and participating in constituency politics, was through the ILP. Second, the trade union wing, concentrating its attention on domestic labour problems, was content to let the ILP make the running in developing the party's foreign policy attitudes.

Whatever glosses Lenin, Kautsky and the International—not to mention militant rank-and-file ILPers—were prepared to put on the Labour Party's position, the Parliamentary Labour Party functioned in the pre-war period as little more than a docile Left wing of the Liberals. Twenty-four out of thirty-one Labour MPs elected in 1906 owed their seats to Lib–Lab pacts, and a further twenty-one Lib–Lab MPs were elected entirely under Liberal auspices. When Liberal fortunes slumped in the January 1910 election, Labour strength increased only by virtue of the Lib–Lab bloc's decision to take the Labour Whip, and of the resultant strength of forty-six, only six were opposed by a Liberal. The December 1910 election which produced the war Parliament returned forty-eight Labour MPs, again all but six of whom owed their seats to open or secret Lib–Lab pacts.

This, then, was the Labour Party whose representatives on the International had committed it to a policy of social revolution in the event of war! Such a commitment, had it ever been submitted to a

Labour Party Conference, would certainly have been rejected over-whelmingly—if it had ever been allowed by the Conference Arrangements Committee to reach the agenda.

The ILP's specialisation in foreign affairs, however, did produce powerful Labour challenges to the Liberal Government's foreign policy. Labour spokesmen made the running in persistently challenging the Foreign Secretary, Sir Edward Grey, to come clean about Britain's secret alliance with France, the terms of which were hidden not only from Parliament but also from most of the Cabinet. In a foreign affairs debate in December 1911, Ramsay MacDonald, Leader of the Labour Party, charged that under Grey's policies Britain was 'heading straight for war'. Philip Snowden, another ILPer and the party's shrewdest foreign affairs spokesman, urged that 'the only possible way of averting a great European war is to bring about a better understanding with Germany. That is impossible so long as Sir Edward Grey is at the head of the Foreign Office.' The Labour Party Conference of 1912 endorsed the ILP position in a resolution, moved by Keir Hardie, which protested against 'the anti-German policy pursued in the name of the British Government by Sir Edward Grey', which was declared to be 'the cause of increasing armaments, international ill-will, and the betrayal of oppressed nationalities'.

Disarmament and the arms race were further preoccupations of the ILP. During the two years immediately preceding the war it gave wide publicity to the growth of the private armaments industry, tracing its commercial connections at home and overseas and its network of overlapping directorships. The principal fruits of these investigations were Walton Newbold's *The War Trust Exposed*, G. H. Perris' *The War Traders*, and H. N. Brailsford's *The War of Steel and Gold*. These, with Norman Angell's historic work challenging the Great Illusion that modern war could be commercially profitable, had considerable influence. Some of the more spectacular researches into the machinations of the arms manufacturers were gathered together in a pamphlet by Philip Snowden, *Dreadnoughts and Dividends*, in which Snowden took for his text the statement of a former Treasury official, Lord Welby: 'We are in the hands of an organisation of crooks. They are politicians, generals, manufacturers of armaments, and journalists. All of them are anxious for unlimited expenditure, and go on inventing scares to terrify the public and to terrify Ministers of the Crown.'

One result of these exposures of the military-industrial complex of the day was that many Labour activists were partially inoculated against calls to war and official justifications for war. There is no doubt that the ILP's crusade against the arms drive materially contributed to the strength of the anti-war party when war did break out.

It was the small Marxist-oriented British Socialist Party, a new incarnation of the SDF, which first alerted the British Labour movement to the dangers inherent in the Austrian declaration of war on Serbia. On 28 July the party's Executive published a statement branding Austria the aggressor and congratulating continental Socialists on the action already being organised to keep the peace. For the Labour Party, Keir Hardie hurried to Brussels for the emergency meeting of the International Socialist Bureau. On 30 July the Parliamentary Labour Party, in a unanimous statement, expressed the hope that 'on no account will this country be dragged into the European conflict in which, as the Prime Minister has stated, we have no direct or indirect interest', and called on Labour organisations to 'watch events vigilantly so as to oppose, if need be, in the most effective way, any action which may involve us in war'. The sentiments were irreproachable, but there is no indication that the Parliamentary Party had the vaguest notion of what would constitute 'most effective' action.

The Liberal and Socialist daily press opposed Britain's entry into the war, and the *Daily Herald* and *Daily Citizen* called for immediate mass demonstrations. The ILP's Manchester-based weekly *Labour Leader* carried on 30 July a front-page editorial by Fenner Brockway headed: 'The War Must Be Stopped—and We Must Stop It.' The European Labour movement, it said, 'is the guardian of peace. It is fifty million strong, and if it will only act unitedly it will make war impossible.'

No nation which is divided against itself [the article continued] can expect to wage war successfully with another nation. On the Continent, where the armies are Conscriptionist, this is particularly true, and it is an open secret that thousands of the soldiers serving the German, French and Austrian Governments by compulsion are

Socialists and view their task with loathing and abhorrence. Victories cannot be won with armies of that nature . . . No Socialist conscience would approve the war which is looming before us if it came upon us. We have the power to stop it. We must do so. How? By demonstrating in such numbers and with such fervour all over Europe that the various Governments will be made to realise and fear the strength of the anti-war party . . . What is the National Executive of the Labour Party doing to bring the British movement into line with the movement on the Continent? Let it get to work at once.

There were some who thought the *Labour Leader*'s agitation unduly, even hysterically alarmist, among them W. C. Anderson, the ILP's chairman. 'Despite all signs to the contrary', he wrote, 'there will, I believe, be no war; nothing, at any rate, in the nature of serious or extended warfare'.

On 1 August the British Section of the International issued a 'Manifesto to the British People', signed by Keir Hardie, chairman, and Arthur Henderson, secretary. More impassioned than the Parliamentary Party's statement, and containing much more of Hardie than of Henderson, the manifesto was none the less devoid of any specific recommendations for Socialist action. The workers were urged to prevent war; they were offered no advice on how to set about it. But the ringing phraseology paid emotional dividends, and the manifesto's impact was heightened by the simultaneous news of the martyrdom of Jaurès.

The long-threatened European war [ran the manifesto] is now upon us. For more than one hundred years no such danger has confronted civilisation. It is for you to take full account of the desperate situation and to act promptly and vigorously in the interests of peace. You have never been consulted about the war.

Whatever may be the rights and wrongs of the sudden, crushing attack made by the militarist Empire of Austria upon Serbia, it is certain that the workers of all countries likely to be drawn into the conflict must strain every nerve to prevent their Governments from committing them to the war.

Everywhere Socialists and the organised forces of Labour are taking this course. Everywhere vehement protests are made against the greed and intrigues of militarists and armament-mongers.

We call upon you to do the same here in Britain upon an even more impressive scale. Hold vast demonstrations against war in every industrial centre. Compel those of the governing class and their press who are eager to commit you to co-operate with Russian despotism to keep silence and respect the decision of the overwhelming majority of the people, who will have neither part nor lot in such infamy. The success of Russia at the present day would be a curse to the world.

There is no time to lose. Already, by secret agreements and understandings, of which the democracies of the civilised world know only by rumour, steps are being taken which may fling us all into the fray. Workers, stand together therefore for peace! Combine and conquer the militarist enemy and the self-seeking Imperialists today, once and for all.

Men and women of Britain, you have now an unexampled opportunity of rendering a magnificent service to humanity, and to the world!

Proclaim that for you the days of plunder and butchery have gone by; send messages of peace and fraternity to your fellows who have less liberty than you! Down with class rule! Down with the rule of brute force! Down with war! Up with the peaceful rule of the people!

Arrangements were already being made for the 'vast demonstrations' demanded by Hardie and Henderson. A Trafalgar Square meeting was arranged for Sunday 2 August under the auspices of the British Section of the International. On 31 July the ILP head office sent out fifty telegrams to the largest of its branches in England and Wales, calling on them to organise anti-war meetings in their own town on the same Sunday, and the party's Scottish Divisional Council Executive sent similar instructions to Scottish branches. Meetings were held in almost every city and major town in Britain, many of them jointly with trades councils, BSP branches, Free Church councils and peace societies. James Maxton, then chairman of the ILP's Scottish Divisional Council, claimed that there were more than a hundred meetings in Scottish towns and industrial centres alone.[2] The *Labour Leader* on 6 August carried reports from thirty-two meetings in England and Wales.

Nearly 15,000 attended the Trafalgar Square demonstration, which the *Manchester Guardian* described as 'far larger than the most important of the suffrage rallies'. Banners and red flags floated above the mass of heads, and speeches were punctuated with verses from *The Red Flag* and the *Internationale*. 'The Church will not lead in this holy war against crime and bloodshed', said Keir Hardie from the plinth of Nelson's Column, 'so the task is left to the workers.' Robert Williams, Transport Workers' secretary, assured the Parliamentary Labour Party of full support in the country for anti-war activity in the House of Commons. J. Stokes, chairman of London Trades Council, called for a neutral Britain. George Lansbury promised that the spirit of Jaurès would live on until the goal of freedom was reached. Will Thorne declared that only the workers could wage war and only the workers could prevent it. The ever-romantic and ever-optimistic Cunningham Graham enthused: 'I have never before seen the people of England so firmly set against intervention as they are today. The spirit is passing from man to man, woman to woman, town to town, county to county.'

By acclamation the crowd endorsed a resolution drawn up by Hardie and Henderson and moved in the Square by Henderson. The text had already been circulated by the ILP and was used as the basis for resolutions passed at many of the provincial meetings:

> This demonstration, representing the organised workers and citizens of London, views with serious alarm the prospects of a European war, into which every European Power will be dragged owing to secret alliances and understandings which in their origin were never sanctioned by the nations, nor are even now communicated to them; we stand by the efforts of the International Working-Class Movement to unite the workers of the nations concerned in their efforts to prevent their Governments from entering upon war, as expressed in the resolution passed by the International Socialist Bureau; we protest against any step being taken by the Government of this country to support Russia, either directly or in consequence of any understanding with France, as being not only offensive to the political traditions of the country but disastrous to Europe, and declare that as we have no interest, direct or indirect, in the threatened quarrels which may result from the action of Austria in Serbia, the Government of Great Britain should rigidly decline to engage in war, but should confine itself to efforts to bring about peace as speedily as possible.

Probably many more than 100,000 Socialists and Labour supporters demonstrated that Sunday afternoon. But the following day

2—OO

Sir Edward Grey told the Commons that Britain's 'understanding' with France committed her to declare war on Germany. It was a matter of 'national honour'. Only a proclamation of unconditional neutrality could keep Britain out of the war, and our commitment to France, he claimed made such a proclamation impossible.

Bonar Law, for the Conservatives, promised that the Government could rely on the 'unhesitating support' of His Majesty's Loyal Opposition for 'whatever steps they think it necessary to take for the honour and security of the country'. John Redmond, for the Irish Nationalists, promised the sympathetic support of the Irish people. But the consensus was shattered by the Labour Leader, Ramsay MacDonald. Grey, he told the House bluntly, was wrong. 'I think the Government which he represents and for which he speaks is wrong. I think the verdict of history will be that they are wrong . . . Whatever may happen, whatever may be said about us, whatever attacks may be made upon us, we will take the action that we will take of saying that this country ought to have remained neutral, because in the deepest parts of our hearts we believe that that was right and that that alone was consistent with the honour of the country and the traditions of the party that now are in office.'

Thus MacDonald established his reputation as a pacifist opponent of the war. It was not deserved. On this, as on so much else, he was equivocal. Only three days later he told a meeting in his own constituency, Leicester: 'Whatever our view may be on the origin of the war, we must go through with it'; and a month later he wrote to the Mayor of Leicester, in a letter intended for public reading at a recruiting meeting: 'Victory must be ours . . . We cannot go back, nor can we turn to the right or to the left. We must go straight through . . . I want the serious men of the Trade Union, the Brotherhood, and similar movements to face their duty. To such men it is enough to say "England has need of you"; to say it in the right way. They will gather to her aid.'

Perhaps, as many have speculated, MacDonald's outspoken attack on Grey and the call for British neutrality were part of an ill-timed bid for the leadership of an anti-war group which at first looked to be potentially more broadly based than the Labour Party. Lloyd George and others in the Cabinet, as well as a large section of Liberal backbenchers, were known to be critical of Grey and rumoured to be on the point of breaking with the Government. Perhaps MacDonald mistook the fervour of the Sunday rallies for a national mood, insensitive to the fact that wider public opinion, swayed by the press, was already swinging in favour of war. Whatever his intention, the speech made him overnight the most hated man in the land. Throughout the war years he was a public pariah and a Parliamentary leper. Horatio Bottomley, editor of *John Bull*, published a photostat copy of MacDonald's birth certificate as documentary proof that he was indeed a bastard. The torrent of abuse drove MacDonald back into the arms of the ILP activists, men who in the immediate pre-war period had learnt to despise his equivocation and distrust his devotion to gradualism but were now willing to forgive him everything on the premise that a man so abused by their enemies could not be as bad as they had feared—a premise for which certain later Labour leaders were to have cause to be grateful.

Britain made her declaration of war on 4 August, the day after MacDonald's public attack on Grey. On 5 August the Labour Party hierarchy met in a series of three meetings to determine its line. The Joint Board of the National Executive, the Parliamentary Party and the TUC met first, followed by the full National Executive and finally by the Parliamentary Party.

The Joint Board meeting had been convened a few days earlier with the object of forming a National Labour Peace Emergency Committee to co-ordinate action against British intervention. But the events of 4 August had nullified that intention, and instead of a Peace Emergency Committee the Joint Board appointed a War Emergency Workers' National Committee. The principal object of the Committee was to keep a vigilant eye on labour interests in the event of the war leading to economic collapse, rising prices and mass unemployment. But it was evidently intended that the Committee should also agitate for peace. Arthur Henderson told the *Daily Citizen* that it would 'take all necessary steps for the promotion of an early and permanent peace'.

The meeting was dominated by the trade union bloc, and only the miners spoke out for a more radical role for the Committee. The South Wales miners had just provoked the wrath of the patriotic press by turning down flat an Admiralty request that they forgo two of their three days August holiday to ensure that the navy was well supplied with coal during the crisis. A day or two earlier the Miners' Federation had declared its willingness to organise a miners' strike against the war if unions in other countries involved would undertake to do the same, but nothing had come of the idea.

The National Executive meeting produced a formal declaration on the causes of the war and on the party's immediate responsibilities. The conflict had been provoked by 'Foreign Ministers pursuing diplomatic policies for the purpose of maintaining a balance of power'. Britain's own policy of 'understandings with France and Russia only' had been bound to strengthen Russia in Europe and Asia, and thus endanger good relations with Germany. Grey, 'as proved by the facts which he gave to the House of Commons, committed, without the knowledge of our people, the honour of this country to supporting France in the event of any war in which she was seriously involved, and gave definite assurances of support before the House of Commons had any chance of considering the matter. The Labour movement reiterates the fact that it has opposed the policy which produced the war.'

On future action, the Executive stood by that part of the International's Stuttgart resolution calling for 'intervention to bring the war promptly to an end' by acknowledging its 'duty to secure peace at the earliest possible moment on such conditions as will provide the best opportunities for the re-establishment of amicable feelings between the workers of Europe'. This, rather feebly, was to be done by 'watching for the earliest opportunity for taking effective action in the interests of peace'. In the meantime, while watching, all Socialist and Labour organisations were urged to 'concentrate their energies' on putting into effect the programme of the new War Emergency Workers' National Committee for 'mitigating the destitution which will inevitably overtake our working people while the state of the war lasts'.

The National Executive statement followed faithfully the line of MacDonald's speech two days earlier, but the decisive meeting was that of the Parliamentary Party, dominated as it was by the trade union group and bound by invisible chains to the Liberal Party. At the outset, several members ventured to criticise MacDonald's attack on Grey, uneasy, no doubt, at the depth of hostility it had aroused in the press. Their primary concern was for Labour's respectability. Already an avowedly pro-war group within the party had begun to take shape. At the opposite end of the spectrum, the seven ILP members were against the war, though J. R. Clynes and James Parker were soon to support it. Between the two groups were the bewildered and the uncommitted, plus a dominant body of opinion which, while it made no profession of enthusiasm for the war, was not prepared seriously to consider obstructive action or direct resistance.

MacDonald, as party leader, tried to persuade the meeting to endorse the National Executive's statement. He met with sullen opposition from the trade union bloc. They resented the 'ILP tone' of the statement, and argued that meek endorsement of it would leave the Parliamentary Party open to the charge of being subject to the dictates of an outside body. When MacDonald failed to win majority support for his proposal that the statement be read in the Commons that evening as the official view of a united Labour Party, he rightly interpreted this as a vote of no confidence in his leadership, and thereupon resigned. The cause of his resignation was officially published as 'disagreement with some of his colleagues on certain aspects of the European crisis'. Into his place stepped the secretary of the British Section of the Internationl, Arthur Henderson—Free Churchman, total abstainer, a liberal and humane trade unionist and middle-of-the-roader who argued that the iron fact of war made the apportionment of blame irrelevant in the face of vital considerations of national unity and safety.

News of Germany's violation of Belgian neutrality came too late to influence the party's decision, but when it arrived it was a godsend to those who felt obliged to provide a moral rationalisation of their political somersault. Many who at first remained sympathetic to MacDonald and the anti-war minority went over to the majority position when the full story was told, with no detail spared, of 'the rape of little Belgium's wives, mothers and daughters'. Politicians and newspaper proprietors who had campaigned with demoniacal energy against Home Rule for Ireland became overnight dedicated evangelists of the rights of small nations. The war had already become endowed with what all modern wars must have if they are to enjoy enthusiastic public support, namely a moral sanction, an air of Holy Crusade.

This sanctification did not take place until after a Labour majority had resolved, despite the party's earlier pronouncements, to support the war; but it eased and speeded the process by which the Labour Party moved from an embarrassed, resigned acceptance of British intervention to total endorsement of the Government's position, leading it to throw itself with complete, if not exactly gay abandon, into the struggle for a military victory.

The first step was the calling of a truce in the class war. The Management Committee of the General Federation of Trades Unions, meeting within a week of the outbreak, pronounced Britain blameless and pledged its support to the Government. Many of the separate union executives circulated their branches and advised against industrial action. Strikes in progress at the outbreak of war were, for the most part, abruptly terminated, without consultation with the rank-and file, and often on the employers' terms. G. D. H. Cole, who supported Labour participation in the war-effort and was unsympathetic[3] towards the ILP and the anti-war minority, deplored this unconditional surrender on the industrial front. 'At any moment', he wrote in the *Daily Herald* on 20 August, 'the Government and the capitalists whom they represent will be able to abrogate all the laws on the plea of "national emergency". If Labour continues throughout the war to allow gains won by industrial warfare in times of international peace to be filched from it, it is laying up a store of misery and hardship in the future. All the old battles will have to be fought over again, and instead of being further on the road to emancipation, Labour will have lost ground.'

But Cole's view did not prevail. On 24 August, in conference together, the Parliamentary Committee of the TUC, the Management Committee of the GFTU and the National Executive of the Labour Party resolved 'that an immediate effort be made to terminate all existing trade disputes, whether strikes or lock-outs, and whenever new points of difficulty arise during the war period a serious attempt should be made by all concerned to reach an amicable settlement before resorting to a strike or lock-out'. The number of industrial disputes fell from ninety-nine in the month prior to the war to fifteen in the month following Britain's entry, and from 836 in the first seven months of the year to 137 in the last five. The truce lasted through the autumn and winter, and was only partially lifted in the spring of 1915 when it became clear that many employers, mainly in the smaller trades and in commerce, had taken advantage of the war to reduce wages or staff, and to push up profits.

'Economically as well as politically, Labour was taken altogether by surprise' by the war crisis. 'If the deliberations of the International had given the workers but doubtful guidance for their political action in the crisis, there had been still less an attempt to forecast the industrial situation that would be created or the action that Labour ought to pursue . . . Industrially, as well as politically, the mind of the workers was in a state of bewilderment when war broke out. The supremely important decision as to Labour's industrial policy was therefore taken on the impulse of the moment, without much forethought or foresight.'[4]

Labour's declaration of industrial peace served only to divide still further the political arm of the movement, since it produced a body of critics which supported the leadership in its attitude to the war but was bitterly critical of its surrender of independence on the industrial front. These criticisms were soon given a sharper cutting edge when the party faced the question of its attitude to army recruiting.

Under the terms of the war-time party truce the Liberal Government and Conservative Opposition decided jointly at the end of August to initiate a national recruiting campaign. The Labour Party was invited to join, and a majority of the Parliamentary Party favoured participation. This view was conveyed to the National Executive of the party on 29 August, and after heated debate and with ILP dissent, the National Executive resolved

> That in view of the serious situation created by the European war the executive committee of the Labour Party agrees with the policy of the Parliamentary party in joining in the campaign to strengthen the British Army, and agrees to place the central office organisation at the disposal of the campaign, and further recommends the affiliated bodies to give all possible local support.

Arthur Henderson joined Asquith and Bonar Law as joint presidents of the Parliamentary Recruiting Committee, and was appointed a Privy Councillor. Three more Labour MPs, James Parker, Frank Goldstone and J. Pointer, also joined the committee. The decision unreservedly to co-operate with the capitalist parties was attacked not only by the ILP, which held that recruiting was no job for Socialists, but by a considerable body of pro-war opinion which urged that Labour should have maintained its independence and run its own recruiting drive, as the British Socialist Party decided to do.

The decision to make the party's organisational machinery available for recruiting was justified on the ground that voluntary recruitment was preferable to the likely alternative, conscription. Henderson, speaking to a meeting at Walsall on 10 September, argued that the Labour Party, as a determined opponent of conscription and all forms of compulsory military service, had a special obligation to 'make the voluntary system commensurate with the present national needs'. The TUC used the same argument in its 'Manifesto to the Trade Unionists of the Country', published at the beginning of September. This declared that the TUC leadership was 'gratified at the manner in which the Labour Party in the House of Commons has responded to the appeal made to all political parties to give their co-operation in securing the enlistment of men to defend the interests of their country', and went on to assert that 'in the event of the voluntary system of military service failing the country in this its time of need, the demand for a national system of compulsory military service will not only be made with redoubled vigour, but may prove to be so persistent and strong as to become irresistible. The prospect of having to face conscription, with its permanent and heavy burden upon the financial resources of the country, and its equally burdensome effect upon nearly the whole of its industries, should in itself stimulate the manhood of the nation to come forward in its defence, and thereby demonstrate to the world that a free people can rise to the supreme heights of a great sacrifice without the whip of conscription.' We shall shortly see what came of that argument.

In their efforts, however, to assure a suspicious press and public of Labour's unquestionable and unquestioning patriotism, the party leaders were handicapped by the loud and militant pacifism of the ILP minority. On 15 October, therefore, the party published a new manifesto 'to clear away, once and for all, misconceptions which have been circulated as to the attitude of the British Labour movement'. It was signed by a majority of Labour MPs, the Parliamentary Committee of the TUC, the Management Committee of the GFTU and other union leaders. The manifesto represented Labour's most fully considered apologia for its support of the war.

Abandoned altogether was the claim that the war arose from

international rivalries, secret diplomacy or the foreign policy of Sir
Edward Grey. Instead, all blame was placed squarely on German
resistance to Britain's proposals for mediation between Austria and
Serbia, on German preparations to invade France, on German
violation of Belgian neutrality, and on Germany's 'peremptory,
domineering ultimatum to Russia'. All this proved that 'the German
military caste were determined on war if the rest of Europe could not
be cowed into submission by other means . . . Nothing, not even
national honour and good faith, was to stand between Germany and
the realisation of its ambitions to become the dominant military
power of Europe, with the Kaiser the dictator over all.'

The Labour Party, the manifesto explained, recognised that
Great Britain, having exhausted the resources of peaceful diplomacy, was bound in honour, as well as by treaty, to resist Germany's
aggression by force of arms. 'The party realised that if England had
not kept her pledges to Belgium, and had stood aside, the victory of
the German army would have been probable, and the victory of
Germany would mean the death of democracy in Europe.

> Working-class aspirations for greater political and economic power
> would be checked, thwarted, and crushed, as they have been in the
> German Empire. Democratic ideas cannot thrive in a State where
> militarism is dominant; and the military State with a subservient and
> powerless working class is the avowed political ideal of the German
> ruling caste. The Labour Party, therefore, as representing the most
> democratic elements in the British nation, has given its support in
> Parliament to the measures necessary to enable this country to carry
> on the struggle effectively . . .
>
> The policy of the British Labour movement has been dictated by a
> fervent desire to save Great Britain and Europe from the evils that
> would follow the triumph of military despotism. Until the power
> which has pillaged and outraged Belgium and the Belgians, and
> plunged nearly the whole of Europe into the awful misery, suffering,
> and horror of war, is beaten, there can be no peace. While the conflict
> lasts England must be sustained both without and within; combatants
> and non-combatants must be supported to the utmost. The Labour
> movement has done and is doing its part in this paramount national
> duty, confident that the brutal doctrine and methods of German
> militarism will fail. When the time comes to discuss the terms of

peace the Labour movement will stand, as it has always stood, for an international agreement among all civilised nations that disputes and misunderstandings in the future shall be settled not by machine guns but by arbitration.

Thus in all essentials the Labour leadership, with the majority of the party behind it, gave total endorsement to the Liberal Government's view of the war. This harmony between what the orthodoxies of the International would have labelled class enemies found organisational expression as Labour representatives at local and national level were brought into innumerable offices and committees, so becoming directly involved in the business of the State at war. In March 1915 Henderson accepted the chairmanship of the National Labour Advisory Council, a Government creation intended as a vehicle for enforcing the industrial truce which had shown signs of breaking down and was now being given legal sanction under the 1915 Treasury Agreement. Thus, in Cole's words, Henderson 'was attempting to double the parts of leader of the Labour Party in the House of Commons and *de facto* industrial adviser to a Government in which Labour was not represented'.

That situation lasted only two months. In May 1915 Henderson joined Asquith's new three-party Coalition as President of the Board of Education. Two other Labour MPs, William Brace and G. H. Roberts, were given junior posts. As with its counterparts in France and Belgium, a party which a few short years before had endorsed a commitment to make war the occasion for the overthrow of capitalist class rule was now represented in a capitalist War Government. Little wonder that Keir Hardie died, on 26 September, worn out and deeply disillusioned. 'The working-class movement, trade union and Socialist alike, is contemptuously passed over', he had written despairingly in the *Labour Leader* on 6 August 1914. 'Ten million Socialist and Labour voters in Europe, without a trace or vestige of power to prevent war! . . . Our demonstrations and speeches and resolutions are all alike futile. We have no means of hitting the warmongers. We simply do not count.'

REFERENCES

1 H. N. Brailsford, *The War of Steel and Gold*, 1914
2 *Labour Leader*, 6 August 1914
3 Cole had some sharp things to say about the anti-war Socialists in *Labour in War-Time*, published in 1915. But from 1916 to the end of the war he campaigned vigorously on behalf of conscientious objectors and for a negotiated peace
4 G. D. H. Cole, *Labour in War-Time*, 1915

Chapter II

Across the Roar of Guns

THE ILP dissociated itself from what it regarded as a shameful apostasy on the part of the Labour movement. It denounced both the war and Labour's support for it in equally forthright terms. The breach quickly became bitter and apparently unbridgeable. Repeated attempts were made by the Right wing to proscribe the ILP. Among those who urged this course was a young trade union organiser named Ernest Bevin. It was to Henderson's credit that, despite his later acquiescence in the persecution of the most active war resisters, he fought to keep the heretical ILP within the fold, and so preserve the coalition nature of Labour's political organisation.

The ILP made its declaration of independence on 13 August when it published in the *Labour Leader* a defiant counterblast to Labour's capitulation, all the weightier for being drafted by W. C. Anderson who was doubling the role of a member of the ILP's National Administrative Council with the chairmanship of the Labour Party's National Executive Committee.

> Each country in turn, largely through the influence of its Jingo press [said the manifesto] has been stampeded by fear and panic. Each country has tried to outstrip other countries in the vastness and costliness of its war machinery. Powerful armaments' interests have played their sinister part, for it is they who reap rich harvest out of havoc and death. When all this has been done, any spark will start a conflagration like the present . . .
>
> We are told that international Socialism is dead, that all our hopes and ideals are wrecked by the fire and pestilence of European war. It is not true.
>
> Out of the darkness and the depth we hail our working-class comrades of every land. Across the roar of guns, we send sympathy

44

and greeting to the German Socialists. They have laboured unceas-
ingly to promote good relations with Britain, as we with Germany.
They are no enemies of ours, but faithful friends.

In forcing this appalling crime upon the nations, it is the rulers,
the diplomats, the militarists who have sealed their doom. In terms
of blood and bitterness the greater democracy will be born. With
steadfast faith we greet the future: our cause is holy and imperishable,
and the labour of our hands has not been in vain.

Long live Freedom and Fraternity! Long live International
Socialism!

Some 400,000 copies of the manifesto were distributed within a
fortnight. From being a relatively obscure provincial weekly unknown outside the Socialist movement, the *Labour Leader* began to
achieve national notoriety for its outspoken opposition to the war.
It had few competitors. The Scottish *Forward* was more tentative
in its tone, and the *Daily Citizen*, ailing and due to cease publication
a few months later, followed Labour's official line, calling on its
readers to 'stand together in defence of the motherland'. George
Lansbury's *Daily Herald*, which dropped to weekly publication
during the war, backed the ILP line, but it lacked the panache of its
more sectarian Manchester rival.

Through the pages of the *Labour Leader* the ILP attacked the
popular justification of the war as a crusade for the relief of 'Little
Belgium', and argued that Britain would have been better placed
to work for the rights of small nations by remaining neutral.
'Belgium certainly has a grievance against Germany', said the
Labour Leader on 6 August, 'but, as we have before suggested, in a
war of this kind her neutrality was almost certain to be outraged by
one side or the other. Her one hope lies in the pressure of outside
nations when the war is over and treaties are being signed; Great
Britain could have rendered her an immeasurably greater service by
standing aside until the Powers of Europe had broken themselves
against each other, and by then insisting on the maintenance of her
independence. Great Britain could have played the noble part of
peacemaker. She could have waited until the time was opportune
and then have offered her services as mediator. Our Government
has denied Britain that part. She had disgraced her in the eyes of all

the generations of the future.' The doctrine of 'positive neutralism'
enunciated on the Left in the 1950s was nothing new.

The ILP ridiculed Labour's defensive assertion that German
militarism was the chief enemy of democracy and socialism. Hardie
and MacDonald, both writing in the *Labour Leader* on 27 August,
argued that Russian autocracy, with which Britain was allied, was a
worse threat to Europe than German militarism. 'When the war is
over', wrote Hardie, 'it will be Russia that will carry off the laurels,
and, probably, a good instalment of German militarism will have
become part of our own institutions.' 'Russia in arms with us to
free Europe from an autocracy, whether political or military, is a
grim joke!' wrote MacDonald. Both men overestimated the strength
of German Socialism, which Hardie pictured as being on the verge
of 'bringing the military class to subjection' until thwarted by war;
both underestimated the potential of the Russian revolutionary
movement.

The *Labour Leader* found gifted exponents of the case against the
war, and made a regular feature of their essays. Charles Trevelyan,
the Liberal MP who had resigned his Government post as Parliamentary Secretary of the Board of Education on the outbreak of
war, wrote that 'the rulers, the diplomats, the militarists, have failed
because their fundamental faith is distrust of human nature'. The
only hope now lay with the growing political strength of the working
classes. Bertrand Russell asked: 'What would Christ do if he were
now on earth among the Christian nations? He would denounce the
scribes and pharisees—the lawyers and bishops—who hound on
those who look to them for guidance. He would go to the opposing
armies and say "resist not evil", "love your enemies—lay down your
arms and have faith in a power that is greater than artillery". And
the armies would cease their combat for a moment, to crucify him
between the lines, lest the devil's work should cease.' H. N. Brailsford wrote: 'He who conceives that by war the world can be freed
from militarism, little peoples permanently secured from aggression, and the sway of public law established, deludes himself and
errs. One may by force prove that one coalition is temporarily
stronger than another. One can prove nothing else.' And Herbert
Morrison, the circulation manager of the *Daily Citizen*, wrote: 'The
International is dead: long live the International! The British
Labour movement is dead: long live the British Labour move-

ment! . . . I think the people have gone wrong. I think the people's movement has gone wrong. I think the institutions which the people's movement has created have gone wrong . . . These are trying times for those of us who are capable of resisting the militarist chloroform.'

As part of its effort to disperse the chloroform cloud, the *Labour Leader* returned with a vengeance to its recurrent theme of the evils of private arms manufacture. In its issue of 20 August it revealed that four directors of the Nobel Dynamite Trust, one of the 'Big Five' partners in what was known as the Armaments Ring, were Germans. Three German banks were major shareholders. Other blocs of shares were held by four senior officers in the British Army, one French officer, five German officers and two brothers-in-law of the Prime Minister—Harold Tennant, Under-Secretary at the War Office, and Lord Glenconner, an officer of the National Service League. The Trust, reported the *Labour Leader*, sparing its readers no detail, not only had extensive interests in, and interlocking relationships with, several British arms firms, including Vickers, but also had major interests in four German arms factories and lesser interests in many more, including the already notorious firm of Frederick Krupp. Vickers in turn owned Henry Whitehead and Co., whose shareholders' list carried the names of Tennant, six backbench MPs, the Speaker of the House of Commons, twenty-five Peers, two Bishops and a Dean. Whitehead's had supplied the Austrian fleet with the torpedoes being used against British ships, and the British firms of Yarrow and Thorneycroft had supplied the Austrian fleet with most of its engines and boilers. As Philip Snowden commented acidly of the arms combines, 'These are the people whose internationalism is unquestioned. The Armaments Ring has been busy equipping the various nations who are at war, and guns made in the same factory and ships built in the same yard will be used against each other in this conflict.'

The ILP opposed the industrial truce and fought Labour participation in the Parliamentary Recruiting Committee's campaign. On the latter question it issued a statement to branches justifying its stand. The real purpose of the recruiting campaign, it suggested, was justification of the war; any appeal for recruits should come from the party's own platforms, not from platforms shared with Labour's enemies; no such appeal could be justified, anyway, until army pay was raised, pending which, recruiting amounted to 'touting for sweated labour'; above all, Labour should be determined 'not to get inextricably mixed up and confused with our opponents'. The ILP's National Administrative Council evidently thought little of Henderson's argument that participation in an all-party drive for voluntary recruitment was the only alternative to conscription. 'Much as we detest universal military service,' said the NAC, 'that plan would be less discreditable than the general hunting and harrying of young men now taking place.' The advocates of conscription were soon to make good use of this argument.

The *Labour Leader* denounced the Labour Party's support of the recruiting campaign as 'a grave betrayal of the principles of the Party and an outrage upon its traditions and hopes', language which brought a rebuke from W. C. Anderson. His plea for tolerance was attacked in the paper's correspondence columns on 17 September by a young man named Clifford Allen, who found tolerance of war 'nothing less than revolting'. 'In political affairs', Allen asserted, 'you have got to be dogmatic and hold actions and policies to be right or wrong . . . We Socialists are far too broadminded . . . We need to spread light and sanity amongst the unenlightened . . . This means to some extent flying in the face of the Labour Party. Never mind, our ultimate loyalty to it in social and industrial matters will be all the stronger—it will be like the meeting of husband and wife after a temporary but typical estrangement.'

Despite its little domestic rows, the ILP maintained an astonishing degree of unity in propagating its bitterly unpopular anti-war line. The *Labour Leader* could report on 10 September, more than five weeks after the outbreak of war and nearly a month after the ILP's declaration of dissent from the Labour Party view, that not a single resolution supporting the war had been received from branches, though it conceded that there had been 'a few quite insignificant resignations'. The seven-man Parliamentary Party was less solid, Clynes and Parker moving over to the official Labour position. But the ILP as a whole was less divided than most other constituent parts of the Labour movement. There was a small but vocal anti-war party among the trade unions, particularly among some of the larger trades councils. The Fabian Society had on the one side its critics of the war, like Bernard Shaw, and on the other

its pro-war patriots like H. G. Wells, who dismissed the ILP as
'the shabbiest scum of Socialism'[1]. Even the rigidly Marxist British
Socialist Party was divided, H. M. Hyndman, the leader, enthusiastically supporting the war and advocating conscription,
while a large part of the rank-and-file took the ILP view. Hyndman
was eventually disowned at the BSP annual conferences of 1915 and
1916, and he left the party to form a jingoistic National Socialist
Party. The BSP henceforward acted in alliance, despite frequent
sectarian bickerings, with the ILP.

The ILP, of course, shared the common illusion in the autumn
of 1914 that the war would be short, sharp and over by Christmas.
In taking a line that was bound to provoke an immense amount of
national resentment it certainly did not foresee the appalling extent
of the war, a four-year marathon of atrocity that was to change
history. The ILP clung to the hope that, after a few convulsive
months of madness, the world would return to normal and International Socialism would resume its march. It conceived its task as
a holding operation for sanity. At no time did its leaders contemplate
any attempt to use the war to provoke a revolutionary situation, and
its Parliamentary group, under MacDonald, was concerned to keep
the party's activities on the safe side of the line separating constitutional opposition from direct resistance and rebellion. They
resisted militant rank-and-file pressure to vote against the war
credits, deciding that 'no useful purpose would be served by carrying opposition to the war to that length; and a protest in any case
would have been ineffective, and we felt that so long as the war
continued it would havē been both foolish and inhuman to deprive
our armies of the necessary equipment to carry it on with adequate
supplies'[2].

The Labour Left had no monopoly of dissent on the war issue.
The Liberal Left also was critical of the decision to take Britain into
the war, and a small part of it went almost as far as the Parliamentary
ILP in its criticism of the Liberal Government and its declared war
aims. Two Cabinet members resigned at the outbreak of war: the
veteran Gladstonian Lord Morley, and the Liberal trade unionist
John Burns. A small knot of Liberal backbenchers declared against
the war, including four Quaker Members—Arnold S. Rowntree,
T. E. Harvey, J. Allen Baker and J. W. Wilson—and four men
associated with the new Union for Democratic Control—Joseph

King, Arthur Ponsonby, Richard Lambert and Charles Trevelyan. For the first few weeks of the war this group was able to produce evidence of fairly strong support for their views from many of the local Liberal Associations, and it was largely from among this section of the Liberal rank and file, the young radicals and the veteran believers in the old slogan of 'Peace, Retrenchment and Reform', that a young Liberal solicitor named Scott Duckers formed an abortive 'Stop-the-War Committee' in the autumn of 1914. But the bulk of Liberal opinion, after initial hesitations, swung behind the Government, accepting official assurances that the war was being waged in defence of Liberal principles.

Mention has been made of the Union of Democratic Control. This was in effect a coalition of ILP and Liberal critics of the war, and it quickly came to play a crucial part both in agitating for an early negotiated settlement and in campaigning against con-scription. The UDC was the brain-child of Charles Trevelyan, who had followed Lord Morley and John Burns by resigning his own post as a junior minister at the outbreak of war. Trevelyan came from a distinguished Liberal-Whig family: his great uncle was Lord Macaulay, and his father was Sir George Otto Trevelyan. Co-founder of the UDC with him was another product of the Whig tradition, Arthur Ponsonby, who had been private secretary to the anti-Imperalist Liberal Prime Minister, Sir Henry Campbell-Bannerman. The secretary and treasurer was E. D. Morel, who, with Roger Casement, had won public honour before the war by exposing the Congo rubber atrocities. Morel resigned from the Liberal Party at the outbreak of war and threw himself into the task of building the UDC. In July 1916 he published a pamphlet, *Truth and the War*, which argued that Britain was no less re-sponsible than Germany for the events which had led to war. More than 30,000 copies were sold, but when Morel sent a copy to the French writer Romain Rolland in Switzerland, he was arrested and charged under the Defence of the Realm Act (DORA) with unlawfully transmitting printed matter to a neutral country. For this crime he suffered six months in jail. Snowden later suggested in his *Autobiography* that prison life broke Morel's health and contributed to his early death in 1924, after he had served briefly as a Labour MP during MacDonald's first administration.

Trevelyan, Ponsonby and Morel formed the UDC shortly after the outbreak of war, and in November 1914 issued its first manifesto. Ramsay MacDonald had joined their executive committee, and so had Norman Angell, author of *The Great Illusion*. The manifesto declared the Union's intention of mounting public pressure for 'democratic control of foreign policy', as opposed to the secret diplomacy of the immediate pre-war years. The first step towards this end was an early negotiated settlement of the war on the basis of four cardinal points: first, the principle of self-determination; second, the ratification of treaties by Parliament; third, the abandonment of the balance-of-power principle and its replacement by the idea of a 'concert of nations' which would set up an international council and machinery for guaranteeing peace; and fourth, drastic measures of multilateral disarmament, coupled with the nationalisation of the arms industry. This bold but by no means extremist programme met with almost universal abuse. The UDC was accused of being pro-German, and the *Daily Express* made the inevitable allegation that it was financed by German gold. Despite the slanders and the organised breaking up of its public meetings, the Union made remarkably good headway and could boast nearly a hundred branches by its first birthday. Most of these were in ILP country—industrial Scotland, Lancashire and Yorkshire, the Midlands and South Wales—but the influx of radical intellectuals, mostly middle class, broadened the base of the anti-war movement. The young Fenner Brockway described the men of the UDC as 'bourgeois to their fingertips', and commented that 'they might have been lifted out of any gathering of gentlemen of England'[3]. But MacDonald was shrewd enough to see in these gentlemen potential recruits to a post-war Labour Party, and part of the UDC's historical importance lies in its usefulness as a bridge between the old progressive party and the new. One commentator has gone so far as to describe the UDC as 'to a large extent the decisive factor in the decline of the Liberal Party and the rise of the Labour Party after the war, the Liberals who became active in the UDC during the war years leading the way for many more who passed over into the Labour ranks in the early 'twenties'[4].

Of at least as much importance was the fact that the UDC provided the diverse elements who were opposed to or critical of the war with a clear-cut, cohesive programme which both reached out to their idealism and remained anchored within the area of practical politics. The UDC's programme was adopted *in toto* by the ILP at its first war-time annual conference, in April 1915, and by several fringe groups on the Left in the spring and summer of 1915. A large part of the programme was adopted by the conference of Allied Socialist Parties which met in London on 14 February of the same year. Later it made more influential converts: President Woodrow Wilson of the United States built his Fourteen-Point Peace Programme on the ideas formulated in the UDC manifesto.

★ ★ ★

While Left-wing Socialists and a remnant of radical Liberals were carrying through a political opposition to the war, the traditional Christian pacifist movements were mobilising for their own peace crusade. In December 1914 the fragmented peace groups within each of the major religious denominations came together in the Fellowship of Reconciliation, described by a sympathetic Quaker as 'an organisation which works by prayer and the propagation of a right spirit, which eschews political action and is not in any immediate hurry to count up results'. The FoR formed 165 branches during the course of the war, and recruited 8,000 members. It held devotional meetings and discussion circles, published pamphlets expounding a New Testament basis of pacifism, issued a quarterly *News Sheet* and a monthly journal, the *Venturer*, and co-operated with the No-Conscription Fellowship in campaigning against, and later encouraging resistance to, the Military Service Acts. Despite its distrust of politics, the FoR's first Annual Report contained a fierce denunciation of the industrial system—'unchecked competition leading to sweated labour and dishonest practices'—and the organisation later went on record in specific opposition to capitalism and imperialism. It took root in several countries overseas, notably in the United States, where its journal, *The World Tomorrow*, was edited by Norman Thomas, later leader of the Socialist Party and several times Socialist candidate for the Presidency. Except when its energies were absorbed almost entirely by the anti-conscription campaign, the FoR concentrated on the unrewarding task of preaching peace to the Churches, and made abortive efforts to organise a World Conference of Churches on Peace.

The spearhead of the Christian pacifist movement was, inevitably, the numerically small but articulate and highly organised Society of Friends—the Quakers. In November 1914 its executive committee, the quaintly named 'Meeting for Sufferings', issued to all local meetings a Declaration on the War. It began by quoting the historic testimony of the Society that 'all war is utterly incompatible with the plain precepts of our Divine Lord and Lawgiver, and with the whole spirit and tenor of His Gospel, and that no plan of necessity or of policy, however urgent or peculiar, can avail to release either individuals or nations from the paramount allegiance which they owe unto Him who said "Love your enemies". To carry out such a profession consistently is indeed a high attainment, but it should be the aim of every Christian.'

The Declaration then proceeded: 'Whilst reaffirming this statement of our faith we cannot shelter ourselves behind any traditional tenet. We are in the presence of living issues. Today many of our fellow-countrymen are impelled to enlist by a sense of chivalry towards the weak and by devotion to high national ideals. Today again the members of our Society, especially the younger men, are entering upon a time of testing. We can well understand the appeal to noble instincts which makes men desire to risk their lives for their country. To turn from this call may seem to be a lower choice. In many cases it means braving the scorn of those who only interpret it as cowardice. To not a few it involves the loss of emmployent. The highest sacrifice is to contribute our lives to the cause of love in helping our country to a more Christlike idea of service. Those who hear the call to this service, and who respond to it, will be helping their nation in the great spiritual conflicts which it must wage. Already arrangements are being made by Friends to give opportunities in the stricken districts of Europe for the alleviation of disease, misery and starvation. We see danger to principle in undertaking any service auxiliary to warfare which involves becoming part of the military machine.'

The officially sponsored Quaker war-work committees were the War Victims' Relief Committee and the Emergency Committee for the Relief of Germans, Austrians, Hungarians and Turks in Distress. The former offered overseas service to young Quakers who could not in good conscience volunteer for the army but nevertheless felt impelled to do something to mitigate the ravages of war. Its service groups worked in France, rebuilding devasted villages, restoring damaged water supplies and manning emergency civil hospitals. About 200 members of the Committee were of military age and were required, on the introduction of conscription, to apply to the Tribunals for exemption from military service in order to continue their relief work. One or two refused to allow their work for the Committee to be classified by the Tribunals as 'alternative service', and chose the lot of the 'absolutist' conscientious objectors: prison. The second body, the Emergency Committee, employed only a few men of military age. Its work was among English women married to expelled or interned Germans, and to alien enemies in internment camps.

But even before the Society's publication of the Declaration on the War, a small group of young Quakers were organising themselves for non-military war service. In September 1914, Philip J. Baker, a Fellow of King's College, Cambridge, began recruiting friends for an unofficial Quaker Ambulance Unit. In October he organised a training camp at Jordans Farm, a Quaker centre near Beaconsfield. In November the first hastily trained corps of the Friends Ambulance Unit set out for Dunkirk. One of its members, T. Corder Catchpool, described in a letter home the task that awaited them on arrival.

I shall never in my life forget the sight and sounds that met us. Figure two huge goods sheds, semi-dark, every inch of floor space— *quais*, rails, everywhere covered with the flimsy French stretchers, so that in places you had to step on them to get about—and on each stretcher a wounded man—desperately wounded, nearly every one. The air heavy with the stench of putrid flesh, and thick with groans and cries. Four hundred of these wounded, and one French medical student to attend to them—an English staff officer and an English naval officer helping voluntarily. Half dead as we were with fatigue, we flung ourselves into this work throughout the night, the need was so great. Consider this man, both thighs broken, and he has travelled twenty kilometres, *sitting on the seat* of a crowded railway carriage. Or this one, with his arm hanging by a shred of biceps—or this, with bits of bone floating in a pool of pus that fills up a great hole in his flesh, laughing bitterly when I turn away to vomit, overcome by the stench of sepsis—he may well laugh bitterly—he has lain eight days on the filthy floor in an outhouse of some farm near the front. Or all these, case after case with bullet wounds through the abdomen, septic, fatal—so we work on through the night, hurrying from one to the next . . .[5].

The FAU at first met with little assistance or encouragement from the British military authorities, and for the first few months it worked with the much more co-operative French armies. Later, when the British army began to understand that these volunteers, who paid their own expenses, were prepared to tackle jobs that no one else would touch, relations with the Unit became much more amicable and co-operative. More surprisingly the Unit was at first regarded with some suspicion by the Quaker establishment. Its origins, as we have seen, were unofficial. The Unit was already at work in France by the time the Quaker executive issued its Declaration on the War. There were Quakers who thought that the Unit was compromising the Society's pacifism by its willingness to work in conjunction with the army, organised on para-military lines and sometimes under direct military orders. On the other hand, there were Quakers who, despite the Society's traditional pacifism, felt it their duty to support the war: a third of all Quakers of military age volunteered for army service, or allowed themselves at a later stage to be conscripted. Thus the FAU reported to the Society's Yearly Meeting but was not controlled by or responsible to it until 1916.

In the early months not all its members were Quakers, though when conscription came in the Government insisted that the Unit confine its recruitment to members of the Society. Certainly not all the 1,400 men who at one time or another served with the Unit can properly be classified as conscientious objectors. Some soon volunteered for the army, others put up no resistance to conscription. On the other hand, a small number of the 1,200 FAU members who applied to the Tribunals for exemption from the Military Service Acts refused to accept 'alternative service' and chose to return to Britain and take their stand with the absolutists in prison. Corder Catchpool was one, and he detailed the reasons for his decision in the collection of letters published in 1918, shortly before the end of the war, as the classic *On Two Fronts*. Catchpool was adjutant of the Unit by 1916, but by then he was realising that the 'voluntary units were either dispensed with, or practically absorbed into the regular armies. The wounded no longer lacked help, the Royal Army Medical Corps being often closed to applicants. Men displaced by the services taken over by the Unit . . . were often drafted to the firing line, and complained bitterly that I and my colleagues had sent them there.' Those who had accepted 'alternative service', he believed, were often haunted by a sense of having chosen a spiritually second best. Those, on the other hand, who refused all compromise, had enlisted in the 'highest service I know, the formation of a world fellowship of men prepared to die rather than take part in the war'.

The Unit, which owed much of its official acceptance to the respect accorded to Sir George Newman, a highly placed official in the Ministry of Health who accepted its chairmanship, set up dozens of hospitals in France, brought over hundreds of motor ambulances, paid for largely out of Quaker collections, manned dressing stations on the front line, made 127,000 inoculations against typhoid in Belgium, fed and clothed refugees, started village industries such as lace-making, distributed milk and purified water, managed recreation huts, carried 33,000 men home in its own two hospital ships, moved 260,000 sick and wounded from the front in its own motor convoys, and another half million in its four ambulance trains. The first expedition of forty-three men was augmented until the Unit's strength stood at more than six hundred. The volunteers received not a penny in pay, only their food rations. The Unit spent £138,000, all raised by voluntary subscription.[6]

The advent of conscription divided Friends in their attitude towards the FAU's work. The Friends Service Committee adopted and advocated the absolutist position. Some two dozen members of the FAU felt, with the FSC and with Catchpool, that Friends in the Unit were being accorded a privileged status by the Government, and they returned to Britain to take an absolutist stand and its consequences—long periods of military and civil detention.

The Unit nevertheless continued to expand, and built a 'General Section' to accommodate men at home, in agriculture, teaching and work endorsed by the Pelham Committee. Tribunals actually offered more men work in the FAU than the Unit could employ in France, and these were absorbed in orderly work in several hospitals, including the Haxby Road Hospital, York (where the building was owned by the Quaker family Rowntree), Uffculme Hospital, Birmingham (owned by the Quaker family Cadbury), the Star and Garter home for incurables at Richmond, Surrey, and the King George Hospital, London. At the latter military hospital the Unit's 110 men were met by a hostile demonstration by other staff on the night of their arrival. Although there were 120 other orderlies, the FAU men were given the dirtiest and most menial jobs, constantly had their food stolen and were sometimes subjected to physical violence. In December 1916, after five months, the FAU withdrew them.

The men who accepted these kinds of alternative service felt that 'the nation needed maintenance and service of all sorts, on usual civilian lines, and admitted in general the right of the State, if it saw fit—under such crises as plague, famine or war—to prescribe what work a man should do. The line of refusal would be drawn by these men if the work prescribed turned out to be in itself immoral, but not till then.''

The critics of the alternativist line, the absolutists, argued that every kind of permitted service was helping the war indirectly, and that by obeying the Military Service Acts to the extent of accepting work prescribed under them, immoral regulations which deserved all-out opposition were being made workable by the co-operation of their victims. This conflict was to be raised in its most acute form in the summer of 1916, and we shall return to it later.

At home, the Society pressed ahead with peace propaganda through its own Peace Committee, the Northern Friends Peace Board and local meetings. Three hundred peace meetings were organised by Quakers between the outbreak of war and Christmas 1914. Although Quakers tended to be somewhat privileged in the sense that their peace views were widely tolerated as a cranky but on the whole harmless religious phenomenon, the persistently sharp edge of their attack eventually brought them into open conflict with the authorities. To the Defence of the Realm regulations was added in 1917 a clause ordering that all pamphlets and publications dealing with the war or the making of peace should pass official censorship before being issued. In December 1917 the Quaker executive resolved to defy the new regulation, which it described as 'a grave danger to the national welfare'. Its statement continued:

The duty of every good citizen to express his thoughts on the affairs of his country is hereby endangered . . . It is for Christians a paramount duty to be free to obey, and to act and speak according to the law of God, a law higher than that of any State, and no Government official can release men from this duty. We realise the rarity of the occasions on which a body of citizens find their sense of duty to be in conflict with the law, and it is with a sense of the gravity of the decision that the Society of Friends must on this occasion act contrary to the regulations and continue to issue literature on war and peace without submitting it to the censor. It is convinced that in thus standing for spiritual liberty it is acting in the best interest of the nation.

The Home Office was informed of the decision, which was subsequently ratified by Yearly Meeting—the Society's annual conference. Friends' committees and meetings continued to issue pamphlets without sending them to the censor. In January 1918 the Friends' Service Committee published a pamphlet called *A Challenge to Militarism*, about conscientious objectors in prison. In February two Quaker ladies were arrested for distributing it at the doors of a Labour meeting at the Central Hall, Westminster. When their trial took place on 18 April evidence was given by Harrison Barrow, the acting chairman, and by Edith Ellis, co-secretary, that the Committee was responsible for the pamphlet. The charge of distributing the pamphlet was then dropped, pending proceedings against the publishers, the Service Committee itself. A new prosecution was brought against Harrison Barrow, Edith Ellis and her co-secretary, Arthur Watts. Barrow had been prospective Mayor of Birmingham in 1914 but had withdrawn rather than put himself in a position where it would be his civic duty to participate in army recruitment. Edith Ellis was the daughter of the Rt Hon John Edward Ellis, MP, a former Under-Secretary for India. Arthur Watts represented the younger Service Committee Friends of military age, many of whom were already in prison as conscientious objectors. The charge of publishing a pamphlet on the war without submitting it to the censor was quickly proven since it was uncontested. Barrow and Watts were sentenced to six months imprisonment, and Miss Ellis to a £100 fine with 50 guineas costs, which she refused to pay and in consequence suffered three months imprisonment. Confirming the sentences on appeal, the Chairman of the Quarter Sessions, Sir A. J. Newton, snorted: 'One can scarcely contain oneself, and restrain one's indignation. The law has been deliberately and wilfully and ruthlessly broken. For the protection of the Empire and of the civilised world it has been decided that a check should be put on the publication of certain literature. Here is a body which deliberately flaunts everybody and every thing. This Bench will not sanction any such proceedings.' Thus was the Empire and the State protected against the seditious Society of Friends.

The political peace movements met the censorship problem with more panache, if rather less high principle. Finding that the Press Bureau rarely raised objections to the matter submitted, they took to issuing their pamphlets heavily rubber-stamped on the cover with the words 'PASSED BY THE PRESS CENSOR', 'This', explained Philip Snowden, 'gave an importance and authority to the leaflet which it would not otherwise have had, and most people read that inscription to mean that the matter had been approved by the Government[8].'

* * *

These, then, were the shock troops of the war-time peace movement: a minority at the Left end of the political spectrum, and a minority at the Left end of the Non-conformist Christian tradition. Their philosophy—or theology—of resistance is best conveyed by their own spokesmen. Perhaps the most powerful and certainly the most popular exposition of the Christian pacifist attitude to the war was an article in the *Labour Leader* on 24 September 1914 by Dr. Alfred Salter, physician, bacteriologist, former member of London County Council and later a Labour MP. The paper published it with an editorial disclaimer to the effect that it was 'not necessarily the view of the ILP'. It met with such a remarkable response that it went through several reprintings, and more than one and a half million copies were distributed in Britain alone. It was translated into most European languages, including German, and even into Chinese. Some eighty people were at one time or another imprisoned for distributing it in Australia, New Zealand, the United States of America and South Africa.

Dr Salter called his article 'The Religion of a C.O.', and it requires quotation at length.

Behind all human actions and motives there is a philosophy or creed, and behind all actions and motives that affect us deeply there is a religion. What a man thinks or does at times like these depends on what his religion is. Every man has a religion, though he may not know it.

There are only two main religions in the world, though each of them has many forms: 1. The religion which trusts in the power and ultimate triumph of material forces—faith in materialism. 2. The religion which trusts in the power and ultimate triumph of spiritual forces—faith in God.

The materialist religion believes in the big battalions, the millions of armed men, the weight of battleships, the superiority of artillery, the efficiency of organisation, the adequacy of food supplies, the stability of financial resources. Count up your ships and your men, your horses and your chariots, your money and your allies, and put your trust in them. The scene in which you have now to act is one in which God does not count. Force alone matters. That is the gospel of materialism, which, for the time being, seems to be the accepted doctrine of Europe, and the doctrine which is being preached from nearly every pulpit in England.

The other religion is the simple faith that the only thing that matters is the doing of God's will; that whatever happens or threatens, the last word is with Him. For the man who believes in God there is only one sure means of defence, one true line of safety, one clear path of duty—obedience to God's command. The position in which we may be placed may be a difficult one, the combat may seem very unequal—one weak voice against a roaring mob, a few unarmed visionaries against the bristling battalions of the State, a group of obscure nobodies against all the weight and splendour and authority of an Empire. But this religion teaches that the cause of right wins in the long run in spite of odds against it, in spite of temporary defeat, in spite even of apparent annihilation. This religion believes that Truth, ignored, martyred, crushed it may be for the time, will emerge triumphant when the glory and pomp and power of Empire are vanished and forgotten. Assyria, Babylon, Egypt, Persia, Rome, Spain, were all mighty world-powers that conquered by relying on material force. By each of these in turn the claims of love, of mercy, of brotherhood, of the sanctity of human life, were treated with scorn as contemptible weaknesses, and the advocates of such claims were suppressed or laughed out of court. All these military Empires in their day and generation were omnipotent. Nothing could stand against them. All have perished and gone—but the word of the Lord endureth for ever.

In considering our duty as citizens and politicians, then, our actions are really determined by our religion.

My religion is the Christian Religion. I may misunderstand it, but I must speak as I have been given light. If in my bottommost heart I want to know what I should do under any given circumstances, I must ask myself what is God's command on the subject, and what would Christ do in my place. In the matter of this war I must try and picture to myself Christ as an Englishman, with England at war with Germany. The Germans have overrun France and Belgium, and may possibly invade England by airship and drop bombs on London. What am I to do? Am I to answer the Prime Minister's call, make myself proficient in arms, and hurry to the Continent to beat the Germans off?

Look! Christ in khaki, out in France thrusting His bayonet into the body of a German workman. See! The Son of God with a machine gun, ambushing a column of German infantry, catching them unawares in a lane and mowing them down in their helplessness. Hark! The Man of Sorrows in a cavalry charge, cutting, hacking, thrusting, crushing, cheering. No! No! That picture is an impossible one, *and we all know it.*

That settles the matter for me. I cannot uphold the war, even on its supposedly defensive side, and I cannot, therefore, advise any one else to enlist or to take part in what I believe to be wrong and wicked for myself. A country, as an individual, must be prepared to follow Christ if it is to claim the title of Christian.

There is a great place waiting in history for the first nation that will dare to save its life by losing it, that will dare to base its national existence on righteous dealing, and not on force, that will found its conduct on the truths of primitive Christianity, and not on the power of its army and navy. And there is a great place waiting in history for the first political party that will dare to take the same stand and will dare to advocate the Christian policy of complete disarmament and non-resistance to alien force . . .

This classic expression of Christian pacifism was followed by an equally definitive statement of political opposition to the war. It appeared on 1 November in a pamphlet provocatively titled *Is Germany Right and Britain Wrong?* The pamphlet carried the text of a speech made to a Lancashire ILP meeting by Clifford Allen, the man who at twenty-five was soon to become the undisputed, even venerated leader of the war resisters. At the outbreak of war he had already attracted the attention of Labour leaders by his able advocacy of Socialism while an undergraduate at Cambridge. Ramsay MacDonald, on becoming chairman of the company formed in 1912 to launch the first Labour daily newspaper, the *Daily Citizen*, invited Allen to become secretary. In October 1913, when the paper was one year old, Allen became its General Manager, in which capacity he had full charge of the *Citizen*'s business operations. When Britain entered the war, Allen, backed by his circulation manager, Herbert Morrison, held to the ILP position, but those responsible for editorial direction put the *Citizen* behind the war. Allen expressed his dissent in a letter to the paper, published on 27 August.

> We Socialists [he wrote], if not the whole Labour movement, must condemn this war, even if we stir up the spirit of jingoism, and despite the undeniable fact that war will continue, protest we never so loudly. We must protest for one reason alone—the saving of the self-respect and reputation of the Socialist movement. If we stand by now—however wisely—we can never again lift our voices in the cause of peace and internationalism. A jingo spirit stirred, our meetings wrecked, even our heads broken, will only serve to emphasise that the one movement which will always—come what may—condemn war (above all diplomatists' war) is the Socialist movement.

The war divisions weakened the *Citizen*, and in April 1915 a legal judgment ended the paper's short life by a ruling that ordinary trade union funds could not be used to support it. Allen was appointed the company's liquidator. He received a friendly letter of commiseration in June 1915 from Arthur Henderson, now a member of the Government, which within a year was to be responsible for the most savage persecution of Allen and his friends.

In *Is Germany Right and Britain Wrong?* Allen wrote:

> The ILP has emphasised repeatedly the folly, the miserable stupidity of 'the workers of the world' who are gulled and gulled again

into voting for the very masters against whom they strike; who are cajoled into sweating out their wretched existence to produce the wealth and the consequent power of those who strip them of their manhood and womanhood; who parrot-like repeat the prayers of national religions which allow of a national life prohibitive of every Christian virtue; who shout for a war which they do not want, and whose victims they will be. Fooled when they have all the power; intoxicated with the imaginary justice of this war; ready to suffer unutterable anguish in this or any other war. What war, indeed, has there ever been whose righteousness has not be proclaimed by both sides, what war has ever been waged when the capitalist has not hurled the workers to a noble death for a just cause? . . . Our own leaders state that this war is just. Did they imagine for one moment that the Government would not take every precaution that some holy pretext should arise as the cause of a war they had made inevitable? A government would be mad to go to war in these days unless it had public opinion behind it. These capitalists are too wily for us. In Germany they have shewn the war to have a just cause, and the majority of Socialists are with them. In France they have taken the Socialists into their counsels, and have made it seem that the German is such a menace to civilisation that the German comrade must be slain, whilst the British Socialist is crouching in the trench to murder the German Trade Unionist . . .

The cause of Internationalism has suffered a rude shock. The International Socialist Movement has crumbled at the first really critical strain put upon it. Socialists in every country have been fooled by their respective governments. The German Social Democrat is butchering the French Socialist, the British Socialist hears the cry of anguish and hatred of the German comrade he is bayoneting to a fearful death. Where is now our proud boast of the solidarity of the workers? The battle cry of the International is silent. The Democracies of Europe have proved helpless.

Can you picture the next International Socialist Congress, the next meeting of the leaders of the 'workers of the world'? I think I can see in this humiliation the great purging by fire of the half-formed socialist character. We have discovered our weakness, we have perhaps learnt one great lesson—that Socialism must be something of a religion to us before it can have any meaning in times of real stress. Socialists must take their part in politics, but they have been too easily swayed by ordinary political conceptions, they have not yet ceased to be influenced by the capitalist habit of tinkering with the political game.

The international spirit must lead us to prevent the annihilation and dismemberment of Germany, should she be beaten. Her spirit of splendid vigour has produced the sternest philosophy, the most virile art, the most scornful literature, and some of the greatest scientific discoveries of the world. (By the way, I know nothing more amusing than the way in which the average journalist is today claiming a knowledge and long-time understanding of Nietzsche as complete as the Kaiser's intimacy with the Almighty.)

This great national spirit must be preserved for Germany whatever she may suffer in her quite natural but secondhand imperial ambitions. Her remarkable organising ability must be used for its rightful purpose. We Socialists must sit at her feet and learn the lesson of discipline and constancy.

The great International may lie in the dust, but its spirit will revive, and Germany's national spirit be saved.

Foul slanders are circulating. Tales of atrocities—always German —are on our lips. Let us beware; let us reserve judgment so that we may never pass sentence. Our passions are being stirred but not our sense of shame! The destruction of Rheims evoked a louder cry of horror than the destruction of tens of thousands of our sons on the field of battle.

War itself is an atrocity, and are we to stand surprised at its natural consequences? In the name of religion, men and women have been thrown to the lions, in the name of modern commerce the Belgians have torn the limbs of Congo natives; if you let loose the dogs of war, you must take the consequences. If you are going to be brutish, be brutish thoroughly, you can't play at being soldiers. Listen to the capitalist asking in each country for the war to be conducted humanely! Are there no atrocities in times of peace for which he is responsible? Is it not a far more terrible thing to see a little child starve in times of plenty than even to witness the natural excesses of war?

We must refuse to be surprised by war being conducted as war, not like a game of skittles.

Think of Germany's position. The menace of Russia and Pan-Slavism on the one side and a revengeful France, Russia's ally, on the other. Would you not call Germany mad if she was not well defended?

But something more! Britain's shadow clouds the background,

pursuing a foreign policy which threw Europe eventually into war, because it was shrouded in uncertainty. Men are more afraid of uncertainty than of certainty and a thief with a bludgeon . . .

We have got to face the only possible outcome of our Socialist faith: I mean the question of non-resistance to armed force. Don't let us deceive ourselves. The sacredness of human life is the mainspring of all our propaganda. In my opinion, there cannot be two kinds of murder. People say that it is incumbent upon us to hold aloft the sanctity of international morality. Who set up the standards of international morality? Interested nations. But even if all that is true, whatever the circumstances, once force is used, there is only one way of upholding international morality and that is, by individual and national immorality, by murder. Are we to seal this great morality by untold human anguish and by letting loose all men's foulest instincts? Are the bulwarks of this so-called international morality always to be built with torn, crushed human bodies? Is the song of international morality to be the cries and oaths of human lives wasted in anguish on the battlefield?

To Salter and to Allen, to the Christian and to the agnostic, the common springboard of action was an inflexible faith in what both chose to call 'the sacredness of human life and personality'. This was the common denominator which united religious and secular objectors. In the year 1914 it was a hard, almost an irrational and romantic faith. Men who held it could not be allowed by a Government at war to walk the streets in freedom. They were national enemies.

REFERENCES

1 G. D. H. Cole, *op cit*
2 Philip Viscount Snowden, *Autobiography*, 1933
3 Fenner Brockway, *Inside the Left*, 1944
4 G. R. Crosby, *Disarmament and Peace in British Politics 1914–1918*, 1957
5 T. Corder Catchpool, *On Two Fronts*, 1918
6 Meaburn Tatham and James E. Miles, *History of the Friends Ambulance Unit*, 1921
7 John W. Graham, *Conscription and Conscience*, 1922
8 Philip Viscount Snowden, *op cit*

Chapter III

The Conscriptionists

FOR MORE than a decade before the war, conscription had been an increasingly important issue in British politics. As Europe built up its conscript armies, Britain was urged to do likewise, both in defence of the homeland and to provide armed backing in the world struggle for markets.

While the flames of patriotism were still feeding greedily on the fuel of the Boer War, there was published in 1901 the first popular statement for a British conscript army. It was written by George Shee, a self-confessed 'Liberal Imperialist', and called *The Briton's First Duty: The Case for Conscription*. Shee's flyleaf text was Nelson's message: 'England expects that every man will do his duty.' After declaring his faith that 'God has seen fit to favour us above all other nations', Shee argued:

> Just as necessity made every man a warrior in order to defend the community in the early 'struggle for existence', so necessity calls for the armed service of every citizen in order to preserve the enormous accumulation of the fruits of industry from the aggression of jealous competitors in the new 'struggle for existence'—the struggle for the markets.

Shee warned that invasion was imminent, though the likely aggressor was named as France rather than Germany. But, like many subsequent advocates of conscription, he allowed his enthusiasm for the military life as a good in itself to run away with him. The following passage gives the game away:

> I am convinced (and I have seen the results in many Continental countries) that the advantages of military training—*for a short period*, be it understood—are so great from the physical, moral, intellectual and educational point of view that, to paraphrase a celebrated saying, if

66

the necessity for it did not exist, it would be the highest wisdom to invent it.

Shee's book found enough fellow-enthusiasts to father a National Service League, founded in 1902 with the Duke of Wellington as President and Shee as secretary. The League's programme underwent constant changes, veering from conscription for two years to compulsory training for four months. The word conscription, however, was soon found to be an embarrassment, and thereupon dropped. When the League published an abridged version of *The Briton's First Duty*, the original subtitle, *The Case for Conscription*, became *The Case for Universal Military Training*. Shee even claimed that the word conscription in the original edition had been inserted by the publishers against his will[1].

Early supporters of the League included Lord Newton, Field-Marshal Lord Wolseley, Rudyard Kipling, the Duke of Argyll and the Duke of Westminster. The Church, too, was properly represented. The Bishop of Chester was a founder-member, and a remarkable Christian defence of war and military training was set forth by Canon J. H. Scrine in one of the League's leaflets:

But is war and the training for it 'un-Christian'? There is the point, and we meet it. War is not murder, as some fancy; war is sacrifice. The fighting and killing are not of the essence of it, but are the accidents, though the inseparable accidents; and even these, in the wide modern fields where a soldier rarely in his own sight sheds any blood but his own, where he lies on the battle sward not to inflict death but to endure it—even these are mainly purged of savagery and transfigured into devotion. War is not murder, but sacrifice; which is the soul of Christianity.

The conscriptionists' first political opportunity came when, in 1903, a Royal Commission was appointed under the presidency of the Duke of Norfolk to study and report on the organisation of the army—the old Volunteer Forces and the Militia. The National Service League lobbied the Commission in favour of a conscript army on the continental pattern, and that, broadly, is what a majority report recommended in May 1904. But the Balfour Government flatly rejected its advice. When Lord Newton, for the National Service League, pressed the Commission's case in the House of Lords, he was defeated by fifty-nine votes to twenty-one.

The arguments ranged against conscription were several. First there were those expressed in a minority report of the Norfolk Commission: quality was more valuable than quantity in a fighting force. Then there was the question of expense: the Secretary for War, H. O. Arnold-Forster, claimed that the Commission's recommended one year of compulsory service would add £25,900,000 to the Army Estimates. More important were the strategic arguments; first, that the introduction of conscription in Britain would alarm our neighbours and accelerate the arms race, and second, that Britain's defences were adequately safeguarded by an enormous, growing and costly navy. But the most important argument was the simple one that conscription would never, at least in peace time, be tolerated by the British people, who regarded it as a foreign monstrosity, a revival of the old, barbaric press-gangs writ large. Mr Winston Churchill expressed the point well enough: conscription 'would no doubt be of some use in providing occupation for members in another place who had not got much to do, but it cannot be said seriously to enter into the practical politics of the country[2]'.

So the National Service League set itself the task of converting public opinion, of making conscription practical (i.e. electorally popular) politics. It published a stream of leaflets and a monthly *National Service Journal* (later called *The Nation in Arms*), organised public meetings and set up branches. In 1905 it picked up its most valuable recruit, Field-Marshal Lord Roberts, the immensely popular veteran of the Boer War and of half a century's skirmishes. 'From my own experience and from the evidence given before the Duke of Norfolk's Commission,' he told a London Chamber of Commerce meeting on 1 August, 'I, for one, consider that there is now no option but to introduce universal training and service for home defence.' Four months later he became the League's President, and the last ten of his eighty-two years were given over to a crusade for conscription—or 'universal military training' as he was taught to call it by the League's public relations men.

After the Liberal landslide of 1906, the conscription question began to take on a party-political colour. Three MPs had lent their names as supporters of the League on its foundation in 1902, two of them Conservatives and one Liberal. The 1906 election brought into the Commons forty-three League supporters, all but a handful of whom were Conservatives. The Opposition front benches were not yet ready to commit themselves, but their backbenchers were. The first onslaught came when the Government presented its reformed forces scheme in 1906, establishing the Territorial Army. Three times the League's supporters in the Lords initiated debates for compulsion, none of them successful. A Liberal backbencher, Captain Kincaid-Smith, sought leave in 1908 to introduce a Bill to establish compulsory training in the Territorials. The Bill failed by 250 votes to thirty-four. Almost all the thirty-four were Conservatives. When Lord Newton introduced a similar Bill in the Lords in 1909 it was defeated by only twenty votes—123 to 103.

Paradoxically, while the conscriptionists made almost no headway in winning over public opinion during the first half-dozen Conservative years of the century, they began to make real progress during the era of radical social construction which followed the 1906 Liberal landslide. The reason is not hard to find. In 1907 Lord Northcliffe began a campaign for conscription in his *Daily Mail*, the largest and most powerful popular newspaper in the country. Day after day it raised the bogy of invasion and preached national service as the only sure instrument of national defence.

But where the League and its fellow travellers needed a real breakthrough was among the organised Labour movement, now immensely influential and opposed almost *en masse* to any kind of conscription, partial or total. In 1909, however, Labour's solid front began to crack. First, in March, Labour MP Will Thorne advocated a scheme of universal short-term military training on the Swiss pattern—fourteen to forty-eight days' full-time service each year[3]. Then, in December of the same year, a more formidable Socialist spokesman, Robert Blatchford, contributed a series of articles to the *Daily Mail* which demanded full conscription in terms more forthright than that paper's editorials had ever dared use.

A diversion is necessary at this point to explain the traditional British socialist attitude to conscription from which Thorne and Blatchford departed. In the counsels of the International, the British movement was odd man out. The continental Socialist movements not only accepted conscription, they welcomed it. Their concept was of a 'Citizen Army', democratically organised and subject to popular control. In their view, a ruling class which conscripted and armed its workers was doing the Socialist movement a favour, for such action served to arm the masses for revolution. A broadly based conscript army was felt to be a much less dangerous instrument of domestic tyranny than a small, highly trained, permanent force. European Socialists who fought to carry radical anti-war policies within the International were enthusiastic defenders of conscription or compulsory military training. Jean Jaurès, who after his assassination became an international symbol of pacifist socialism, was an advocate of the Swiss system of short-term conscription, if not of his own country's more full-blooded version.

But in Britain any kind of conscription was anathema to the greater part of the Socialist movement, particularly to the ILP and the Labour Party. The ILP was never, after all, a revolutionary body in the sense that the European Marxist movement was revolutionary. It never craved a 'Citizen Army'. Steeped in two parts of Methodism to every one of Marx, its non-conformist, liberal and humanist traditions were stronger than its revolutionary rhetoric. And besides, the British movement was not faced with a *de facto* situation of conscript armies defending vast land frontiers, as were its continental counterparts. British socialism could afford the luxury of debating conscription in the abstract.

But one small section of the British movement did adopt the continental viewpoint, and that was Hyndman's Social-Democratic Party, subsequently the British Socialist Party and eventual nucleus of the Communist Party. Hyndman agitated, with the Tory leaders, for an increased navy, and went one better by demanding conscription. Blatchford, veteran editor of the most popular Socialist weekly of the day, the *Clarion*, organiser of the *Clarion* cycling clubs and author of best-selling *Merrie England*, shared Hyndman's enthusiasm for military strength and his xenophobic hatred of Germany.

In December 1909 Blatchford wrote to the *Daily Mail*, offering them a series on conscription. 'So serious and so imminent is the danger and so onerous and severe is the task that danger imposes on us,' he wrote, 'that the question of national defence should take precedence over every other question at present before the country.' The Right-wing *Mail* jumped at the chance of recruiting so able and influential a socialist propagandist to its own favourite cause, and offered Blatchford ten articles. He used them to propose an immediate Bill for two years' compulsory service, a Bill for elementary military training of all schoolboys over the age of ten (in his book *My Life in the Army*, published the following year, he appears to advocate the extension of this training to schoolgirls), and vast increases in naval expenditure. 'Volunteering,' he wrote, 'is no use . . . We shall have to arm and train the manhood of the nation, or other nations whose manhood is armed and trained will wipe us out.' The *Daily Mail* published reprints by the hundred thousand.

That Blatchford's militarism was an expression of his conception of socialism is clearly shown in this extract from *My Life in the Army:*

> No man who has never drilled with a regiment, or marched with a column, or taken part in the evolutions of a brigade can imagine the spirit of collectivism of which I write. To him the idea of a corporate mind and soul is unthinkable. Let him do the bayonet exercise in close order front and rear rank back to back; let him run in from the firing line and from rallying squares; and he will begin to understand what the words 'regiment', 'nation' and 'community' mean . . . Dr H Miller Maguire [a contemporary writer on military affairs] said to me once: 'Peace or no peace, I'd have every man trained to arms. If there was never to be another fight I'd drill every male thing. By George, I'd have universal military training in heaven!'

This was going somewhat further than the pro-conscription European socialists. As for Shee, so for Blatchford, military service was a good in itself. The author of *Merrie England,* who continued to the last to allot himself a place on the 'anarchist-communist' wing of the socialist movement, was disowned by most of his comrades, and even by some who were by no means his comrades: Winston Churchill described him as 'a ridiculous Jingo'[4].

But few readers of the *Daily Mail* were ideological socialists or libertarian Liberals, and public opinion began to show evidence of shifting towards at least the moderate conscriptionist party—those content to advocate short-term training. In the January 1910 general election the Tories won 127 seats. Many new Members were declared conscriptionists. The National Service League's list of Parliamentary members and supporters jumped from the forty-three of 1906 to 155.

As the naval arms race between Britain and Germany spiralled upwards, demands for national service became more frequent and more broadly based. Even the ineptitude of Lord Roberts in praising

German militarism and publicly describing the Kaiser's imperialist and pan-European ambitions as 'an excellent policy' which Britain should emulate, did no more than temporarily dent the League's popularity among the upper and upper-middle classes. In 1911 even Lord Haldane, Secretary for War and architect of the reorganisation of the army on determinedly voluntarist lines, was hinting that in changed circumstances compulsory service might become necessary.

On four occasions in 1912 the conscriptionist Tory backbenchers in the Commons either forced debates on compulsion or introduced the subject in debates on other military matters. Another full-dress debate took place in the Lords in February 1913. On 16 February Lord Roberts spoke at a meeting in Bristol for which there were 20,000 applications for tickets. Moves were even made at Cambridge University to make military training a condition of graduation. A National Service (Territorial Force) Bill was introduced in the Commons on 13 March, and the debate, which was not allowed by its sponsors to proceed to a vote, was notable for a critical contribution from Keir Hardie.

In March 1914 the Prime Minister turned down a deputation from the National Service League. In the same month Lord Willoughby de Broke relieved the growing tedium of the campaign by introducing in the Lords a proposal for the conscription of 'gentlemen' only, as an example to the lower classes. This was defeated by fifty-three votes to thirty-four, despite the support of the Bishop of Bangor, who thought it a step in the right direction, and of Lord Lucas, who believed it to be 'the most thoroughgoing example of the rich serving the poor since Christ first preached the principle nineteen centuries earlier'. In contrast, on 11 May, a Conservative Member in the Commons, Mr Samuel Samuel, proposed that funds allocated by the Treasury to slum clearance would be better diverted to conscription, which would 'create for the poorer classes of this country a training, and put them, at a period of their life when they are most likely to suffer deterioration in their physique and their morals, in a position to have a period of healthy exercise with good food, which would build up their constitution and do more for them than any amount of slum clearance'.

This, then, was the situation at the outbreak of war in August. Some two-thirds of the Parliamentary Conservative Party were

avowed conscriptionists, though the leadership was still uncommitted. A large majority of Liberal Members were voluntarists on
principle, though a significant minority, including Liberal Imperialists on the Right and David Lloyd George on the Left favoured
schemes for compulsory training. The Liberal Government held
the view that naval supremacy plus a highly trained professional
army afforded Britain adequate protection against invasion, but it
was not collectively opposed on principle to compulsion and many
of its leading figures conceded that 'changed circumstances' might
make a case for conscription. Finally there were the forty-odd
Labour Members, anti-conscription to a man with the exception of
Will Thorne's tentative support for compulsory training, and the
Irish Nationalists who shared the Labour view and were implacably
opposed to any Westminster-enforced conscription of Ireland. Outside Parliament, the organised Labour movement was solidly
hostile, the middle class was apprehensive but undecided, and the
upper classes, along with the Northcliffe press, were enthusiastic.
A popular referendum would certainly have swept any proposals
for compulsion into limbo. But in political circles the conscriptionists were making the running.

★ ★ ★

War fever at first drowned the conscription clamour. The colourful
panoply of recruiting machinery—bands, posters and tales of
military derring-do—pulled in volunteers at the rate of 300,000 a
month during the first three months of the war, in addition to men
recalled from the Reserve and Territorials called to the colours. It
was as much as the War Office could do to feed, clothe, accommodate
and arm them.

Kitchener put the Government's position plainly in a speech to
the Lords on 25 August:

> The Empires with whom we are at war have called to the colours
> almost their entire male population. The principle which we on our
> part shall observe is this, that while their maximum force undergoes a
> constant diminution, the reinforcements we prepare shall steadily and
> increasingly flow out until we have an army in the field which, in
> numbers not less than in quality, will not be unworthy of the power
> and responsibilities of the British Empire.

But lest that should be interpreted as an absolute and binding commitment to the voluntary system, Kitchener added ominously:

> I cannot at this stage say what will be the limit of the forces required or what measures may eventually become necessary to supply and maintain them . . . But if the war should be protracted, and if its fortunes should be varied or adverse, exertions and sacrifices beyond any which have been demanded will be required from the whole nation and Empire, and where they are required we are sure they will not be denied in the extreme needs of the State by Parliament or the people.

The conscriptionists understood his message: the voluntary system would be retained and defended while it delivered the goods, but, as Lord Haldane had hinted in 1911, 'if circumstances change . . .' Voluntarism, in short, was to the Liberal leadership an expedient, not an inviolable principle.

Kitchener's statement gave rise to questions in the Commons which enabled Asquith to state plainly that the Government was not at that stage planning conscription. For a time, during the political truce and first recruiting campaign, the conscriptionists for the most part held their hand, though Mr Claude Lowther did unsuccessfully urge the Government to 'consider the advisability of providing rifles and instructors for forces raised for home defence by private individuals' and to make it 'obligatory for every man in the country between the ages of eighteen and thirty years to devote at least two hours daily to drill and rifle practice during the duration of the war'.

Christmas came and went, and it became grimly apparent that the war would be a long drawn-out struggle, devastatingly wasteful of manpower and ammunition. By the new year the rate of recruitment was down to 120,000 a month. Wives of married men serving in the trenches of the Western Front, living alone on minimal dependants' allowances, began to voice their resentment of the young unmarrieds who stayed at home earning relatively good money—or where they didn't, the Northcliffe press voiced it for them.

In the course of a debate in the Lords on army reinforcements on 8 January, Lord Haldane, now Lord Chancellor, admitted that the Government had an 'open mind' on the subject of conscription. 'In time of peace,' he declared, 'I have always told your Lordships that I thought that to resort to compulsory service would be a bad thing, and at this time now I do not think it would be a good thing. Unless it becomes a final necessity, which it has not as yet, it should not be resorted to . . . But at a time of national necessity any other consideration must yield to national interest and we should bar nothing in the way of principle if it should become necessary.' And again: 'Given a great national emergency I think it is your duty to resort to (compulsion)—Therefore I do not want to take up any attitude based on abstract principle about it.'

So openly to profess an open mind is to invite vigorous activity from those bent on closing it in their favour. The National Service League declared the truce over and went to war against the voluntary system. 'I cannot think,' said G. W. Currie, Conservative Member for Louth, on 8 February, 'that any form of compulsion which the Government should think of adopting could compete in point of degree of tyranny with the many appeals that will be possibly made if larger numbers of men are required to be raised, and of the two kinds of tyranny, or compulsion, or whatever the word may be, I should infinitely prefer the one to the other.' This was a shrewd argument. It took the wind from the sails of those libertarians who were complaining about the bullying, highly pressured methods of recruiting officers. When, later in the year, opponents of conscription complained that the voluntary system itself had become 'practical compulsion' and 'illegal conscription', they were met with the retort: 'Then legalise it!'

On 11 March Asquith denied the need for an 'investigation' into conscription. On 20 April Lloyd George, as Chancellor of the Exchequer, told the Commons: 'The Government are not of the opinion that there is any ground for thinking that the war would be more successfully prosecuted by means of conscription.' This statement was subsequently to be resurrected and quoted many times by anti-conscriptionists when Lloyd George became the popular champion of compulsion. Eighteen years later he explained in his *War Memoirs* that his words were 'determined by the fact that as yet the voluntary system was continuing to yield as adquate a flow of recruits as could be absorbed by our training and equipping facilities at that date'.

In particular, the real shortage was of shells, not of men, and by March this had become the occasion of a major crisis within the War Cabinet. Lloyd George wanted to transfer responsibility for

munitions supply from the War Office to a separate Ministry of
Munitions, and was threatening resignation if he failed to get his
way. Kitchener, affronted, threatened resignation if Lloyd George's
proposals were accepted. Asquith devised an uneasy compromise,
forming a Shells Committee under Lloyd George's chairmanship,
loosely attached to the War Office.

These growing national divisions hastened the end of the first
war-time Government. Working-class suspicion; dissensions in the
War Cabinet; a campaign by Northcliffe directed against Kitchener,
War Office incompetence, the shell shortage and the voluntary
system; a growing restiveness on the part of the Tory opposition;
and finally, and decisively, a fit of prima donna temperament by
Winston Churchill at the Admiralty; all these combined to bring
down the Liberal Government. On 19 May Asquith announced the
formation of a Coalition.

The Conservative Party was by now solidly and officially conscriptionist: the leadership had followed where its backbenchers
led. Into the Cabinet came Lord Curzon, who had been second only
to Lord Roberts in the National Service League; Lord Newton,
another League leader; Sir Edward Carson, Lord Balfour, and
Andrew Bonar Law. All were keenly aware that Tory supporters in
Parliament and in the country were looking to them to secure a
'more vigorous prosecution' of the war, and a willingness to
champion conscription was fast becoming the measure and token of
determination to fight through to total victory. The fear that
coalition would produce an immediate Cabinet majority in favour
of conscription was one of the decisive factors which persuaded the
Labour Party to allow its leader to accept Asquith's invitation to
join the Government. Henderson went in as Secretary to the Board
of Education. Junior posts in the Government went to two other
Labour MPs, William Brace and G. H. Roberts.

The conscriptionists seized their new chance. Now began a step
by step campaign, brilliantly conceived and executed, by which the
voluntarists and pacifists were manoeuvred into corner after corner
from which escape was impossible. Not for the first, and certainly
not for the last time, liberals and libertarians were out-smarted and
out-politicked by their more ruthless adversaries.

When Asquith resumed his seat after telling the Commons of the
Government reorganisation, General Sir Ivor Herbert was on his

feet, urging that this was a good time 'to take stock of what we have got in the way of men, and of the manner in which they may be most usefully applied'. To this end he proposed the establishment of machinery preliminary to the introduction of compulsory service, including 'a census and registration of the whole male population, noting and verifying the capacity of each one'. He had many supporters. One after another Tory backbencher rose to put the case for conscription and national registration: the working classes would prefer 'universal service' to a voluntary system under which 'it is only the willing horse who goes, while the loafers and shirkers stay at home'; conscription was justified 'not only by the necessity of having more men . . . but on the better and higher ground of equality of service'. One enthusiast thought the Government should encourage individuals to go and raise private armies from among the South African Basutos. Another declared that the rich should make the supreme sacrifice, for King and Country, of abandoning the luxury of motor travel and sending their chauffeurs forthwith into the army. H. J. Tennant, Under-Secretary for War, replied in terms appropriate to a coalition of voluntarists and conscriptionists: compulsion was 'foreign to the British nation, to the British character and to the genius of our people', but (in a phrase of classic prevarication) 'I do not deny it may be possible that there may arise a time when such a policy may be desirable'.

The Cabinet Conservatives took up Herbert's proposal for a national registration scheme. So, too, did Northcliffe's newspapers, which were now pursuing a daily vendetta against Kitchener, blaming him not only for the shells 'scandal' but also for his resistence to Northcliffe's own repeated suggestion that he publicly declare, over and above the politicians' heads, a military need for conscription. On 8 June the Prime Minister, in answer to a Parliamentary question from Herbert, indicated that registration was 'receiving the careful consideration of the Government'. On 21 June, Tennant declared that registration was 'a not undesirable policy at all, as it may perfectly well keep the door of voluntarism open'. On 29 June the Government introduced its National Registration Bill.

The President of the Local Government Board, Walter Long, described it as 'a grand voluntary movement to secure knowledge of the forces which the country possesses'. Few believed him. The Bill was almost universally understood to be the first step to compulsion and that impression was not dispelled either by Long's explicit denial that it 'contains in some mysterious and concealed fashion the policy of conscription for the army', or by Asquith's own assurance that no action on conscription was contemplated. Sir Thomas Whittaker moved its rejection as a patent first move towards compulsion and Sir W. H. Cowan declared that that was precisely why he was supporting it.

The debates on the Bill, between its introduction and first reading on 29 June and the passing of the third reading on 8 July, were notable for major and contrasting speeches by Philip Snowden and Arthur Henderson which only too clearly underlined the critical division within the Labour movement and the Parliamentary Labour Party. Snowden denounced not only the Registration Bill but the Coalition Government itself, which he declared to have been engineered by Lord Northcliffe—'the man who destroyed the last Government and continues to dictate the policy of this Government'. The Bill fulfilled to the letter the demands made by Northcliffe in *The Times* and the *Daily Mail*. But, said Snowden, Northcliffe was not the Bill's only begetter. Lord Milner, chairman of the National Service League had boasted a few days earlier, at the League's annual dinner, that 'the most eloquent exponent of national service' (Curzon) was now in the Cabinet. He had gone on to urge members to work 'diplomatically', not for the full programme of the League but for such moves in that direction as the Registration Bill promised. 'This is a surrender by the Government to this agitation which has been going on outside the House for all these months', Snowden concluded, 'and the appetite grows by what it feeds on. They have succeeded in their first demand. This will not be the last. There is no doubt about it that if this Bill becomes an Act, and if this register be compiled, then at once a violent press agitation will be begun for the use of the material of this register for the purpose of enforcing compulsory military service.'

Henderson was angry at Snowden's bitterly phrased attack on the Government of which he had just become a member. 'We may have our opinion as to the reason of the change of Government, and the method by which that change was brought about,' he declared, but the Coalition should be given the chance to exercise its responsibilities. The Bill should be judged on its merits rather than on its parentage. Voluntary recruiting had been a splendid success, reflecting 'the highest possible credit upon our country, and especially upon the men who offered their lives in the first instance in order that they might serve their King and Country in the great and righteous cause we are prosecuting on foreign territory'. National Registration would 'enable us to obtain that very knowledge and information that we essentially need if we are going to complete the war on the voluntary principle'. Henderson's speech, and the line-up of the whole debate, provoked a Liberal MP, Mr R. C. Lambert, to the dazed observation that 'the Tory party seems to have adopted bureaucratic Socialism, and the Socialist party to some extent has joined hands with it'.

Snowden was right: 'The appetite grows by what it feeds on.' Less than three weeks after the National Registration Bill became law (by 259 votes to 161 on second reading) the conscriptionists prepared a further onslaught. On 28 July Asquith solemnly warned the Commons and the country that the war looked like becoming a contest of endurance. On the same afternoon Lloyd George, whose Shells Committee had now become a separate Ministry of Munitions, repeated his familiar warning of munitions shortages and made the industry's labour force his scapegoat. Captain Guest suggested that the two statements together made an excellent case for compulsory military service. Josiah Wedgwood agreed, and demanded a dynamic lead from the Prime Minister: 'In times of war you have got to sacrifice the individual to the community. You have got to have a dictator, if possible; a man who will direct. I do not care whether he takes risks or makes mistakes, but for God's sake give us a leader who will lead without fear of consequences.'

Tennant parried for the Government with the standard facing-both-ways formula: no necessity for altering the voluntary system had been demonstrated, but the door to conscription would not be closed.

When the results of the register were collated it was found that some 5,000,000 men of military age were not serving with the forces. Substracting those in vital occupations and the medically unfit, it was estimated that between 1,700,000 and 1,800,000 men available to serve had not volunteered. Efforts to bring them in were intensified. Women presented white feathers, symbols of cowardice, to men of enlistment age brazen enough to walk the streets in civilian clothing. Posters warned young fathers of the day that would surely come when their children would demand to know what they had done in the Great War. And in the music halls, representative wives and sweethearts sang 'We don't want to lose you—but we think you ought to go! . . .'

Recruiting committees, in defiance of War Office instructions not to mention conscription, bolstered their appeals to patriotism with threats of forthcoming compulsion. 'Volunteer—or be fetched' was their message. Illustrating this point, James Hogge, anti-conscription Liberal Member for East Edinburgh, read the following letter to the Commons on 5 July, written by a recruiting major to potential recruits:

> Dear Sir,—Unless you have some good and genuine reason for not enlisting, which I am agreeable to investigate, I advise you to offer to join the Army before you are made to. This is an entirely private and friendly piece of advice. Compulsion may not be so far off as you think. I am only waiting the word to call up every man of eligible age, and, as you see, I have you on my list. It is possible that you may be one of those to whom this advice does not apply—there are some such to whom this letter is unavoidably addressed—but if you are, I can only tell you that I have good reason to believe that you will be mightily sorry in the end if you wait until you are fetched. Not only that, but if it comes to fetching, those who are fetched will not be asked where they would like to go.—Yours truly, Major [name withheld], Recruiting Officer.

Continued Labour opposition to conscription was causing impatience among French Socialists, who feared that the 'pacifism' of British Labour was weakening the Allied cause. Accordingly, two Labour MPs, John Hodge and Adolphe Smith, spent the summer recess visiting French Socialist leaders, assuring them that Labour was giving energetic backing to the war and to voluntary recruitment and emphasising their conviction that 'the pacifist element was a very small moiety of the whole[5]'.

More important developments took place during the recess. Following national registration, Asquith gave way to pressures for the appointment of a Cabinet Committee to investigate the manpower situation and the financing of the war. In evidence to the committee, Kitchener, long under pressure from the conscriptionists, declared his opinion that only some form of compulsion would enable the army to maintain seventy full-strength divisions in the field, his minimum requirement. He favoured a ballot scheme, a modern version of the old Militia Ballot which Sir Henry Campbell-Bannerman had dismissed 'as conscription tempered by the roulette-table'. Kitchener, who liked to see himself as above politics, declared himself angry at the party strife on the conscription issue. He had intended, he said (according to Lloyd George in his *War Memoirs*) 'to choose his own time for rushing it on the country as a non-party measure of military emergency'.

Lloyd George also gave detailed evidence to the Committee. He submitted that his own Ministry of Munitions had succeeded in ending the shortage of shells and small arms. It was no longer true that Britain had more forces in the field than she had the capacity to arm—indeed, the reverse situation was beginning to apply. It was time to introduce conscription on the French model. Every able-bodied man should be made liable to serve. 'With this general and basic authority', he advised, 'you could work the rest all right[6].'

On 2 September, the committee issued its report. It declared (1) that one hundred rather than seventy divisions should be the target, (2) that the men were available, and (3) that they could not be obtained by the voluntary system. Recruiting, said the report, had dropped to 80,000 a month. Even that figure could only be maintained 'by repeated canvassing of individuals, by every form of social, and in some cases of economic pressure upon all classes of men (except munition workers) from seventeen to forty-five whether married or single, whether usefully employed or not, and whether or not they can be spared from their trade or district'.

On 15 September, when Parliament resumed, Asquith moved the seventh vote of credit for the war, bringing the total war budget to date to £900,000,000. The army was absorbing £2,000,000 a day and the navy £600,000. What had little more than a year earlier seemed an adequate force of 150,000 men had risen to just short of 3,000,000. But casualties already totalled more than 380,000, and the war front was widening. Recruiting, the Prime Minister added, without revealing the content of the Cabinet Committee's report, was dropping.

The National Service League made a telling contribution of its own to coincide with the recall of Parliament. It issued a statement, published prominently in all the daily newspapers, bearing the signatures of thirty MPs and twenty-two Peers, all of whom were on active service. More signatures were promised.

> We, the undersigned, [it read] being at the moment engaged in the service of our King and Country on sea or on land, are of the opinion that the time has come when every fit man, whatever his position in life, must be made available, as and when his country calls him, for the fighting line, or, if sufficiently qualified, for National Service at home.

Both the timing and the content of the statement suggested inside knowledge of the divisions in the Cabinet which had opened—or reopened—on presentation of the Cabinet Committee's report. The opponents of conscription were arguing, with a touch of desperation, that conscription was impracticable because volunteers would refuse to share the trenches with conscripts: 'While a separation of conscript and volunteer armies was unworkable their mingling would be disastrous.' The League's statement was a forceful answer to that argument. Lord Curzon also declared that his own investigations in the field showed a strong resentment among volunteers that men at home had not been conscripted, and Lloyd George subsequently wrote in his *War Memoirs* that 'the army in the field felt strongly that those at home who would not come out otherwise should be fetched'.

Although the Cabinet Committee's report was not published it was an open secret that the Cabinet was acutely divided. Northcliffe's *Times* represented the division as one of drift versus action. Said a leader on 18 September:

> The true line of division, in so far as it is yet possible to classify public men, lies between those who cling, often half unconsciously, to the old Parliamentary game of vanishing party politics and those who see clearly that nothing matters in these days except to beat the Germans. In this division the question of national service is only one factor. Great efforts will certainly be made, and are already being made, to represent it as the apple of discord in a harmonious Cabinet. But the truth is that the divergence of opinion among politicians, which is doubtless reflected in the Cabinet itself, covers a very much broader ground. It is the divergence in effect between the policy of

drift and the policy of action, the policy of hoping for the best and the policy of ensuring it, the policy of always being too late and the policy of looking ahead in time.

Northcliffe's own propagandising on behalf of conscription was bitterly attacked by the Irish MP, John Dillon. The proprietor of *The Times* and the *Daily Mail* had 'done all in his power to obstruct the voluntary system', refusing to publish Kitchener's recruiting calls, ridiculing the work of the recruiting sergeants and 'inciting men to refuse to enlist until they are fetched'. 'Many men in Ireland', Dillon added, 'have been sent to jail for less than Lord Northcliffe has done. Many newspapers in Ireland have been suppressed without protest from us for less than the *Daily Mail* has done . . . If it were not for the connections and power of Lord Northcliffe he would have been in jail long ago[7].'

The League and Northcliffe together were always powerful advocates, but the single most important factor in swinging public opinion towards conscription in the latter half of 1916 was the public advocacy of David Lloyd George. A host of historians and biographers, notably Beaverbrook in *Politicians and the War*, have described the transformation of Lloyd George from the social reformer who had risked his political career and even his neck by denouncing the Boer War, and who had thought seriously in that last week of July 1914 of opposing Britain's entry into the Great War —the transformation of this champion of radical dissent into the man who first galvanised the munitions industries into double production, then pleaded with the tongue of angels for universal conscription, and finally ousted his former leader and assumed aggressive, militant autocratic control of Britain at war. As we have seen, Lloyd George had favoured a compulsory system for some time. But it was not until the late summer of 1915 that he felt it politically expedient to direct almost his entire public energies towards this end. Lloyd George irrevocably cast his lot with the conscriptionists that September. He did so because he had become certain they would win.

* * *

The TUC met that same September. Although large majorities were registered for resolutions which in effect endorsed the Government's war policy, a rash of resolutions urging resistance to conscription were also on the agenda. Many were in terms which threatened to commit the TUC to a major battle with a Government in which Labour was represented. The TUC Parliamentary Committee resolved the situation by submitting its own resolution, carefully worded to combine the maximum of opposition to conscription with the minimum commitment to action. It was passed unanimously.

> We, the delegates to this Congress, [it said] representing nearly three million organised workers, record our hearty appreciation of the magnificent response made to the call for volunteers to fight against the tyranny of militarism.
>
> We emphatically protest against the sinister efforts of a section of the reactionary press in formulating newspaper policies for party purposes and attempting to foist on this country conscription, which always proves a burden to the workers, and will divide the nation at a time when absolute unanimity is essential.
>
> No reliable evidence has been produced to show that the voluntary system of enlistment is not adequate to meet all the Empire's requirements.
>
> We believe that all the men necessary can, and will, be obtained through a voluntary system properly organised, and we heartily support and will give every aid to the Government in their present efforts to secure the men necessary to prosecute the war to a successful issue.

On 28 September Asquith pleaded for an end to the conscription controversy as the whole question was receiving the careful and anxious consideration of the Government. A full statement of intent was promised in the immediate future. On the same day a secret Labour conference of MPs and trade union leaders was addressed by both Asquith and Kitchener. The Secretary for War put forward his arguments for conscription by ballot. The Prime Minister left many of his hearers with the impression that he planned to resign if conscription were decisively carried within the Cabinet.

The real purpose of the conference, however, was to explore means of giving effect to the TUC's resolution against conscription. The outcome was a 'Socialist National Defence Committee', with C. W. Bowerman, MP for Deptford, as secretary and Henderson as a consultative member. The committee seems to have become immersed immediately in a struggle between doves and hawks, and when its manifesto was published on 6 October it was clear the hawks had won:

Fellow-countrymen!—Never, in our thousand years history, has this country been in such deadly peril. But for the pluck and public spirit of the men who have volunteered for our defence the fate of Britain would be the fate of Belgium, of Poland, of Armenia. To the Army we owe our lives, the honour of our women, the safety and sanctity of our homes. To defend the Motherland tens of thousands have died, and many more have escaped death only at the cost of wounds or disablement.

Britons! The places of those heroes must be filled. We cannot, we dare not, leave those who are fighting for us without adequate reinforcements. At least half a million more men are wanted immediately to strengthen the forces of our fellow-countrymen in France, Belgium, Gallipoli, Mesopotamia, or to take the place of those on garrison duty, at home, in India, or elsewhere.

There are hundreds of thousands of young, vigorous and capable men who can be spared for this glorious duty, who are still not in khaki. If they hesitate any longer they will be for ever shamed. If they refuse to respond to their country's call, the nation must and will claim them on other terms.

Fellow-countrymen! There cannot be rights without duties. Freedom cannot exist where men are not prepared to defend it. The defence of the country is the elemental duty of every capable citizen. Where the country calls all must respond. It is not contrary to the principles of democracy, not out of harmony with the bases of trades unionism, to enforce on all citizens that national solidarity implied in the duty of national defence. The men who shrink now will assuredly be compelled to play the game or be treated as national blacklegs . . .

Fellow-citizens! The Government's silence is ambiguous, mischievous, and dangerous. Let them speak out. Let them permit Lord Kitchener to speak. Let us know where we are and what we have to do. The British people will answer the call. Britain half-armed and using half her strength cannot conquer Germany, which has mobilised the entire nation for the struggle. National service is not only a duty but a right.

So much for a TUC resolution unanimously opposing conscription!

The Cabinet resolved its divisions by agreeing on a final test for the voluntary system. Lord Derby was commissioned to plan and direct a new recruiting drive, making use of the returns on the national register. The voluntarists congratulated themselves on having won an eleventh-hour reprieve. The conscriptionists had more foresight. They knew that the Derby Scheme must fail, as earlier high-pressure schemes had failed, to bring in all available men; and they knew that so long as a substantial body of young men in inessential occupations avoided military service the case for compulsion would win converts. They also held the trump card: Lord Derby himself, now cast in the public role of the last hope of voluntarism, was a declared conscriptionist. As far back as 1901, even before publication of Shee's *The Briton's First Duty* or the birth of the National Service League, Derby (then Lord Stanley, Financial Secretary to the War Office), had written:

> Conscription may be a nasty pill for some to swallow; but what is in a name? Let us call it universal service . . . Let us ask our fellow-countrymen . . . to be ready at all times and in all places to guard and defend the national flag.[8]

National registration had resulted in a scheme of categorisation supervised by a committee under the chairmanship of Lord Lansdowne. Men of enlistment age were grouped according to a Board of Trade assessment of their usefulness and availability. Into Group 1 went those in essential civilian occupations. Group 2 consisted of men in trades and occupations from which 'a few' could be spared. Into Group 3 went those in trades from which 'a large proportion' could be spared. Group 4 consisted of the 'unstarred' men—those in 'unnecessary' occupations, virtually all of whom could be spared.

Under the Derby Scheme, recruiting officers made a personal canvass of all men of enlistment age. They were pressed to 'attest' their willingness to join the army when called upon to do so, and to signify the sincerity of their attestation by taking the military oath. Those who attested were to be called up age-group by age-group, the single men first and the married thereafter. All who took the military oath were presented with commemorative arm-bands. To

give the scheme a royal send-off, the King published a special appeal
'To My People'.

Tribunals were hurriedly set up in each locality to hear applications for exemption from attestation, or requests for transfer from
one Group to another. Such applications could be made only by
employers on behalf of their employees. The employer was required
to convince the Tribunal that the man for whom exemption was
pleaded was 'individually indispensable'; that every effort had been
made to replace him with a man over enlistment age, or a woman;
that the man's work was itself of 'national importance', and that the
employer had granted all reasonable facilities for enlistment.

On 2 November the Prime Minister, explaining the working of
the scheme, stated his own position thus: he had no principled
objection to conscription, but it would only be resorted to if there
were 'something in the nature, I will not say of universal, but of
general consent', and if Lord Derby's scheme, the last fling of what
was still quaintly called voluntarism, failed. He promised a full
evaluation of the scheme as soon as it closed, on 30 November. On
the basis of that evaluation the Cabinet would decide the future basis
of recruitment. Asquith went on to give a pledge which the conscriptionists were to seize on joyfully and make the central plank of
their final attack. 'I am told by Lord Derby and others,' said the
Prime Minister, 'that there is some doubt among married men who
are now being asked to enlist, whether, having enlisted, or promised
to enlist, they may not be called upon to serve while younger and
unmarried men are holding back, and not doing their duty. Let them
at once disabuse themselves of that notion. So far as I am concerned
I should certainly say the obligation of the married man to serve
ought not to be enforced or held to be binding upon him unless and
until—I hope by voluntary effort, if it be needed in the last resort,
as I have explained, by other means—the unmarried men are dealt
with.'

This declaration, with its explicit threat that conscription would
be resorted to if the Derby Scheme failed to bring in the requisite
numbers, was just what the War Office and its recruiting officers
had been angling for. They were now able to tell potential recruits
openly what for weeks they had been saying unofficially: 'If you
don't join voluntarily now you'll be fetched in a month or two.' On
13 November, in a speech at Bristol, Walter Long, President of the

Local Government Board, warned: 'Single men may be perfectly certain that if they fail today, at this hour of their country's need, they will be called upon compulsorily to take their place in the ranks. These young men will be sent to the trenches, and if they survive the trenches they will have something to think about for the rest of their lives.' Two days later an advertisement in the *Glasgow Herald* warned, under the royal arms: 'Enlist before 30 November. If you do not, the Prime Minister has pledged himself and his Government that compulsory means will be taken.'

Asquith's speech was dissected and analysed by all parties, and both conscriptionist and non-conscriptionist professed to find in it some support for his own view. But the uncertainty was not to last long. On 11 November Lord Derby circulated a statement to the press:

> Lord Derby is authorised by the Prime Minister to express his surprise that his statement in the House of Commons of 2 November should be considered in any way ambiguous.
>
> The Prime Minister on that occasion pledged not only himself but his Government when he stated that if young men do not, under the stress of national duty, come forward voluntarily, other and compulsory means would be taken before the married men were called upon to fulfil their engagement to serve.
>
> Lord Derby is further authorised to state definitely that if young men medically fit and not indispensable to any business of national importance, or to any business conducted for the general good of the community, do not come forward voluntarily before 30 November, the Government will, after that date, take the necessary steps to redeem the pledge made on 2 November.
>
> It must be clearly understood that no marriage contracted after the registration day (15 August) will entitle any man to be relegated to the married groups.

Thereafter the most insistent demand of the conscriptionists was, quite simply, that the Prime Minister's pledge be redeemed—with the corollary that the only way to redeem it was to conscript the unmarried men.

Derby completed his report and handed it to the Prime Minister on 20 December. Predictably, it showed that the married men, secure in their assurance that they would not be required to make good their attestation until the single men had been winkled out, had attested in reasonable numbers, while the single men had held back. The net result deducible from Derby's mass of statistics was that the Scheme had made available another 340,000 men out of a total potential of 2,200,000.

The following day, 21 December, Asquith requested Parliamentary authorisation for an additional number of land forces to the tune of one million men. He did not at this stage reveal Derby's figures, which he said he had only had time to glance at the previous evening. His aim, he declared, was to get 'potentially every man, of military age and capacity, not disqualified by physical or domestic conditions, who is available, consistent with making an adequate provision for our other national necessities'.

The Christmas recess began with news that British casualties totalled 528,227 killed, missing or wounded—about a third of them killed or missing. The 'wastage' of men at the front was running at 15 per cent per month.

On 22 December the Home Secretary, Sir John Simon, turned down an appeal from Philip Snowden for remission of sentences of six months hard labour passed on Thomas Ferris and Sydney Overbury of Leeds, prosecuted under the Defence of the Realm Act for publishing a leaflet opposing conscription and the war. This was Sir John's last public act as Home Secretary. On 27 December the Cabinet met for two hours in the morning and adjourned until the following day. On 28 December it agreed the terms of a Military Service Bill to be presented after the recess. Simon resigned in protest, and the public was given its clearest intimation yet of the Government's intention.

On 5 January 1916, Asquith introduced the first Military Service Bill, imposing conscription as from 2 March on all single male subjects between eighteen and forty-one, exempting those employed in civil work of national importance, those who could show they were the sole support of their dependents, the unfit, and those who could show a conscientious objection. Local Tribunals on the Derby Scheme pattern were to be constituted to hear applications for exemption, then Appeal Tribunals, and finally a Central Appeal Tribunal for special cases. The Local and Appeal Tribunals were to sit in public, the Central Tribunal in private. There was a right of appeal from the Local to the Appeal Tribunal in all cases, but appeal could be made to the Central Tribunal only by leave of the Appeal Tribunal.

Asquith quoted the figures made available in the Derby report. He then said: 'Speaking for myself at the moment—for myself alone —as I have said, I do not propose on this larger issue to speak for all my colleagues—I am of the opinion that, in view of the results of Lord Derby's campaign, no case has been made out for general compulsion. I, at any rate, would be no party to any measure which had that for its object. The Bill that I am about to ask leave to introduce is one, I think, which can be sincerely supported by those who, either on principle, or, as in my own case, on grounds of expediency, are opposed to what is commonly described as conscription. This Bill is confined to a specific purpose—the redemption of a promise publicly given by me in this House in the early days of Lord Derby's campaign.'

Sir John Simon led the opposition to the Bill, reminding the Prime Minister that if he had given one pledge to married men he had given an equally binding pledge on 2 November that the Cabinet would not seek to resort to compulsion unless there was general consent in the country. And there was no such consent. 'Does anyone really suppose,' he asked, 'that once the principle of compulsion has been conceded you are going to stop here?'

Philip Snowden put the view of the anti-conscription Labour Members during the debate on the second reading, on 12 January. The record of the Government was such that it could not be trusted. The Prime Minister had pledged that the National Registration Act was not a prelude to conscription. The Bill was a surrender to the conscriptionist members of the Cabinet, to a conspiracy that had been going on for months. There was no guarantee that it would not be the prelude to general conscription. 'If the Minister of Munitions were to succeed the present Prime Minister, should we be assured against a measure of general conscription?' This Bill could permanently fasten compulsory service on Britain, for the duration of the war and after, which is what the conscriptionist leaders wanted.

Arthur Henderson followed, declaring himself 'a convinced and ardent supporter of the voluntary principle'. But he supported the Bill. Compulsion in this 'modified form' did not violate any principle to which he was attached, nor did it menace industrial freedom. 'For over thirty years I have been connected with trade unionism. During the whole of that time I have been associated with those who have never hesitated to apply compulsion. Wherever they thought the welfare of the State, or the welfare of a single class, or the welfare of a trade demanded it, they were ready to use this instrument. I have voted . . . to enforce temperance reform by legislation. We have all advocated compulsion to secure the extension of trade unionism, and many of us have advocated measures of the most drastic social reorganisation—measures which could only be enforced by compulsion on the largest and widest possible system. If we have done this to improve the health of the people, to regulate their social habits, to break down the barriers of class, to equalise the distribution of wealth, surely we cannot object to do it to save the nation, and not this nation alone, but the little nations to whom we are pledged, who know that nothing but our victory can save them from foreign domination . . . Those who fear that compulsion will remain after the war are those who have no faith in our victory. This war is to end in peace, and not in any long-drawn cycle of armaments and counter-armaments, suspicion, aggression and revenge.'

On 17 January the Bill went to the House in Committee for clause by clause ratification and amendment. One addition had already been secured by Quaker Members T. Edmund Harvey and Arnold S. Rowntree in private session with Asquith, providing that 'any certificate of exemption may be absolute, conditional or temporary, as the authority by whom it was granted think best suited to the case, *and also, in the case of exemption on conscience grounds, may take the form of an exemption from combatant service only, or may be conditional on the applicant being engaged on some work which in the opinion of the Tribunal dealing with the case is of national importance.*' The glaring ambiguities of this clause were to be responsible for a great deal of trouble and suffering a few months later.

Philip Snowden moved an additional clause to safeguard the persistent objector from the death penalty under the Army Act, Section XII (1). Sir F. E. Smith declared that the War Office would not inflict the death penalty in such cases, but when Snowden pointed out that the danger lay with men not admitted as genuine by their Tribunals and therefore not legally recognised as conscientious objectors, the clause was allowed. But again, as will be seen, the wording was not precise enough to prevent conflicting interpretations by the War Office and by the objectors' organisations.

Joynson Hicks proposed that exemption be granted only to Quakers and members of religious bodies which included an objection to all war among their fundamental tenets. Deriding what he called the 'Slackers' Charter', he further proposed that exemption be withheld from men who had joined such bodies since 15 August 1914, immediately after the outbreak of war. The clause was subsequently withdrawn.

George Barnes, despite his support of the Bill, urged that absolute exemption should be granted to Socialist as well as religious objectors. Charles Trevelyan warned that 'many thousands' would refuse any connection with war, and proposed complete exemption, not subject to any Tribunal's view. R. L. Outhwaite, Liberal Member for Hanley, also voiced the fear that Socialists would not be properly treated by Tribunals, and brought forward an amendment to allow exemption to a claimant who made a statement of his conscientious objection on oath before two Justices of the Peace. The amendment was supported by Snowden, who criticised the working of the Tribunals under the Derby Scheme, alluded to the Australian and New Zealand prisons 'filled with conscientious objectors rejected by Tribunals[9]', pointed out that opposition had obstructed the working of the Munitions Act in South Wales and had prevented the application of conscription to Ireland, and warned that total opposition would be forthcoming from the 'ten thousand members of the No-Conscription Fellowship'.

The new Home Secretary, Herbert Samuel, made a speech on which conscientious objectors at first built a great deal of hope. He claimed that a bootmaker, for example, who claimed under Subsection 1(a) of the Act that his trade was so necessary as itself to carry exemption, but failed in that plea, would, if he were a conscientious objector, have his calling accepted and obtain exemption on it. When this apparent ruling was subsequently put to the Tribunals it was almost invariably ignored.

The Bill's first reading was passed on 6 January by 403 to 105. By 12 January, with the abstention of the Irish Nationalists on the exclusion of Ireland from the Bill, the opposition had shrunk to 39 (41 with two tellers) on the second reading. And only 36 (plus two tellers) opposed the third reading on 24 January. The seven ILP

MPs all opposed the Bill. Of the full Parliamentary Labour Party, including the ILP, 15 opposed it[10] and 16 supported it[11] (including the three Labour members of the Government). Several Liberals swung to the Government after opposing it on the first reading. Of the persistent opponents, four—Joseph King, Arthur Ponsonby, Richard Lambert and Charles Trevelyan—were associated with the Union of Democratic Control, and four—J. Allen Baker, T. E. Harvey, Arnold S. Rowntree and J. W. Wilson—with the Society of Friends. A further group sat as Independent Liberals in opposition to the Coalition: Dr C. Addison, Sydney Arnold, John Burns, Sir W. P. Byles, H. G. Chancellor, W. Clough, A. G. C. Harvey, J. M. Hogge, R. D. Holt, Edward T. John, Leif Jones, B. Kenyon, Sir E. H. Lamb, D. M. Mason, R. L. Outhwaite, Arthur Sherwell and J. H. Whitehouse. Sir John Simon also carried his opposition into the divisions. Some of these, notably G. J. Wardle and Will Thorne in the Labour Party, and Dr C. Addison from the Independent Liberals, later went over to the Government position.

On 25 January the Bill had its second reading in the Lords, where Lord Courtney of Penwith moved to alter 'objection to the undertaking of combatant service' to 'objection to undertake any service or engage in any action in support of the war, or to the undertaking of combatant service'. The Bishop of London opposed the amendment, declaring that conscience was of little consequence until it was 'educated'. The Government refused to accept the amendment and it was not pushed to a division. The debate closed with what proved to be an empty assurance from Lord Lansdowne that the Government wished to enable the Tribunals to give absolute exemption where necessary. On 27 January 1916, the Bill received the Royal Assent and became the law of the land.

* * *

Asquith's principle defence of the conscription of the unmarried was that it was necessary to safeguard the married men. He quoted the ballad in which Henry V, on the eve of Agincourt, instructs his 'Lord Derby':

> Go 'cruit me Cheshire and Lancashire
> And Derby hills that are so free;
> No married man or widow's son—
> No widow's curse shall go with me.

But no sooner were the unmarried men safely gathered in than a clamour began for general conscription. The married men who had attested pleaded that before they were called up the single men in essential work should be taken and the resultant vacancies filled by the married. The single men, for their part, resented what they saw as discrimination against them. Each group became the fanatical advocates of the conscription of the other. Within a matter of weeks demands for universal compulsion were being made in all quarters, outside and inside the Cabinet.

Asquith had specifically denied the need for general conscription. But Simon and Snowden had forecast that it would quickly follow once the principle had been yielded. They were right. On 6 April Asquith promised an announcement on the 18th. On the 18th he had to confess that the Cabinet was deeply divided, and the statement was postponed to the following day. By then the disagreements were still unresolved, and Asquith committed himself to the observation that if agreement proved impossible 'the result must be the break-up of the Cabinet'.

So strong was the tide now running for general compulsion that when the Government did announce on 27 April certain limited extensions of the first Act the Commons refused to look at its half-measures. So on 3 May, after secret sessions of both Houses—rare, even in wartime—the Government introduced a Military Service (General Compulsion) Bill.

Lloyd George was its inspiration and architect.

> Is it inconsistent [he asked] with the principles of democracy that the State should demand the services and help of every man to defend its life when it is at stake? There never yet has been a country faced with a great military peril that has ever saved itself without resort to compulsion. Never! It is true of autocracy, it is even more true of democracy. Every healthy body has demanded the help of its members to defend itself. Thank God Britain is not a paralytic that cannot command the services of every citizen.
>
> Where is the principle? I have a personal interest in finding it out, for I have been told that I am a traitor to Liberal principles because I supported conscription. I cannot find it.

To which William Pringle, delineating the schism which was to break the Liberal Party, replied with bitter irony:

We have been worshipping false gods! We have been living in Egyptian darkness in regard to this! It is not until now that this new Moses has come to lead us to the promised land that we have found out the true secret of Liberalism and democracy! Why, the contention is beneath contempt.

The Bill was again supported by Henderson, who represented it as a choice between conscription and a German victory. The hard core of thirty-six opposed its second reading. On 25 May it received the Royal Assent, and Sir William Robertson, Chief of the Imperial General Staff, wrote gratefully to Lloyd George: 'For this Bill the Empire's thanks are due to you—alone.'

Even this measure of general compulsion by no means satisfied the dedicated conscriptionists. By December 1916 Lloyd George had succeeded in his long intrigue to oust Asquith and take his place at the head of a Coalition pledged to a 'fight to the finish'. A new National Service Scheme, later re-organised under a separate Ministry of National Service, sought out volunteers from among the unfit and ineligible to take the places of men fit for military service but hitherto exempted on occupational grounds. In April 1917 a Military Service (Review of Exceptions) Act was passed, by which the Government sought a further million men by drastically tightening up the provisions concerning occupational exemptions, and by reviewing such exemptions already given by the Tribunals.

Three months later a further Act was passed which made certain categories of alien resident in Britain liable for service or alternatively subject to deportation to their country of origin. This raised acute problems for the large number of Russians in Britain, most of whom were political refugees from the Tsar. Several hundred of the 30,000 Russians of military age had active Bolshevik or Menshevik revolutionary connections and were opposed to the war. One of the organisers of a No-Conscription Fellowship branch among these exiled revolutionaries was George Tchitcherine, who was arrested and interned in Brixton Jail for five months before being deported to Russia. By the time he arrived in Moscow the Russian Revolution had taken place, and Tchitcherine graduated almost straight from Brixton Jail to the office of Foreign Minister.

A further Act in January 1918 gave almost total powers to the Director-General of National Service to cancel occupational exemptions, but not exemptions given on conscience grounds. Finally, a Bill was introduced by Lloyd George in April raising the upper age limit to fifty-one and making provision for further raising it to fifty-six in the event of national emergency. Provision was also made for executive cancellation of all exemptions, including those to conscientious objectors, and for conscription of the clergy for non-combatant duties—to which the Church could hardly object with much moral conviction, since nine out of ten pulpits had for four years been turned into high-pressure recruiting platforms. Most controversial of all, however, was the Act's provision for extending conscription to Ireland in return for an early Home Rule Bill.

Among those who opposed this last Act were Asquith and Henderson, now out of the coalition. Both urged that the extension of conscription to Ireland would be unenforceable, and they were right. The Irish Church denounced the Bill and openly preached non-cooperation. Eamonn De Valera penned an historical appeal to the United States to speak out against 'one of the greatest crimes ever committed by a strong nation upon a weak . . . introduced by a Government that has ceased to enjoy the confidence of the people, but which the exigencies of war make it inexpedient to remove; passed by a Parliament that has long outrun its course, and has long ceased to be representative of public opinion; . . . enacted for Ireland by an alien assembly in which Irish representatives are utterly powerless to protect Irish nationals.' De Valera was arrested and interned before his appeal was finished, but Irish opinion was not to be silenced so easily. The Government was forced to withdraw this part of its intentions, and withdrew also its bribe of early Home Rule. As T. P. O'Connor told the Commons a year later, on 3 April 1919, Lloyd George 'did not add one Irishman to the British Army by his Conscription Act. He stopped recruiting altogether for the Army, but he did the work of recruiting for the Sinn Feiners. He sent tens of thousands of men who were wavering into the revolutionary camp, and he gave the last and deadliest blow to the constitutional movement.'

With the exception of the Irish clause, to which there were 116 opponents in the House of Commons, the anti-war party in Parliament put up only token resistance to the extensions of the first two Military Service Acts. 'Once the principle and practice of conscription had been accepted by Parliament,' wrote Philip Snowden

THE PRIME MINISTER'S PLEDGE

To Married Men is now being redeemed by Parliament. But let the young unmarried men themselves redeem that Pledge by joining under the Group System **TO-DAY.**

DO NOT FORCE YOUR COUNTRY TO FORCE YOU TO FIGHT, BUT COME OF YOUR OWN FREE WILL

MILITARY SERVICE ACT 1916

EVERY UNMARRIED MAN of MILITARY AGE

Not excepted or exempted under this Act

CAN CHOOSE ONE OF TWO COURSES:

(1) He can ENLIST AT ONCE and join the Colours without delay:

(2) He can ATTEST AT ONCE UNDER THE GROUP SYSTEM and be called up in due course with his Group.

If he does neither, a third course awaits him

HE WILL BE DEEMED TO HAVE ENLISTED

under the Military Service Act

ON THURSDAY, MARCH 2nd, 1916.

HE WILL BE PLACED IN THE RESERVE, AND BE CALLED UP IN HIS CLASS, as the Military Authorities may determine.

Top left: The last appeal for volunteers before the death of the voluntary system. *Top right:* Two choices; join up or be fetched. The Military Service Act explained in a War Office poster. *Below:* Platform party at the N-CF National Convention, Memorial Hall, London, November 1915: Clifford Allen is standing and on his right is Aylmer Rose. Seated on his left are Fenner Brockway, C. H. Norman, and Sutherland Campbell.

Repeal the Act

FELLOW CITIZENS,

Conscription is now law in this country of free traditions. Our hard-won liberties have been violated. Conscription means the desecration of principles that we have long held dear; it involves the subordination of civil liberties to military dictation; it imperils the freedom of individual conscience and establishes in our midst that militarism which menaces all social progress and divides the peoples of all nations.

We re-affirm our determined resistance to all that is established by the Act

We cannot assist in warfare. War, which to us is wrong. War, which the peoples do not seek, will only be made impossible when men, who so believe, remain steadfast to their convictions.

Conscience, it is true, has been recognised in the Act, but it has been placed at the mercy of tribunals. We are prepared to answer for our faith before any tribunal, but we cannot accept any exemption that would compel those who hate war to kill by proxy or set them to tasks which would help in the furtherance of war.

We strongly condemn the monstrous assumption by Parliament that a man is "deemed" to be bound by an oath that he has never taken and forced under an authority he will never acknowledge to perform acts which outrage his deepest convictions.

It is true that the present Act applies only to a small section of the community, but a great tradition has been sacrificed. Already there is a clamour for the extension of the Act. Admit the principle, and who can stay the march of militarism?

Repeal the Act. That is your only safeguard

If this be not done, militarism will fasten its iron grip upon our national life and institutions. There will be imposed upon us the very system which our statesmen affirm that they set out to overthrow

What shall it profit the nation if it shall win the war and lose its own soul?

Signed on behalf of the No-Conscription Fellowship:

CLIFFORD ALLEN, Chairman.
EDWARD GRUBB, Hon. Treasurer.
A. FENNER BROCKWAY, Hon. Secretary.
W. J. CHAMBERLAIN, Hon. Organiser.

W. H. AYLES,	MORGAN JONES,	
A. BARRATT BROWN,	C. H. NORMAN,	} Committee
JOHN P. FLETCHER,	LEYTON RICHARDS (Rev.),	

8, Merton House, Salisbury Court, Fleet St., London, E.C.

LONDON : AT THE NATIONAL LABOUR PRESS LTD. : ALSO AT MANCHESTER.

A leaflet that meant prison for its signatories.

in his *Autobiography*, 'there was no logical ground for opposition to its extension to all classes of men within the age limit. The extension of conscription to all classes was likely to advance the movement for peace by negotiations, which by this time had achieved considerable force in the country.' Of the legislation raising the call-up age to fifty-one, Snowden added: 'We offered practically no opposition to this measure on the ground that conscription having been accepted, if the men were really needed for the effective prosecution of the war, no reasonable argument could be advanced against recruiting able-bodied men up to fifty-one, most of whom up to that time had confined their practical support of the war to "killing the Germans with their tongues". I even went so far as to suggest rather ironically to the House of Commons that recruiting had begun at the wrong end. As the old men had made the war they ought to have been the first to be called upon to fight it, and I suggested that recruiting might have begun by taking the old men of eighty and gradually working down the age scale as men were required.'

REFERENCES

1 Denis Hayes, *Conscription Conflict*, 1949
2 Parliamentary Report (Hansard), Commons, 6 March 1902
3 *National Defence*, March 1909
4 Quoted without source by Denis Hayes, *op cit*
5 Report by Hodge and Smith to the Parliamentary Labour Party, October 1915
6 David Lloyd George, *War Memoirs*, 1938
7 Parliamentary Report (Hansard), Commons, 15 September 1915
8 Article in the *Bloemfontein Friend*, quoted by Denis Hayes, *op cit*
9 Australia in particular was something of an embarrassment to British conscriptionists. Popular referenda on conscription showed a majority against any such measure, and the Government compromised by resorting to compulsion for home service only, with conscripts debarred from active service overseas. This was a particularly bitter blow to the National Service League, which had boasted of its success in pushing the Governor-General into introducing national service in 1911. Now, appropriately enough, the Australian experience had a boomerang effect on conscriptionists. Lloyd George, in his *War Memoirs*, was compelled to

explain away Australia's failure thus: "Australia, in no wise behind them (the rest of the Empire) in loyalty, valour and pugnacity, somehow failed to carry a repeated referendum for this purpose, as the issue got mixed up with political and personal feuds with which the Commonwealth was rent". The full story is told in *The Story of Conscription in Australia*, by Leslie Jauncey, London, 1935.

10 W. Abraham, W. Adamson, W. C. Anderson, J. R. Clynes, F. W. Goldstone, W. Hudson, F. W. Jowett, J. R. Macdonald, J. Parker, T. Richards, T. Richardson, P. Snowden, J. H. Thomas, W. Thorne and G. J. Wardle.

11 G. N. Barnes, C. W. Bowerman, W. Brace, W. Crooks, C. Duncan, F. Hall, A. Henderson, J. Hodge, J. O'Grady, G. H. Roberts, J. E. Sutton, J. W. Taylor, R. Toothill, S. Walsh, A. Wilkie, W. T. Wilson.

Chapter IV

Against Conscription

THE British Labour movement had been throwing its weight against conscriptionist arguments with almost ponderous predictability since the early years of the century. The ILP wing of the Labour Party had done battle with the continental Marxist concept of Citizen's Armies, and had identified itself, in mood if not in hardline policy terms, with the pacifist sentiments of its founder, Keir Hardie. The trade union wing was more sensitive to the threat of industrial than military conscription, and opposed the one largely because it saw it as a back door approach to the other. Hardie had summarised the Socialist objection to conscription in a foreword to an ILP pamphlet, *A Case Against Conscription*, published in April 1913.

> All forms of militarism [he wrote] belong to the past. It comes down to us as a relic of the days when kings and nobles ruled as well as reigned, and when the workers were voteless, voiceless serfs. Militarism and Democracy cannot be blended. The workers of the world have nothing to fight each other about; they belong to a Common Caste; they have no country to fight each other about; they have no country. Patriotism is for them a term of no meaning. It connotes nothing to which they can link themselves. If it means defence of home, hearth and freedom, then Capitalism is the enemy which is menacing these, and Capitalism knows nothing of patriotism or nationality.
>
> South Wales mineowners supply the Germany Navy with coal to strengthen its power when it begins the invasion of Great Britain, and German manufacturers will supply France with guns wherewith to defeat the German Army. Capitalism, be it repeated, knows no country, has no patriotism. Militarism strengthens capitalism by perpetuating the fiction that there must be enmity and animosity

between nations. International social democracy says no—that the interest of all workers of all countries are identical—and demands co-operation and not war, fraternity, not military rivalry . . .

Compulsory military service is the negation of democracy. It compels the youth of the country, under penalty of fine and imprisonment, to learn the art of war. That is despotism, not democracy. No liberty-loving people will tolerate having these old forms of servitude forced upon them. Conscription is the badge of the slave.

This is what ILP activists believed. Other parts of the Labour Party coalition were for the most part prepared quietly to acquiesce in its Left Wing's sentiments. But the reality of war left no room for passive acquiescence, and the Labour leadership's decision to support the war soon made its opposition to conscription difficult to carry through with any consistency or conviction. True, it made the attempt. Henderson justified Labour participation in the recruiting campaign as the only practical alternative to conscription, and so did the TUC in its recruiting manifesto of September 1914. But active agitation against compulsion was largely left to the ILP. Its annual conference at Norwich on 3–6 April condemned by 243 votes to 6 the Labour Party's participation in the recruiting drive. Three months later, meeting at Keswick in July, the National Administrative Council of the ILP reaffirmed its opposition to conscription and called upon party members to resist its imposition. 'While recognising the right of every individual member to act as his or her conscience dictates', ran the resolution, 'the NAC will do all in its power to defend those members who individually refuse to submit to compulsion'. Three months later again, in October, the NAC went further still, calling on the men of the party to resist the operation of conscription should it be established, realising as it did so the seriousness of a call to disobey the law of the land, particularly in time of war. Unanimously the members of the NAC pledged themselves to do what they were asking the rank and file to do.

Official Labour's opposition to conscription would probably have evaporated very early in the war had not some form of industrial compulsion become a growing threat throughout 1915. Industrial conscription was advocated from several quarters as a remedy for the chaos and disorganisation in the munitions industry, which resulted in a chronic and prolonged shortage of shells. Lloyd George privately blamed Kitchener for his incompetent handling of munitions organisation and publicly blamed the industry's labour force, which he accused of drinking too much. For a time, in the spring of 1915, his energies were devoted to a Welsh Nonconformist-style crusade against the Demon Drink. He persuaded the King to back his campaign with a Royal Proclamation, and advocated nationalisation of the breweries, to be followed by a system of beer rationing. The brewers were only saved by the timely formation of the Coalition Government, whose Conservative members were certainly not disposed to support so radical and socialistic a scheme.

The largest munitions complex in Britain was on the Clyde. As a recent historian of the Clydesiders and their politics has observed, 'The Clyde was an industrial centre absolutely vital to the efficient prosecution of the war in shipbuilding, heavy armaments, armour plating, guns and munitions, and consequently the last place where industrial unrest and stoppages could be allowed; yet practically no account was taken of the politics, the individualism and parochial tendencies of Glasgow which conditioned the attitude of many of its inhabitants towards the war[1].'

In the workshops of the Clyde, the Independent Labour Party, the British Socialist Party and the syndicalist Scottish Labour Party contended for the political souls of a vast labour force which felt little concern for the 'bosses' war'. The ILP's outspoken pacifism, which cost it so much elsewhere in Britain, actually increased its strength on the Clyde. ILP, BSP and SLP militants held most of the local union posts, and they angrily repudiated the industrial truce agreed by the union leaders in London. Even as the truce was being signed, the Clyde's engineering workers put in for a 2d-an-hour rise. When the dispute with both the employers and the embarrassed union leadership was at its height in January 1915, the firm of J. and G. Weir of Cathcart brought in a number of American workers to whom they paid a higher rate and a bonus. The Weir men came out on strike, followed by those at the giant Albion and Parkhead works. To avoid prosecution under the war regulations forbidding unofficial strikes, the men described their action as 'withholding labour', and formed a 'Labour Withholding Committee'. The strike ended only when the Board of Trade persuaded the employers to make a penny-an-hour offer, coupled with some vague assurances on the employment of American labour.

Coming at a time when patriotism in the rest of the country was at a peak, the Clyde strike was bitterly resented. 'At the height of the patriotic fervour, when it seemed treasonable to sabotage the war effort, the country was swayed by an irrational feeling, always liable to erupt while the voluntary system of enlistment lasted, which aroused violent class hatred through the feeling that none of the workers were bearing the same share of sacrifice as the troops in the front line[2].' The hatred was exacerbated by the Clydesiders' confession that they cared little or nothing for the war. Typical of the dozens of resolutions passed on shop floors was one moved by John Maclean at a BSP meeting: 'This War has been brought about by the intrigues of the capitalist and landlord interests of all countries involved; and the workers of the world will obtain no advantages out of the War until they can stop the War at the earliest possible moment.'

Accusations that the strike leaders were pro-German and had been financed by German gold hardly impinged at all on the consciousness of the Clydesiders, and certainly did nothing to deflect them. The Labour Withholding Committee was not disbanded at the end of the strike but re-formed as the Clyde Workers Committee under the chairmanship of Willie Gallacher. The union leaderships were now faced with a permanent institutionalised shop-floor challenge to their authority. A series of disputes followed throughout the summer and autumn of 1915 as Lloyd George carried through a ruthless reorganisation of the industry.

In December Lloyd George embarked on a tour of factories to explain the workings of the 1915 Munitions Act. Glasgow was at first not on his itinerary, but the Clyde Workers Committee eventually persuaded him to address a mass meeting in the great St Andrews Hall on the afternoon of Christmas Day. It turned out to be one of the most extraordinary public meetings of the war. Three thousand people crammed the hall, most of them crying for Lloyd George's blood. The platform was draped with Union Jacks, which hid steel barricades. A girls' choir dressed in khaki began singing patriotic songs, whereupon the shop stewards of the Clyde Workers Committee struck up with the *Red Flag*. Lloyd George, trying to explain his Munitions Act, was greeted with shouts of 'Get your hair cut!' He struggled through half his speech, a mixture of appeals and threats, and finally lost his patience and stormed off the platform. John Muir, of the Clyde Workers Committee, took his place and appealed incongruously for a Christian Socialist Revolution and peace. The meeting ended in a wild march to Glasgow Green and more calls for revolution.

The next morning's papers carried a report of the speech Lloyd George had not been allowed to make, with no mention of the fact that it had not been made, and no mention of the disturbances. To the world outside Glasgow it seemed that the Welsh wizard had walked into the den of lions and emerged unscathed. Only the ILP's Glasgow-based weekly, *Forward*, published a full account of the meeting. The Home Office immediately stepped in and impounded the whole edition. The paper's offices were occupied by the police, and *Forward* was not permitted to resume publication for five weeks.

Its place was taken by the *Worker*, a broadsheet edited by John Muir, published by the Clyde Workers Committee and printed on the ILP Citizens Press. It ran to only four editions, being suppressed for an article urging workers to resist conscription. Muir, the editor, and Tom Bell, the printer, were arrested for sedition. Muir refused to reveal the identity of the author of the article, an ILP man with a wife and family.

This was only the start of a determined Government offensive against the leaders of what middle-class Britain bitterly called the Red Clyde. Six members of the Clyde Workers Committee, including David (later Lord) Kirkwood, were deported to Edinburgh, placed in the charge of the Chief Constable and confined indefinitely to within a five-mile radius of the city. John Muir, Tom Bell, Willie Gallacher, John Maclean and J. McDougall were all sent for trial. So was James Maxton, who, in a speech at Glasgow Green protesting against the deportations, called on munitions workers to down tools and refuse to help the war effort. They all appeared before Lord Strathclyde and received six-month sentences, except for Maclean and Maxton who defended themselves in revolutionary speeches. Maclean got three years and Maxton twelve months. For a while, the Clyde Workers Committee was broken.

The full story of the Clyde disorders, the nearest approach to a revolutionary situation that the Government had to contend with during the war, has been well told elsewhere—objectively by Robert Keith Middlemas in *The Clydesiders*, and entertainingly and colourfully by the late Willie Gallacher in *Revolt on the Clyde*. It has been outlined here, not so much because of its intrinsic importance to the anti-war movement but because it provoked a rising demand for industrial conscription, which in turn antagonised even the loyalist sections of the trade union movement and so prolonged Labour's resistance to conscription of any kind.

Lloyd George himself toyed with the idea of conscription for the munitions industry. In a speech at Manchester on 13 June 1915, when the Clyde was on the boil and the drink controversy was still alive, he declared bluntly: 'We do not want any more recruits for the army. We are getting too many men for the army. We are getting more men than we can equip. What we want is not compulsion for the army, but compulsion for the workshop.' Northcliffe's *Daily Mail* and *Times* campaigned enthusiastically for 'factory conscription'. The *Saturday Review* declared on 21 August that 'National Service is required as much for the effect it will have upon miners and munition workers as for the part it will play in the actual raising of the armies', and in September *London Outlook* published an article by Lieut-Col W. H. Maxwell complaining that 'Trade Unionism, that shelter for slinking shirkers, is imperilling our existence, and by its action a rot of our national soul has set in.' His solution: 'One remedy, and one alone, can eradicate this state of rot—martial law will cure it.'

Parliamentary voices pressed the same case. Sir Frederick Banbury, Conservative MP for the City of London, demanded an additional clause to the Defence of the Realm Act to make it 'lawful to enlist men compulsorily for any work that may be required for the defence of the realm, and to bring such men under military discipline[3]'. In the very first debate which followed Asquith's formation of a Coalition Government, Captain F. E. Guest, Liberal MP for East Dorset, declared that a coalition was better placed than any single-party Government to face the electoral unpopularity that could result from the imposition of 'industrial national service[4]'. Sir Leo Chiozza Money, the eccentric Fabian-Liberal MP for Northampton, called for industrial conscription not only in the munitions factories but thoughout industry, not only for men but also for women, and not only for the war but also for the peace[5].

It was calls such as these that Bruce Glasier had in mind when he wrote the ILP pamphlet *The Peril of Conscription* which went into several editions in the summer of 1915. In his lyrical, nineteenth-century prose the veteran Socialist propagandist wrote: 'The spread of Socialist teaching has revolutionised things. New and gorgeously winged hopes of social equality have taken shape. Labour, conscious of its titanic might, has risen upright . . . Trade Unionism has assumed a new and alarming significance . . . Men from the the mine, the railway, and the factory, are displacing Peers' sons and wealthy manufacturers in Parliament. My readers, do you not grasp the meaning of it all? Think you, do not the ruling classes, the people of rank and great possessions, feel and deeply resent this state of things which is paralysing their power and threatening their very existence? Think you, does no desire, no hope of regaining their lost dominion over the workers and the nation any longer remain in their hearts? The lust and pride of power—power to command others to serve and obey—is not that the passion which above all others has afflicted the world with tyrants and slaves, conquest and oppression, since the world began? And save by reviving the yoke of militarism that lust must remain unsatisfied and that pride perish.'

When the Trades Union Congress met at Bristol on 7 September the *Daily News* made the timely comment, concerning the advocates of conscription, that 'some of them desire it as the only weapon against the growing powers of Trade Unionism'. Certainly it was this suspicion rather than any leanings towards pacifism which prompted Congress to declare against conscription—while nevertheless reiterating its unequivocal support for the war.

Delegates at the TUC voiced the fear that a conscript army would be used to break strikes, as Briand had used conscripts to smash the French national rail strike of 1910. There had been ominous signs during the summer that such secondary uses for the army were not altogether absent from the Government's mind. Early in the year the notorious Dockers' Battalion had been established at Liverpool, blessed by the dock employers, some trade union officials, Lord Derby and Lloyd George himself. The President and Vice-President of the National Union of Dock Labourers were sergeants in the battalion, which was issued with khaki uniforms and made subject

to military law. The battalion met with fierce hostility and resentment from the great majority of dockers, who refused Lord Derby
a hearing when he came to Liverpool to allay their suspicions. Derby
insisted that the battalion would never be used for strike-breaking.
But he added that since it would be run 'in conformity with Union
rules and military discipline' he would not 'look on it as a strike-
breaking battalion if it came to be used to do the work of men who
were fighting their own superior officials and by so doing had been
delaying goods going to the front[6]'. Small wonder that the dockers
were suspicious. Troops, after all, had already been used by the Isle
of Man authorities to unload a vessel during a strike on 19 February.
An industrial strike at Northampton had been broken by the introduction of 'blackleg' labour from the Army Service Corps at the end
of February. Territorials had smashed a strike at Foden's motor
works in April, the Royal Engineers had displaced joiners on strike
at Edinburgh in the same month, and troops had been brought into
the Birkenhead Gasworks during a strike of municipal employees.
Labour anger was hardly allayed by the fact that this sequence of
events began when Henderson was labour adviser to the Government, and continued after he had joined the Cabinet.

On 28 September, in reply to a Parliamentary question, Asquith
admitted that in the previous three months he had received some
four hundred resolutions opposing conscription from various
Labour bodies. In October the ILP launched its final onslaught
with 'Stop Conscription' meetings across the country addressed by
Fred Jowett, Sylvia Pankhurst, George Lansbury and others. But
by now the Derby Scheme was in full cry, and those who had eyes
to see and ears to hear knew that some form of compulsion had
become virtually inevitable. During the Christmas recess the
Cabinet agreed the terms of the first Military Service Bill, to be
presented to Parliament immediately on its resumption.

A special Labour Conference was called in London on 6 January
to debate the party's attitude to the Bill. It declared emphatically
that no case had been made out for any measure of compulsion,
even of a limited and temporary nature. The Parliamentary Labour
Party was urged, while co-operating wholeheartedly in the war
effort, to oppose the Bill at every stage.

But even as Conference resolved to fight on to the last, moves
were being made behind the scenes to clip the wings of Labour's

opposition. At Henderson's insistence, the Cabinet agreed to insert a clause in the Bill specifically repudiating any intention to introduce industrial conscription. This effectively knocked aside one of the main props in the argument of the non-pacifist objectors to compulsion. The other prop, faith in the voluntary system of recruitment, had already been knocked aside by the failure of the Derby Scheme to bring in the desired number of recruits. Labour's revolt collapsed. Half the Parliamentary Party supported the Bill. Although the Labour Party Annual Conference, meeting at Bristol on 26 January, voted overwhelmingly in opposition (by 1,716,000 votes to 360,000), it was a ritual vote: the Bill had already passed through both Houses of Parliament and gone to the King for the Royal Assent.

The ILP made a last desperate effort to thwart the inevitable by whipping up support for a resolution pledging the Labour movement to agitate for repeal of the legislation. The margin by which it was defeated was remarkably small—649,000 votes to 614,000, with heavy abstentions. For the bulk of the Labour movement the battle was over, and they were content to have gone down fighting. The important thing now was to co-operate with the Government in winning the war. The alternative was open and defiant resistance, a course intolerable to the majority who supported the war. Even the ILP, rapidly becoming more isolated and ineffective within the Labour movement, shrank from organising such a campaign, and settled for a support role behind the lines which the No-Conscription Fellowship now came forward to man.

★   ★   ★

When the war was just three months old the editor of the *Labour Leader* wrote himself a letter, which he published in his paper on 12 November. It had been suggested by his new wife, Lilla, whom he had married only two or three weeks before. 'Dear Sir,' Fenner Brockway addressed himself, 'Although conscription may not be so imminent as the press suggests it would perhaps be well for men of enlistment age who are not prepared to take the part of a *combatant* [italics in the original] in the war, whatever the penalty for refusing, to band themselves together so that we may know our strength. As a preliminary, if men between the years of 18 and 38 who take this view will send their names and addresses to me at the address given below a useful record will be at our service. Yours etc., A. Fenner Brockway, Red Row, Mellor, Marple Bridge, Stockport.'

The return posts brought three hundred replies. Lilla Brockway acted as clerk-secretary and dispatched cards inviting nominations for a National Committee. By a process of guided democracy a five-man founding committee was quickly established under Clifford Allen's chairmanship. Brockway was appointed honorary secretary, and the other three founders were James Hindle Hudson, a school-teacher who subsequently became a Labour MP, C. H. Norman, an ILP pamphleteer who was soon to face torture in prison, and the Rev. Leyton Richards, soon to be general secretary of the Fellow-ship of Reconciliation. The No-Conscription Fellowship was in business.

Other more or less established dissenters joined the National Committee. Among them were Bertrand Russell, already at forty-two one of the world's eminent philosophers and mathematicians, temporarily deprived of his Fellowship at Trinity College, Cam-bridge because of his opposition to the war. There was sixty year old Edward Grubb, veteran Quaker campaigner and former organ-ising secretary of the Howard League for Penal Reform, and Dr Alfred Salter, the distinguished bacteriologist who had written *The Religion of a C.O.* Then there were two young men who, like Hudson and Salter, were to become Labour MPs after the war: Walter Henry Ayles and Morgan Jones; Francis Meynell, the subse-quent founder of the Nonesuch Press; Will Chamberlain, the Labour Party's press director in the inter-war years; Bernard J. Boothroyd, later 'Yaffles' of *Reynold's News*—all joined the National Committee during its first year. So, for a brief period, did James Maxton, then Glasgow district organiser of the ILP and later its national chairman.

The N-CF publicly announced itself on 3 December in a leaflet signed by its chairman, Clifford Allen.

Whilst there may not be any immediate danger of conscription [it said] nothing is more uncertain than the duration and development of the war, and it would, we think, be as well if men of enlistment age who are not prepared to take a combatant's part, whatever the penalty for refusing, formed an organisation for mutual counsel and action. Already, in response to personal appeals, a large number of names has been forwarded for registration, and many correspondents have expressed a desire for knowledge of, or fellowship with, others who have come to the same determination not to fight. To meet these needs 'The No-Conscription Fellowship' has been formed, and we invite men of enlistment age who have decided to refuse to take up arms, to join. Intending members should send their names (with any small subscriptions to cover expenses they may be able to give) to the secretary, who will inform them of any fellow-members residing in the same district. Later, groups might, perhaps, be established; certainly we shall have the information for united and decisive action if it becomes necessary.

As the leaflet implied, it was the intention of the N-CF's founders to limit membership to men of enlistment age—those likely to be called upon to face conscription themselves. Although this rule was relaxed to bring in a few older men, and even a small band of women, the organisation remained primarily a fellowship of those pledging themselves to resist compulsory enlistment, and this gave it a significance which no merely academic campaign could ever have hoped to achieve. The bulk of its members were ILP Socialists, who made up nearly two-thirds of a total approaching 10,000. The second largest group were Quakers. Then followed small groups of political objectors from such fringe organisations of the Left as the British Socialist Party, the Socialist Labour Party, the Socialist Party of Great Britain, International Workers of the World and other anarchist and syndicalist bodies. On the religious side were small groups of non-Quaker pacifists drawn from most of the established churches and from fundamentalist sects such as Plymouth Brethren and Christadelphians.

The N-CF, in fact, both in its composition and its philosophy, demonstrated more dramatically than any like organisation the close identity of religious and political dissent in British tradition. Its Socialist members tended to voice their objection to the war and to conscription in the language of Nonconformist religion. Christian objectors usually expounded their position in the language of a social—and often distinctively socialist—gospel. Socialist objectors who had cut themselves off organisationally from the chapels their fathers had attended may have become sceptical of the dogmas of the Churches, but they belonged to a generation which found it hard to live without a spiritual substitute. Their background had been shaped by the humanism, sometimes Christian, sometimes secular, of William Morris, Robert Blatchford and Keir Hardie, set against the wider background of the high-minded phrases and ethical poses of the Gladstone era. At its most maudlin, such a background produced John Trevor's Labour Church Movement and the network of Socialist Sunday Schools. At its sharpest it produced the N-CF.

The Fellowship's two principal leaders were themselves products of this confluence of religious and political dissent. Fenner Brockway was born of missionary parents and grandparents, and arrived at his socialism via the Christian social gospel. Clifford Allen went to Cambridge intending to study for the ministry. At university he became an agnostic, but the zeal with which he embraced secular socialism was fervently religious. 'The Socialist movement is a religious movement', he wrote in 1913, 'and economists must bow the head in silence when they see the people's soul stirred by the bitterness of life.' And again, in November 1914: 'We have perhaps learnt one great lesson—that Socialism must be something of a religion to us before it can have any meaning in times of real stress.' By 1916 he was telling the Battersea Tribunal, in his statement of conscientious objection: 'I am a Socialist, and so hold in all sincerity that the life and personality of every man is sacred, and that there is something of divinity in every human being.' Here, in the mouth of an agnostic, is the creed of George Fox and the Quakers.

At first the N-CF's National Committee was content to hold a watching brief and to carry out its promise to link up individual supporters living in the same locality. 'We were constantly assured, even by our friends', recalled Fenner Brockway, 'that the introduction of conscription was impossible; but the membership increased, and informal groups came together in different parts of the country[7].' The secretarial work was soon too much for the Brockways, and early in 1915 the headquarters of the movement was transferred to a London office. Aylmer Rose, a prominent London Fabian, was appointed organising secretary, and Clifford Allen began to devote most of his time to the Fellowship's work.

Even at this early stage there were fierce, sometimes bitter debates within the National Committee. So many decisions of the thirteen-man body were taken by a majority of one that one member dubbed

it 'the Committee of Sixes and Sevens'. The most important controversy concerned non-combatant service in the army. It was
assumed, with good reason, that any conscription Act eventually
introduced would recognise conscientious objection to combatant
service and make provision for non-combatant service in medical
or clerical corps. The Quakers, in their Declaration on the War, had
declared sternly: 'We see danger to principle in undertaking any
service auxiliary to warfare which involves becoming part of the
military machine.' But Fenner Brockway in his initial letter to the
Labour Leader, and Clifford Allen in his statement issued as the
Fellowship's first recruiting leaflet, had emphasised an objection
only to combatant service. Brockway and Allen quickly moved over
to the more uncompromising view of the Quaker party and succeeded in putting the National Committee on record against non-
combatant service and any kind of 'alternative service' within the
jurisdiction of conscription Acts. But a substantial minority of
N-CF members refused to follow them this far and the question
of alternative service divided the Fellowship throughout its
life.

There were equally troublesome and indecisive arguments about
the propaganda role of the Fellowship. Half the National Committee
wanted to run it as a civil liberties body simply opposing conscription. The other half wanted to declare openly for pacifism and
against the war. Again Brockway and Allen threw their weight
behind the latter party. Nor could the Fellowship ever quite make up
its mind whether actively to encourage resistance or to limit itself
to organising and protecting those who arrived independently at
pacifist convictions. The distinction was, of course, unreal; but the
'Committee of Sixes and Sevens' debated it hotly. A 'Statement of
Faith' acceptable to all was hammered out as follows:

> The No-Conscription Fellowship is an organisation of men likely
> to be called upon to undertake military service in the event of con-
> scription, who will refuse from conscientious motives to bear arms,
> because they consider human life to be sacred, and cannot, therefore,
> assume the responsibility of inflicting death. They deny the right of
> Governments to say, 'You shall bear arms', and will oppose every
> effort to introduce compulsory military service into Great Britain.

Should such efforts be successful, they will, whatever the consequences may be, obey their conscientious convictions rather than the
commands of Governments.

The Statement was later amended to incorporate specific opposition to officially prescribed alternative service under the Military
Service Acts. But never at any time did it adequately express the
variety of ground on which conscientious objections were held.
Clifford Allen himself came to be embarrassed by the religious
rather than political emphasis of the Statement, and claimed its
unsatisfactory nature was the result of hasty drafting. He felt it too
much reflected the traditional view of pacifism and conscientious
objection, 'arising from a definite religious belief in a supernatural
authority', and not enough the outlook of the largest section of the
Fellowship's members, whom he described as holding a moral or
political objection. By a moral objection, he wrote, 'they meant that
they entertained fundamental beliefs either about the value of
human personality, or about the relationship of human beings to
each other . . . Some of them were followers of Tolstoy, but the
greater number were Socialists who believed in the Brotherhood of
Man as genuinely as the Christians believed in the Fatherhood of
God. Others, who have sometimes been called political objectors,
resisted conscription not so much because they were convinced that
all war was morally wrong, or because they believed in any supernatural religious creed; they resisted conscription because it seemed
to them a fatal infringement of human liberty; because they feared
that industrial freedom would be menaced by military conscription;
because they believed that the foreign policy of this country made
Britain worthy of at least some measure of blame for the war; or
because they believed that the war had been engineered on both sides
by groups of men representing a capitalist system of society, against
which system they protested. It is impossible to draw any sharp line
between these different groups . . . Nor is it true to say that these
opinions were static[8].'

That, however, was a retrospective view. In the spring of 1915
much of Allen's energies went on developing closer links with the
Quakers, a body which he recognised to be the best organised and
financially much the most prosperous of all anti-war bodies, despite
its to him irritating apoliticism. At a special meeting in his own

office at the ailing *Daily Citizen*, Allen and Brockway met a group of young Friends in April and agreed a scheme for increasing Quaker representation on the N-CF's National Committee. But in May the Quaker's Yearly Meeting decided to set up its own anti-conscription arm, and appointed the Friends' Service Committee. A series of meetings followed between Allen and officers of the FSC, resulting in the formation in July of a Joint Advisory Council on which were represented not only the N-CF and the FSC but also the growing Fellowship of Reconciliation. A confusing and wasteful parallelism of organisation and effort was thus avoided. The JAC met frequently, often several times a week, and most of the important pronouncements of the no-conscription movement were issued in its name.

The Government's national registration scheme, introduced that July, convinced the three bodies that conscription was only a few months away. The FSC recommended Quaker objectors to register, but with the addition—'Whilst registering as a citizen in conformity with the demand of the Government, I cannot conscientiously take part in military service, in any employment necessitating the taking of the military oath, nor in the production of materials the object of which is the taking of human life.' The N-CF adopted the same line.

Through the late summer it threw its weight behind the industrial campaign mounted by the ILP and other sections of the Labour movement. It lobbied the TUC in September, but pinned little hope on its carefully circumscribed statement opposing conscription. More optimism was aroused by the assurance of the militant miners' leader, Robert Smillie, at the Miners' Federation conference on 5 October, that the great Triple Alliance of miners, railwaymen and transport workers would 'fight the right of one class to conscript another class until they have first conscripted the land and capital of the country'. Further but equally groundless optimism was generated by a statement of the executive of the Scottish Advisory Council of the Labour Party calling on Labour in Scotland to prepare plans for a general strike in the event of Government capitulation to the conscriptionists.

In September the N-CF issued its first No-Conscription Manifesto over the signatures of Clifford Allen, Fenner Brockway, Hubert Peet, Robert Mennell, Alfred Salter and Edward Grubb:

The case for and against compulsory military and munition service is being argued by many who, for reasons of age or sex, would not be subject to it. The signatories to this manifesto think it imperative to voice a protest in the name of a large body of men in this country who, though able-bodied and of military age, will—in the event of coercive measures—be bound by deep conscientious conviction to decline these services, whatever the consequences of refusal.

We yield to no one in our admiration of the self-sacrifice, the courage and the unflagging devotion of those of our fellow-countrymen who have felt it their duty to take up arms. Nevertheless, we cannot undertake the same form of service; our conviction is solemn and unalterable.

Whatever the purpose to be achieved by the war, however high the ideals for which belligerent nations may struggle, for us, 'Thou shalt not kill' means what it says. The destruction of our fellow-men—young men like ourselves—appals us; we cannot assist in the cutting off of one generation from life's opportunities. Insistence upon individual obligations in the interest of national well-being has no terrors for us. We gladly admit—we would even extend—the right hand of the community to impose duties upon its members for the common good, but we deny the right of any Government to make the slaughter of our fellows a bounden duty.

We have been brought to this standpoint by many ways. Some of us have reached it through the Christian faith in which we have been reared, and to our interpretation of which we plead the right to stand loyal. Others have found it by association with international movements; we believe in the solidarity of the human race, and we cannot betray the ties of brotherhood which bind us to one another through the nations of the world.

All of us, however we may have come to this conviction, believe in the value and sacredness of human personality, and are prepared to sacrifice as much in the cause of the world's peace as our fellows are sacrificing in the cause of the nation's war.

Some 20,000 copies were distributed—a meagre number compared with the issue that same month of a million copies of the 'Socialist National Defence Committee's' bugle-call to the colours. But with its publication the N-CF overstepped the mark at which it began to disturb the authorities. The Under-Secretary for War,

Harold Tennant, promised angry conscriptionists in the Commons that he would keep his eye on the Fellowship and consider legal proceedings. A few weeks later two Leeds N-CF members, Thomas Ferris and Sydney Overbury, were prosecuted under the Defence of the Realm Act for publishing a leaflet opposing conscription and the war. They each received six months. On 22 December the Home Secretary, Sir John Simon, refused an appeal from Philip Snowden for remission of their sentences. It was virtually his last official act before resigning office in protest against the Cabinet's Christmas conversion to conscription.

Alive to the threat of police raids and a pre-emptive legal attack, the N-CF had begun to organise itself as a semi-underground organisation, consciously modelled on the suffragette and Sinn Fein movements. Shadow officers were appointed to step into the shoes of any who might be arrested. Local branches, now numbering some two hundred across the country, were advised to do the same. Sometimes elaborate precautions were taken to maintain security. 'If only the authorities had suspected the bona fides of the very respectable group of people who framed fanciful pseudonyms and arranged secret means of communication at the Midland Hotel, Manchester!' recalled Manchester Quaker John W. Graham in 1921, with retrospective relish.

On 27 November, with the Derby Scheme at its height, the Fellowship held its first national convention at the Memorial Hall, London, and Clifford Allen, in an impassioned presidential address, flung down his challenge to the Government.

> We represent in this hall [he said] almost every district from Land's End to John O'Groats, and voice the opinion of thousands of men who will under no circumstances submit to this evil thing, should it come about . . . We are going to oppose this system. But there are two kinds of opposition which can be offered to any measure in Parliament or outside. You can oppose a Bill in the House of Commons, and by agitation in the country up to the time that the Bill becomes the law of the land: you can also resist the operation of that Act, should it go upon the statute book. I want it to be clearly known here, speaking on behalf of the Fellowship, that it is the latter of those two kinds of opposition that we intend to offer . . .
>
> Speaking with a full sense of responsibility, I want the Government

and the public to know that our opposition is not going to be a mere political game. As an organisation we have attempted by our abstention from propaganda to avoid interfering with the will of the majority in the State, so far as the prosecution of the war is concerned; but we want to make it perfectly clear that if now the majority in the State (if indeed there is a majority) decides to impose a system which violates men's deepest religious convictions, we are not going to play at opposition . . . There are various kinds of opposition which a Government can engender in a community. It can engender political opposition and social opposition: but the most dangerous form of resistance which a Government can arouse is that which results from religious persecution . . .

If, despite our present determined opposition, and notwithstanding our determined opposition in the future, conscription becomes the law of the land, we are willing to undergo the penalties that the State may inflict—yes, even death itself—rather than go back upon our convictions. Let it be clearly understood that the members of our organisation have not formed the Fellowship in order to shelter themselves from suffering . . . Those of us who have come to this decision are young men, and we have not come to it without a mental and spiritual struggle. We have endeavoured, so far as possible, to clear our minds of mere cant and hysterical thinking; and having done that we have braced ourselves to an unqualified decision . . .

Life is a very precious thing to young men. We cherish life because of the opportunities for adventure and achievement which it offers to a man who is young. We cherish life because of the call it offers to national and international service, and as we come to our decision here in this conference, we do it casting our eyes over many years of opportunity which lie spread out before us. I believe there is no man amongst us who has any lust for martyrdom for martyrdom's sake . . . But once our minds have been made up, I suggest to you that there has come to us a certain joy, because we are able now to put to the practical test the words which we have used so often in the past, and the principles which we have merely proclaimed and debated. I hold that it is a privilege that the young men of our generation should have such an opportunity of bearing witness to the faith that is in them . . . Probably far more powerful propaganda than countless meetings, or countless declarations, will be the testimony of men who are willing to suffer rather than sacrifice their convictions in this matter of peace.

Concluding his address, Allen moved on behalf of the National Committee the following resolution, adopted as the delegates stood in silence:

> We, the delegates and members of the No-Conscription Fellowship, assembled in National Conference, fully conscious of the attempt that may be made to impose conscription on this country, recognising that such a system must destroy the sanctity of human life, betray the free traditions of our country and hinder its social and industrial emancipation, though realising the grave consequences to ourselves that may follow our decision, hereby solemnly and sincerely reaffirm our intention to resist conscription, whatever the penalties may be.

During the week following the convention a series of meetings across the country were broken up by 'patriotic' mobs of civilians and soldiers. In Nelson, Lancashire, members of the Home Defence Corps in uniform broke into a hall during an anti-conscription meeting and ordered everyone out. In Halifax, a band of local Territorials paraded in front of a hall before and during an anti-conscription meeting, and finally entered the hall and brought the meeting to an early close. In Bradford, soldiers surrounded a hall booked by the local branch of the N-CF and prevented an advertised meeting. A women's meeting in London was prevented by threats of organised disturbances. In Glasgow the corporation announced that public halls would not be made available for anti-conscription meetings. The N-CF passed full information on all these cases to Philip Snowden, who raised the civil liberties issue in the Commons on 8 December, complaining of 'a concerted plot being carried out, apparently with the knowledge and approval of the military authorities, to prevent the public discussion of the question of conscription'.

Whether there was any central War Office encouragement for such activities is doubtful. But there is no doubting the role of certain newspapers in openly encouraging the breaking up of such meetings. On 29 November the Union of Democratic Control held a meeting in the Memorial Hall, London. It was well advertised, and the *Daily Express* advertised it better still. Throughout November the *Express* ran a series on the UDC, hinting at foreign control and pro-German sympathies. Every article made a point of emphasising the date, time and place of the 29 November meeting—clear incitements to its more irresponsible readers to move in and break it up.

A group of nearly one hundred, many of them soldiers in uniform, entered the meeting with what the UDC later alleged to be forged tickets. At a convenient point in the meeting they took possession of the platform and waved banners and flags concealed in their tunics. The group was led by the editor of the *Daily Express*, who forcibly took over the chair and offered the floor to a recruiting officer named Captain Parsons. The UDC's platform party, which included Ramsay MacDonald and Arthur Ponsonby, was ejected.

The War Office had sent along a military policeman in plain clothes—'to see what was going on', as Tennant later explained in the Commons. The police spy's report accused MacDonald of provoking the disturbance which led to the attack on the platform by requesting the removal of a group of uniformed soldiers. 'At the same time', the report continued, 'an individual on the platform, whose name I could not ascertain, but whom I could easily identify, said in a loud voice, sufficient to be heard by the military, "Let that accursed military element be got rid of before we start"', or words to that effect, and almost in the same breath three stewardesses, with collection boxes, who not only appeared to be Teutonic, but could be classified as such by their accent, passed similar remarks quite audibly.' For good measure the report maintained that 'the utmost consideration was shown for those ejected', and its author claimed to have spoken to several trade unionists at the meeting who 'all agreed with me that the behaviour of the military, in spite of the extreme provocation they had received at the hands of the stewards and stewardesses, was, under the circumstances, worthy of all praise'.

In the Commons, MacDonald poured scorn on this version of events, and drew from Tennant a formal acceptance of his denial of responsibility. But, Tennant explained, it was his duty to 'back up my military whom I hope I shall never desert in any matter of this kind when any allegation is made against them'.

This was by no means the only skirmish in which MacDonald was involved. At an ILP meeting in Glasgow a week or two earlier the hall was invaded by a rival meeting of the Scottish Patriotic League. Socialist pacifism in Glasgow was more robust than in the

South. John McGovern, later an erratic ILP MP who ended up in Moral Re-Armament, armed himself with a length of lead piping and placed himself, piping in full and menacing view, on the platform beside the nervous MacDonald. 'That', whispered MacDonald, 'is the kind of pacifist I like!' When one of the Patriotic League leaders hammered at the bolted stage door, at the head of a mob, another pacifist Clydesider, Emmanuel Shinwell, went to the door and knocked him out.

The autumn of 1915 was notable for the transitory emergence of another, very different anti-conscription lobby. In a debate on army supply at the end of October a Conservative MP, Sir Norval Helme, introduced what he called the Commercial Committee—'informally associated together in order to watch the commercial interests of the nation', with representation drawn from 'the textile interests of Lancashire, of Yorkshire, and the mineral interests of the Midlands, and also great financial interests'. The Commercial Committee opposed not only conscription but 'over-zealous recruiting', on the ground that it 'endangered vital trades'. Socialism found itself allied in the fight against conscription, with the enlightened self-interest of British capitalists! The alliance was short-lived. Sir Norval Helme's motion putting commerce before army recruitment was not called, and the Commercial Committee was never heard of again.

More enduring was the National Council against Conscription, formed after N-CF deputations at Christmas to the Home Secretary, Sir John Simon, and to Asquith. Its object was to mount an eleventh hour political campaign against conscription. Robert Smillie, the miners' leader, became the National Council's first president, B. N. Langdon-Davies its secretary and F. W. Pethick-Lawrence its honorary treasurer. Clifford Allen, George Lansbury and H. W. Massingham were members of its executive. When the Conscription Bill became law it changed its name to the National Council for Civil Liberties (not to be confused with the present organisation of that name, which dates from the 1930s). The NCCL concentrated on the civil liberties aspect of conscription and published an avalanche of pamphlets directed not only at the conscription laws but also at the workings of the Defence of the Realm Act and the whole bureaucracy of war. Like the N-CF, which it overlapped and with which it co-operated closely, it was subject to frequent police raids and the removal of literature and files. By the end of its first year it could boast 545 affiliated organisations, including eight national trade unions, 98 trades councils and Local Labour Parties, 95 ILP branches and 150 trade union branches. W. C. Anderson MP succeeded Robert Smillie as president in 1917, and Mrs Ethel Snowden, wife of Philip Snowden and organiser of the Women's Peace Crusade, became honorary treasurer.

The N-CF sustained, even intensified its campaign during the final weeks of 1915. But while the Fellowship continued to lobby against the adoption of any kind of compulsion, its Parliamentary friends, having seen the writing on the wall after the inevitable and contrived failure of the Derby Scheme, were now salvaging what they could by lobbying for ameliorative clauses in the Military Service Bill expected to emerge from the Christmas recess. Arnold Rowntree was pressing for a recognition of conscientious objection to non-combatant as well as to combatant service. Another Quaker MP, Edmund Harvey, had already put the Quaker objectors' case to the Commons on 26 October. Calling for exemption for 'those who are called religious or conscientious objectors', he went on: 'I recognise the immense claim the State has upon the lives of all citizens . . . But I do not agree . . . that it is the elementary duty of the citizen to fight for the State. It is the elementary duty of the citizen in an elementary State, but I believe we have reached already, even in this imperfect state of civilisation, a higher conception of the State and of the duties of the citizen . . . It is a matter of the profoundest conviction. We are prepared, if need be, I believe, to lay down life itself in the cause of our fellow-countrymen, but we cannot take life, even at the call of the State itself . . . We cannot disobey the clear command of our conscience; we cannot disobey what we believe to be the eternal laws of God.'

Asquith's final capitulation at Christmas provoked from Fenner Brockway in a *Labour Leader* editorial the savage judgment that 'the Government of this country has inflicted a greater defeat upon us than any German army has inflicted'. The N-CF now turned to making good its threat of organised resistance. A second national convention was held on 8 and 9 April 1916, in the old Quaker headquarters at Devonshire House, Bishopsgate. Two thousand young men of military age, most of them 'deemed to be enlisted' under the

Act, met together representing 198 branches. 'Earnest of face and tense of spirit', wrote an older Quaker observer, 'they met with the knowledge that the world held them in contempt and that persecution hung over them'.

Snowden, Allen and Brockway were billed to speak. The tension inside the hall was heightened by the sound of rioting outside, where a crowd tried to break through the great iron gates and storm the hall. To avoid provoking the crowd, speeches were accorded a visual rather than a vocal ovation: delegates stood and silently waved handkerchiefs or papers. At the dramatic climax of the convention Fenner Brockway read out the names of the first fifteen men to have been arrested as conscientious objectors, each name being received with the same silent form of ovation. Thus 'the assembled conscientious objectors heard the challenge which told of the coming fight, and braced themselves to act. In many a lonely prison cell and dingy dark room the convention was a sacred memory which kept men loyal to a great cause in a dark hour[9].'

Before the convention closed, two thousand men stood to adopt the following pledge:

> We, representing thousands of men who cannot participate in warfare, and are subject to the terms of the Military Service Act, unite in comradeship with those of our number who are already suffering for conscience' sake in prison or the hands of the military. We appreciate the spirit of sacrifice which actuates those who are suffering on the battlefield, and in that spirit we renew our determination, whatever the penalties awaiting us, to undertake no service which for us is wrong. We are confident that thus we are advancing the cause of peace and so rendering such service to our fellow-men in all nations as will contribute to the healing of the wounds inflicted by war.

Militant pacifism was on the march.

REFERENCES

1 Robert Keith Middlemas, *The Clydesiders*, 1965
2 Robert Keith Middlemas, *op cit*
3 Sir Frederick was a veteran conscriptionist. He had pressed on the

Commons a scheme for reviving the Militia Ballot as far back as 8 June 1904.

4 Parliamentary Report (Hansard), Commons, 19 May 1915
5 Parliamentary Report (Hansard), Commons, 19 May 1915
6 G. D. H. Cole, *op cit*
7 *N-CF Souvenir*, 1919
8 Preface to John W. Graham, *op cit*
9 John W. Graham, *op cit*

Chapter V

The Tribunals

IN THE first week of February 1916, young men of military service age began to receive through the post from their local recruiting committee the War Office's Form W 3236, instructing them that they were required to join the colours forthwith, and adding that men who failed to comply would be dealt with as war-time deserters.

The form, as the Secretary of War was to admit in the Commons on 29 February, went out indiscriminately to all on the military register, including not only those who were exempted by the Act but even those who had already tried to enlist and had been rejected. Tennant defended this procedure on the ground that 'it was absolutely impossible for the authorities to know who were or who were not the people who should receive these notices[1]', thereby indicating the inadequacy of the Derby Scheme, the ostensible purpose of which had been precisely to provide such information.

Recipients of W 3236 were expected either to present themselves as ordered or to send documentary evidence of exemption. Acceptable evidence took the form of certificates issued by the Local Tribunals, which were appointed by local authorities early in February in accordance with Local Government Board instructions, set out in a circular explaining the requirements of the Military Service Act.

The Tribunals consisted for the most part of elderly worthies— the butchers, bakers and candlestick makers of the local community. The nucleus of most of them was the tribunal hastily appointed during the Derby Scheme to hear employers' applications for the exemption of their workers. The Local Government Board urged that the new Tribunals be fully representative of the local community—the Derby Scheme tribunals had been widely criticised on this score—and this instruction was generally given effect by the appointment of nominees of the local Liberal and Conservative associations. Proven zeal in furthering recruiting was frequently rewarded by a Tribunal seat. Places were often offered to the parson and to an official of the local recruiting committee. A pro-war Labour man was considered a good catch, and a pro-war Quaker— by no means beyond procurement—even better.

These men (women were occasionally included, and generally surpassed the men in ferocity) were given the immensely responsible task of judging the sincerity of those who claimed a conscientious objection to the war. Appointed by virtue of their social reliability and unquestioned and unquestioning patriotism, they brought to their work a baffled suspicion of all dissenters, total ignorance of the psychology of religious and political idealism, and a class-bred, bitter hostility to Socialism. Coupled with this was lack of experience in any kind of judicial work, and a widespread ignorance of their own powers under the Act. Most Tribunals were bewildered and frightened, as was the central Government, at the avalanche of conscientious objectors who made application to appear before them. They believed that Britain was in danger of losing the war if sufficient men were not forthcoming, and they saw it as their job to ensure that cowards and shirkers didn't get their own way.

The Local Government Board itself did attempt to give faithful expression to Parliament's intention that the genuine conscientious objector be recognised and exempted. Its circular to local authorities on 3 February stated:

> While care must be taken that the man who shirks his duty to his country does not find unworthy shelter behind this provision, every consideration should be given to the man whose objection generally rests on religious or moral convictions. Whatever may be the views of members of the Tribunal, they must interpret the Act in an impartial and tolerant spirit. Difference of convictions must not bias judgment.
>
> The local authority, in making their appointments to the Tribunal, should bear in mind that the Tribunal will have to hear, among the applications, those made on the ground of conscientious objection. Men who apply on this ground should be able to feel that they are being judged by a Tribunal that will deal fairly with their cases.

But this liberal advice was given when the Government still

believed that there would be relatively few conscientious objectors. When thousands brought their applications to the Tribunals the liberalism vanished.

One of the first religious objectors to be heard by the Shaw Tribunal was told by one of its members, a Councillor Hopwood: 'I think you are exploiting God to save your own skin. It is nothing but deliberate and rank blasphemy. A man who would not help to defend his country and womankind is a coward and a cad. You are nothing but a shivering mass of unwholesome fat!' This was addressed to a man of high scientific qualifications, a member of one of the British Association's research committees[2]. Salford Tribunal refused an applicant permission to quote Quaker grounds for pacifism on the ground that 'we cannot listen to arguments'. The chairman of Wirral Tribunal declared: 'I wish the Government had not put this clause about conscientious objectors in the Act at all. I don't agree with it myself.' An applicant before Willesden Tribunal was asked by the chairman, 'Do you believe the blood of Christ cleanses from all sin?' He replied, 'Yes'. Retorted the chairman: 'Then would you not be forgiven if you took part in this war?'

At Sandown Tribunal a Col. Gordon quoted Christ's words: 'I came not to bring peace but a sword.' The applicant replied by quoting the Sermon on the Mount—'love your enemies, bless them that curse you . . . pray for them that despitefully use you'. 'But surely,' replied Col. Gordon, 'that was personal, not national.' 'My position is a personal one', replied the applicant, who was forthwith refused exemption. An applicant at Exeter was told that his objection to taking life was hypocritical since he admitted to eating cheese, which involved 'killing the maggots'. 'Is it the conscience that makes cowards of us all that you are suffering from?' asked the chairman of Ashton-under-Lyne Tribunal of one applicant. Another, who described himself to the West Glamorgan Appeal Tribunal as a member of the N-CF, was told: 'You belong to one of the most pernicious bodies in the country. Its members are going all over the place distilling poison, and are greater enemies to Britain than the Germans.' Such were the voices of men who, according to the Local Government Board, were to be 'of an impartial and tolerant spirit'.

But crass stupidity was by no means the worst fault of the average Tribunal. The most flagrant injustices arose from the wilful refusal of most of these bodies ever to grant the absolute exemption which alone satisfied the consciences of most objectors. The first Military Service Act, as we have seen, was ambiguous on this point. Section 2 (3) stated: 'Any certificate of exemption may be absolute, conditional or temporary, as the authority by whom it was granted think best suited to the case, and also in the case of an application on conscientious grounds, may take the form of an exemption from combatant service only, or may be conditional on the applicant being engaged in some work which in the opinion of the Tribunal dealing with the case is of national importance.' This was variously interpreted to mean that absolute exemption could be granted to all kinds of claimants, *including* conscientious objectors, or to all categories *except* conscientious objectors. The point was clarified in the Local Government Board circular of 3 February, which, while emphasising that 'the exemption should be the minimum required to meet the conscientious scruples of the applicant', nevertheless made clear that 'there may be exceptional cases in which the genuine convictions and the circumstances of the man are such that neither exemption from combatant service nor a conditional exemption will adequately meet the case. Absolute exemption can be granted in these cases if the Tribunals are fully satisfied of the facts.'

This was clear enough, and if Tribunals had acted on these instructions almost all the misery and scandal that was to follow would never have happened. But the Tribunals panicked at the large numbers coming before them. They feared absolute exemption would give the net they were holding too large a mesh. They saw themselves, too often, as an arm of the recruiting machinery, and were encouraged in this view by an Army Council circular of 20 February which urged military representatives, War Office advisory committees and Local Tribunals to 'take all possible steps to obtain men for the Army'.

Accordingly very nearly all the Tribunals continued their refusal to grant absolute exemptions. Some quoted in defence of this decision the Local Government Board's advice to keep degrees of exemption down to the minimum, but many flatly asserted that they would never give absolute exemption to anyone. The Durham Appeal Tribunal told an applicant who quoted both the Act and the circular in support of his contention that the Tribunal was empowered to grant an unconditional certificate: 'We are not bound by any statement made by any Members of Parliament or any circular issued by the Local Government Board.'

Abuses of this kind were cited by Philip Snowden in the Commons on 24 February. Walter Long, the President of the Local Government Board, denied knowledge of such cases. Snowden undertook to provide him with evidence and on 9 March Long conceded that he had found it necessary to write to certain Tribunals reminding them of the provisions of the Act. But still the number of absolute exemptions remained very small indeed, confined almost entirely to members of the Society of Friends.

This rigid attitude was backed by the Central Tribunal, the CO's final court of appeal. Pronouncing on the case of Douglas R. Bishop, a Friend who had stated an 'absolutist' objection to any kind of service, military or non-military, imposed under a Military Service Act, the Central Tribunal ruled as follows:

> The Central Tribunal, after hearing the appellant in person, were satisfied that, apart from his objection to the actual taking of life, his position was that his conscience would not permit him to accept as a condition of exemption that he should undertake any work other than work to which he felt he was called, and that of that call he must be the sole judge. The Tribunal did not consider that this was a form of conscientious objection recognised by the Military Service Act, or one that could be recognised by any organised State.

Thus the Local Government Board and the Central Tribunal were issuing conflicting interpretations of, and rulings on, the terms of the Act. The Local and Appeal Tribunals were virtually free to take their choice. The matter came before the High Court of Justice on 18 April, but confusion was thereby only the worse confounded. A case involving an objector named F. L. Parton was tried by Justices Darling, Lawrence and Avory. Darling gave a firm judgment to the effect that Tribunals could only exempt from combatant service. Lawrence concurred, but Avory could not agree that Tribunals were so limited.

It was imperative for the Government to clear up the matter, and it did so in the second Military Service Act, introduced the following month. Paragraph 4 (3) ran: 'It is hereby declared that the power to grant special certificates of exemption in the case of an application on conscientious grounds under Subsection 3 of Section

2 of the principal Act, is additional to and not in derogation of the general power conferred by that Act to grant an absolute, conditional or temporary certificate in such cases.'

But by this time several hundred objectors had passed through the Tribunals and into the hands of the military. Moreover, even the second Act's categorical affirmation of the Tribunal's right to grant absolute exemption was not allowed to be the last word. The Central Tribunal advised Local and Appeal Tribunals in June that in its view only religious objectors could legitimately claim exemption and, further, in direct defiance of the clarifying clause of the second Act, that genuine objectors to both combatant and non-combatant service should be awarded only conditional exemption bound up with acceptance of 'work of national importance'. The Central Tribunal's advice, though not legally binding on Local and Appeal Tribunals, was conveyed to them in a Local Government Board circular. In the prevailing confusion, its pronouncements assumed an authoritative and final character, not only on the vexed question of exemption but also in the distinction made between religious and Socialist objectors.

> The Central Tribunal [said the circular] have had before them a number of appeals by persons alleging conscientious objection to military service not based on any religious ground. These persons are in most cases members of some Socialist organisation. The cases differ.
>
> In some the objection alleged is based on opposition to the present war; in others on disapproval of the present organisation of society, which the man considers not worthy of defence, though he would fight in defence of a State organised in a way he approves. These opinions, however genuinely and strongly held, do not, in the view of the Central Tribunal, constitute conscientious objections within the meaning of the Military Service Acts.
>
> In the majority of the remaining cases, the Central Tribunal are satisfied that the appellants have a genuine belief that the taking of human life in any circumstances is morally wrong, and the Central Tribunal hold that such an objection is properly met by exemption from combatant service. In some of these last cases the appellant has proved a genuine settled conscientious objection not only to the actual taking of life, but to everything which is designed directly to

Above: Two of Will Dyson's anti-conscription cartoons published in the *Herald* in 1915. *Left: WAR PROFITEER* 'Ah if these ruffians pause to object to me picking their pockets at such a moment as this the country will have to conscript the unpatriotic shirkers.' *Right:* Great Newspaper Proprietor (to leader-writer): 'Dwell on the necessity for a dictator, and—ah—lightly indicate the type of great organiser he should be!' *Below:* C. H. Norman is 'fetched' by the Army: 29 April 1916.

Above: The N-CF National Committee, May 1916. Front row, left to right; C. H. Norman, Dr Alfred Salter, Aylmer Rose, Fenner Brockway, Clifford Allen, Edward Grubb, Will Chamberlain, Catherine Marshall. Standing: left to right; Rev. Leyton Richards, Morgan Jones, John P. Fletcher, A. Barratt Brown and Bertrand Russell. *Below:* Outside the Mansion House Court. A picture taken during the 'Repeal the Act' case against the N-CF National Committee which was to put them all in jail. Standing in the road are Walter Ayles (with bag), Will Chamberlain, A. Barratt Brown, Clifford Allen and Fenner Brockway. Standing behind Chamberlain is J. P. Fletcher.

assist in the prosecution of the war. Such cases, where established, entitle the appellant, in the opinion of the Central Tribunal, to exemption from all forms of military service upon conditions as to performing work of national importance, the terms of which will be found in cases decided by the Central Tribunal.

The Central Tribunal have carefully considered such authorised publications of Socialist organisations as have been laid before them. On the material available they do not find that membership of any such organisation is in itself evidence of a conscientious objection to military service.

The Central Tribunal regard the age of the man alleging conscientious objection as an important factor in the consideration of the question whether his objection is so deliberate and settled as to entitle him to exemption or to the widest form of exemption.

The Joint Action Committee, representing the Friends' Service Committee, the N-CF and the FoR, protested vehemently against the Central Tribunal's highly restrictive interpretation of Parliament's provision for objectors. In a letter to the President of the Local Government Board, quoting the Central Tribunal's statement and commenting on it paragraph by paragraph, the Committee first accused the Central Tribunal of seeking to 'annul the specific declaration of the second Military Service Act that it is within the competence and discretion of Tribunals to give absolute exemption', and then contested the quite arbitrary claim that the Military Service Acts made no provision for Socialist objectors. 'The distinction which is made in this decision between religious and moral grounds of conscientious objection is unsound. A conscientious objection on whatever grounds professed involves in every case an appeal to the ultimate moral authority which the individual recognises. It is impossible to state at what point a man's moral judgment begins consciously to acquire what is commonly known as a religious or spiritual sanction, and it applies an unwarrantable assumption on the part of any body of men that it should issue a categorical pronouncement upon a subject which involves very difficult and contentious metaphysical considerations.'

To the Central Tribunal's recommendation that objectors to all forms of military service be granted exemption 'upon conditions as to performing work of national importance, the terms of which will be found in cases decided by the Central Tribunal', the Committee pointed out that 'these terms include a proviso in one case that the "work of national importance" shall be useful for the prosecution of the war. This renders the exemption thus granted wholly nugatory, inasmuch as work which is "useful for the prosecution of the war", however indirect it may be, does by that description of it become a form of service which a man who objects to war will also reasonably and rightly include within the scope of his objection. Moreover, there are men whose conscientious objection extends to any form of alternative service imposed under a Military Service Act.'

The letter finally protested against the recommendation that the age of the objector should be regarded as an important factor in judging the validity of a conscientious objection. 'That a person's youth should make his statement of his conscientious objection crude and inadequate is only natural, but it does not at all follow that his objection is unsound or immature because he is young. Moreover, if a man be old enough to fight, he is also old enough to have an opinion whether it be right or wrong to fight; and if he is not old enough to have such an opinion, it is a moral outrage to compel him to fight. And if he be compelled into the Army at 18 years of age because he is not considered to have a "deliberate and settled" objection, will he then be allowed to claim release from the Army, say, at 21 years or whatever the age may be at which his conscience may be judged to have reached maturity?'

These three points—the Tribunals' reluctance in all but a very few cases to grant absolute exemption, their frequent refusal to recognise Socialists as genuine conscientious objectors, and their assumption that the eighteen- and nineteen-year-olds were too young to have a settled opinion on the morality of participation in the war—made inevitable a bitter, uncompromising struggle between authority and the dissenters.

★   ★   ★

The confusion that characterised the work of the Tribunals was not lessened by the variety of attitudes and grounds of claim to be found among the conscientious objectors, and before we document this confusion further we must examine the different categories of objector appearing before the Tribunals.

In March 1916 the War Office announced the formation of a new Non-Combatant Corps for conscientious objectors. The NCC, said the announcement, would be an army unit, subject to normal military discipline, but it would bear no arms. Its members would not be required to fight or take life. They would be used in 'the repair of roads and railways, sanitation, the provision of huts and baths for soldiers coming out of the trenches, and the manufacture and provision of many necessaries of life'.

This met the objection of religious COs whose primary concern was to obey the commandment 'Thou shalt not kill'. Some 3,300 of the 16,100 objectors who went before the Tribunals accepted Non-Combatant Corps service. But the No-Conscription Fellowship and the Quakers bluntly stated their repudiation of this compromise in a letter to Asquith dated 14 March:

> We consider it at once our duty to acquaint you with the opinions of conscientious objectors regarding the new Army Order establishing a Non-Combatant Corps.
>
> The Government should understand that the men for whom we speak can, under no circumstances, become part of this corps, which we observe will be under the control of the War Office, and in every sense part of the military machine.
>
> The suggestion that we could afford assistance in the manner indicated shows an entire misunderstanding of our convictions. We have repeatedly attempted to make clear that our position is one of fundamental objection to war on religious or moral grounds, and that no plea of necessity or of policy can justify us in participating in its prosecution.
>
> It will therefore be seen that our objection covers any form of military service, combatant or non-combatant, and also, for all but a few of us, any form of civil alternative, under a scheme whereby the Government seeks to facilitate national organisation for the prosecution of war.
>
> The only transfer from present occupations to which the great majority of the men for whom we speak could consent, would be such as would afford them greater opportunity of working towards the attainment of peace and towards the removal of international and racial hatreds. This, we maintain, is the highest service we can render to our fellow-men, now and at all times.

The letter was signed by Clifford Allen and Fenner Brockway for the N-CF, and by Robert Mennell and Hubert Peet for the Quakers.

Objectors who refused non-combatant service were able to quote the Secretary of War as telling the Commons on 14 March: 'Members of the Non-Combatant Corps will be organised in units to relieve combatant soldiers for service at the front.' This frankness conceded their case: there was no morality and no honour in refusing combatant service oneself while being prepared to relieve another for it. If it was wrong to pull the trigger, it was equally wrong to have someone else pull it for you. This was the position adopted by the N-CF, the FSC and the FoR.

But as we have seen, in very nearly all cases where they granted any exemption at all, the Tribunals exempted COs only from combatant service, or stipulated that exemption was conditional on the applicant accepting 'work of national importance'. This exposed further divisions among COs. Not all who felt compelled to refuse service in the Army's own NCC felt equally compelled on conscience grounds to refuse other kinds of non-combatant service under civil control. Of the 12,800 objectors who declined to join the NCC, 6,300—almost exactly half—accepted one or other of the various kinds of alternative service made available[3]. The remainder at first refused any kind of work, military or civil, prescribed under the Military Service Acts, though 3,750 subsequently accepted the modified prison sentences offered under what was known as the Home Office Scheme. Leaving aside those discharged on medical grounds and those for whom records remained incomplete, some 1,300 refused every compromise offered by the Government and spent the war in prison, mostly under conditions of hard labour. These were the Absolutists. Those who accepted alternative service were known as Alternativists, and those who took the Home Office Scheme as 'Schemers'. The three groups co-existed more or less happily within the N-CF, only occasionally generating friction.

Alternative service took several forms. The Board of Trade appointed a committee under the chairmanship of W. H. Pelham to advise Tribunals about it, and to attempt to bring available work and workers together. The Pelham Committee included the Quaker Liberal MP T. Edmund Harvey and a prominent opponent of the war, Charles Wright. It recommended the following work as being of 'national importance':

Agriculture—Farm labour, market gardening and fruit growing, seed raising, agricultural machinery making and repairs. Agricultural education and organisation.
Forestry—Cutting, hauling and preparing timber.
Food Supply—Flour milling, sugar refining, margerine production.
Shipping—Mercantile marine, shipbuilding and repairing.
Transport—Railways and canals. Docks and wharves. Cartage connected with same.
Mining.
Education.
Public Utility Services—Sanitary services. Local authorities. Fire brigades, civil hospitals, workhouses, infirmaries, asylums.

Many Tribunals chose at first to ignore the Pelham Committee, which they quaintly supposed to be pacifist-dominated, and many COs also refused its good offices on the ground that its certificates of exemption, obtained from the Army Council, stipulated at first that the 'work of national importance' should be 'useful for the prosecution of the war'. This stipulation was later dropped, allowing many more COs to avail themselves of the committee's services in good conscience. Altogether 3,964 did so. Another nine hundred accepted alternative service provided by the Tribunals without reference to the Pelham Committee.

Some tribunals not only ignored but actually obstructed the Committee's work. The Clerk of the Appeal Tribunal at Manchester kept its circulars from the Tribunal chairman. Ignorant, therefore, of its proper function, he made a practice of giving objectors 'noncombatant service under the Pelham Committee', which enabled the Clerk to pass their names to the military for forced recruitment into the Non-Combatant Corps. After some weeks of this practice the chairman was appraised of the real situation by J. W. Graham, and set about recalling the men who had passed through his hands and suffered by his misconception. Some sixty such cases were righted, but in many of them the redress came too late to prevent their arrest and handing over to the army. It took Graham six weeks of unremitting effort to secure the release of just one of them. Eight remained in the army, serving long periods of military detention for refusing to obey orders.

Incapable as they were, by reason of their own inexperience and the confused nature of the briefing they received from the central Government, of fairly judging conscientious objection, the Tribunals' task was made no easier by the inevitable presence of a military representative whose job it was to oppose all claims and to argue the Army's need of each objector. The military representative usually appeared in uniform, and he often dominated the civilian members of the Tribunal. Although not officially a member himself, he almost always sat with the members and remained with them while the applicant was sent out of the room during their consultations. Often it was the military representative who posed the stock question: 'What would you do if you found a German soldier raping your sister?' which produced from one applicant[4] the famous answer: 'I should endeavour to interpose myself between them.' Cases in which military representatives grossly abused their power were raised in the Commons by Philip Snowden and James Hogge. Hogge charged that, where applicants who had been refused exemption were taking their cases on to the Appeal Tribunal, the Local Tribunal was advising the military representative of the grounds of its decision without vouchsafing this information to the applicant, thus giving the military representative a clear advantage when the appeal was heard.

The military representative at Sheffield told an applicant that there was only one way to absolute exemption, and that was death. The chairman of Seaton Delaval Tribunal, after consulting the military representative, told an objector that if he refused noncombatant service he was liable to be shot. The military representative at Manchester Tribunal on one occasion ordered press reporters present not to report a statement of opposition to the war.

Despite the express ruling of the Local Government Board that Tribunal hearings should always be open to public and press, attempts, more or less persistent and successful, to hold the sittings in private, were made at Falmouth, Oswaldtwistle, Helston, Bromley, Mountain Ash, Doncaster, Musselburgh, Sunderland and Swansea. Major John Newman MP appealed on 8 March to the Home Secretary, Herbert Samuel, to 'censor in the public press all reports' of Tribunals, 'in view of the exhibition of lack of manhood and cowardice displayed before Local Tribunals by young men seeking escape from military service on conscientious grounds'. Samuel agreed that 'Sometimes "conscience makes cowards of us all"', and in effect rebuked the press for giving undue prominence to cases before the Tribunals, but confessed that there were 'serious objections to prohibiting publication of the reports'. No one would suspect from this exchange that there was an almost unanimous attitude in the press of bitter hostility towards conscientious objectors. In most of the cases it reported the *Daily Express* referred to all applicants before Tribunals as 'pasty-faces'.

We have already noted the official conviction that a Socialist conscience unsupported by religious faith was a contradiction in terms. The following exchange took place at the Burnley Tribunal on 27 March 1916:

> *Applicant:* 'I am a conscientious objector because I am a Socialist.'
> *Chairman* (the Mayor): 'Don't you know that every Socialist is expected to use a rifle in the street he is in?'
> *Applicant:* 'Oh, no, you are probably thinking about Anarchists.'
> *Chairman:* 'Yes, it is proved that Socialists are allied to Anarchists.'
> *Member of Tribunal:* 'Up to now there is no proof of conscience.'
> *Chairman:* 'He cannot claim to be a Socialist and a conscientious objector.'

The application was refused.

When two members of the N-CF National Committee were brought together before the Birmingham Tribunal and made out identical cases, a conscience was allowed to the Quaker, A. Barratt Brown, but not to the Socialist, W. J. Chamberlain.

Finally, there was the ludicrous inconsistency of the Tribunals. Brentford Tribunal refused absolute exemption to conscientious objectors but granted it to members of the Brewery Company, who were deemed to be engaged on 'work of national importance'. Six months' exemption was granted by Southwark Tribunal to twenty-one single men employed by the Harmsworth Press on *Home Chat*, *Comic Cuts*, and similar literature of national importance. At Market Bosworth all the men employed by the local hunt were granted exemption.

Despite the fact that some of the worst injustices were raised in the Commons by Snowden, Jowett, Anderson and T. E. Harvey, the information having been supplied by the N-CF, public opinion at first showed little sign of concerning itself with the fate of the 'pasty-faces'. But on 22 March Snowden made a long speech citing no fewer than fifty-four Tribunal injustices (afterwards printed by the N-CF as a penny pamphlet under the title *British Prussianism: The Scandal of the Tribunals*). Snowden claimed to be mentioning only one-twentieth of the cases which had been brought to his notice. He was followed, in similarly critical vein, by T. E. Harvey, Philip Morrell, J. W. Wilson, Arnold Rowntree, J. H. Whitehouse and William Pringle. Rowntree had the temerity to remind the Minister of Munitions, David Lloyd George, of his pacifism during the Boer War, and to ask what he would have done if forcibly recruited for it. Lloyd George replied that he would not have hesitated to play a part in helping cure the wounded. 'What is there inconsistent in a man who objects to war doing his best to cure the wounded, to repair the damage of war, and see that the hurt inflicted on humanity is as little as possible? If a conscientious objector tells me that he objects to that, I say without any hesitation that in a case of that kind the real reason is not conscience but fear. Tribunals are entitled to search out rigorously and relentlessly the motives of men when they come forward and plead that they should not take part in the struggle.'

Snowden's massively documented indictment produced a leading article in the *Daily Chronicle*, criticising the 'grave scandal' of the Tribunals, the 'gross military irregularities', 'the brow-beating of men by deliberate misstatements of the law', 'the cheating of some, the kidnapping of others', and the Tribunals' 'inconsistency, their uneven hand, their frank and avowed illegalities'. The Bishops of Oxford and Lincoln both wrote letters of protest to *The Times*. The General Committee of the Free Church Council passed a unanimous protest. Even the *Solicitor's Journal* declared itself shocked by the procedure of 'scratch bodies enjoying a brief tenure of power over their fellows'.

But public opinion remained for the most part indifferent. The sufferings of the troops seemed of infinitely more consequence at a time when the full horrors of trench warfare were just beginning to penetrate the public consciousness. The persecution of a few cranks at home seemed but a drop in the world's ocean of sufferings. The 'Scandal of the Tribunals' made a fleeting appearance in the headlines of the liberal press and was then forgotten. But the public criticism had one beneficial effect. On 23 March the Local Government Board issued a circular to all Tribunals reasserting their competence to grant absolute exemption, and referring disapprovingly to the 'somewhat harsh cross-examinations' which some applicants had undergone. 'Tolerance and impartiality' were again urged on the Tribunals, which were also reminded that they were obliged to hold their sittings in private. Many more paragraphs of advice counselled justice and moderation.

The counsel was little heeded, however, and on 6 April Snowden returned to the attack in the Commons. This time his principal target was the Appeal Tribunals, and he confined himself to their doings during the two weeks that had elapsed since the Local Government Board's circular on 23 March. The Appeal Tribunals had for the most part been hearing appeals against the Local Tribunals' refusal of absolute exemption. Snowden cited cases in which the Appeal Tribunals of the County of London and of Monmouthshire not only rejected these appeals but also cancelled the conditional exemption already granted. The Stoke-on-Trent Tribunal had summarily treated eight objectors together without hearing evidence. The Surrey Tribunal had ruled that 'the Act does not permit exemption from non-combatant duties in the case of a conscientious objector'. The chairman of the West Sussex Tribunal had declared that he had no power to grant absolute exemption. The Middlesex Tribunal admitted that an applicant was genuine, and then dismissed his appeal. The same Tribunal told a Socialist he could not have a conscience if he had no religion. The Midlothian Appeal Tribunal re-heard nineteen cases in which absolute exemption had been granted by the Edinburgh Tribunal. The appeals had been lodged by the military representative, and eighteen of the nineteen were reduced to exemptions from combatant service only. Eight military representatives attended this hearing.

Snowden declared that he had received 2,600 letters in five weeks on the administration of the Military Service Act. Many detailed illegal arrests. One was from a member of a Tribunal in Wiltshire who wrote that he was powerless to prevent his colleagues acting unjustly and illegally. Another quoted a letter from the Plymouth recruiting officer to an applicant awaiting the hearing of his case by

the Appeal Tribunal. 'You had better come and save trouble,' it
said, 'I've had the result of your appeal already.'

★ ★ ★

While the Tribunals did their work, the COs' organisations
organised what resistance they could. The National Council
Against Conscription publicised some of the miscarriages of justice.
The Quaker journal *The Friend* did the same. The N-CF, in
addition to collecting evidence of illegalities and passing them on to
Snowden, began in March 1916 the publication of a weekly organ
The Tribunal, about which much more will be said later. The *Labour
Leader*, fed by its ILP reader-correspondents in every northern
town, exposed irregularities in out-of-the-way places which might
otherwise have escaped attention in London and Manchester.

Improvised attempts were made across the country to provide
opportunities for guidance to be given to the less articulate objectors.
Sometimes these attempts took the form of organised classes, run
by N-CF branches or Quaker groups, or by the two combined. Informal classes were held, for instance, at the Friends' Institute in
Manchester on every night of the week, up to forty potential
objectors attending, to be advised on the procedure of the Tribunals
and the provisions of the Military Service Acts. J. W. Graham, who
'lectured' at this 'school for shirkers and pro-Germans', as one
MP described the classes, wrote: 'We had, of course, to take care
not to produce bogus applicants, as we were roundly accused of
doing by the less reputable newspapers. We were, in fact, honoured
by spies, apparently anxious about their souls. It is possible that the
principal help we gave was in letting the men feel that they were not
alone[5].'

The N-CF was, of course, accused of 'manufacturing conscience',
to which it replied that it was not manufacturing but articulating it.
The classes, which were organised spasmodically in at least fifty
centres throughout the country, taught the more hesitant objectors
to meet such stock posers as the question, 'What would you do if a
criminal assulted your mother?' by answering with a careful statement differentiating between the policeman and the soldier, and
between a testimony against the organised violence of warfare and a
testimony against all force or coercion. Often the classes deliberately set out to expose the weaknesses of certain pacifist arguments,

such as those springing from Biblical literalism, thus discouraging their use before a Tribunal.

But only a tiny fraction of objectors were given this kind of help in framing their case—a few hundred out of the 16,100 who went before the Tribunals. This total figure is Graham's calculation, made in 1922. No central record was kept of applications on grounds of conscience, and an accurate count is rendered impossible by the inadequate nature of the records kept by some Tribunals, as well as by the fact that some men appealed on both conscience and practical grounds, and that others appeared several times before a Tribunal, being granted temporary, renewable exemptions.

The following summary, therefore, owes less to official statistics than to the records and estimates of such bodies as the Conscientious Objectors' Information Bureau. These indicate that of the 16,100 who went before Tribunals probably no more than two hundred received absolute exemption. (The official figure of six hundred, given by Lord Peel on 2 April 1919, is incomprehensible, unless, as Graham suggests, it incorrectly includes FAU members as having had absolute exemption.) Some 640 conditional exemptions were granted to members of the FAU in France, another 440 to men in its 'General Section', and another three hundred to FAU men in British hospitals. 3,964 men took 'work of national importance' under the Pelham Committee, and another nine hundred directly under the Tribunals. 3,300 accepted service in the Non-Combatant Corps. Three hundred took alternative service in the Quakers' War Victims' Relief Committee or the military's Royal Army Medical Corps. An estimated 175 evaded the Military Service Acts altogether by going into hiding, escaping abroad or otherwise keeping out of authority's way. 6,261 refused to accept their Tribunal's verdict either ordering them into the Army or prescribing alternative service. These, the Absolutists and the Schemers, were to bear the brunt of the persecution that followed.

REFERENCES

1 Parliamentary Report (Hansard), Commons, 29 February 1916.
2 This and other cases described in this chapter are quoted from N-CF papers and from John W. Graham, *op cit*, who attended Tribunals in the Manchester area as a Quaker observer.

OBJECTION OVERRULED

3 These figures, and those given at the end of this chapter, are taken from statistics compiled by the Conscientious Objectors Information Bureau in 1921. They differ slightly from the figures published in 1919 by the N-CF, but these latter were admittedly provisional.

4 Said by Kingsley Martin, in his autobiography *Father Figures* to be Lytton Strachey, but at least a dozen veteran COs have claimed, in conversation or correspondence with me, to have originated this one!

5 John W. Graham, *op cit.*

Chapter VI

Deemed to be Soldiers

REJECTED first by his Local and then by his Appeal Tribunal, or admitted to be genuine but refused an acceptable form of exemption, the objector was called up. From the moment he was instructed to report to camp, whether or not he did so, he was 'deemed to be enlisted', and his absence made him liable to prosecution for desertion.

After a few days of such 'desertion' the objector was visited by a policeman, arrested, and taken first to the recruiting office and then to the police station, where he spent the night in a cell. The next morning he was brought before the magistrate. The police or a recruiting officer offered evidence of his liability to serve, and the prisoner again declared his conscientious objection. He was then fined £2 for failing to report under the Military Service Act, and handed over to a military escort, which took him to the barracks to which he had first been ordered to report. There he was required to change into uniform, to sign his paybook and generally submit to routine orders. Such orders were refused, and he was charged with disobeying a lawful command and placed in the guardroom.

This sequence, which after an initial period of confusion quickly became standard, was described in detail in *Handed Over* by J. Scott Duckers, a 33-year-old solicitor who had given legal assistance to several COs. He was a radical Liberal and chairman of the Stop-the-War Committee.

Duckers was one of the small minority of objectors who refused to appear before the Tribunals on the ground that to do so was to admit their jurisdiction in a matter where the individual conscience alone was valid judge. On 26 March 1916 Duckers was called to the colours. He replied that, 'having been opposed on principle to war all my life, and being convinced that Britain's entry into the present conflict was unnecessary and unjustifiable, I do not intend, in any circumstances, to render any form of military service'.

I went on with my business and with meetings as usual [he wrote in *Handed Over*] until on Tuesday, April 11, on walking up the stairs to my office in Chancery Lane, I saw two stalwart men in plain clothes, one of whom accosted me and asked if I were Mr Scott Duckers. I said 'Yes', and he then intimated that they would 'like a word' with me. I knew what this meant, and leading the way into my private room, asked them to sit down and state their business. The spokesman opened a pocket-book and, showing me a card inside, said that he was a police-sergeant of the 'G' Division, and that he wished me to answer some questions under the Military Service Act. I said that I declined to answer any questions and asked if he had a warrant for my arrest. He replied in the affirmative, and pulled a paper out of his pocket. All this was done very pleasantly and courteously by the officer, and knowing that he was simply acting on his instructions, I neither felt nor showed any resentment.

It was amicably arranged that one of the policemen should accompany Duckers in a taxi to Lambeth, where he was due to attend a case, and that, under continuing police escort, he would then go to Bow Street Magistrates' Court. While awaiting the taxi Duckers gave the sergeant a copy of *Liberalism—Its Principles and Proposals*, written before the war by Herbert Samuel. The sergeant was reminded that, as Home Secretary, Samuel was his chief, and Duckers evidently had some satisfaction in pointing out the parts of the book in which the pre-war Samuel had demonstrated the evil and folly of conscription. The officer replied that when they got in the Cabinet people talked very differently, to which Duckers responded: 'You had better be careful. Anything you say now may be used in evidence against you.'

While we were waiting I wrote a letter to my father, spoke on the telephone to my friend, C. H. Norman, sent for two or three persons to come and see me, emptied my pockets of a few things it was no use taking to gaol, and gave final instructions and said 'Goodbye' to everyone in my office. A taxi was procured, and the sergeant and I were soon on our way to Lambeth Police Court. In the cab I had a good look at his warrant, which turned out to be a combined instruction to inquire and authority to arrest or do anything he thought necessary. It was directed to the chief of Vine Street Police Station and issued by the military authorities.

At Lambeth Duckers assisted counsel in defending a conscientious objector. Then, with the police sergeant, he went on to Bow Street Court, 'But we found the police there would not have anything to do with us. It was not their job, and anyway the court was full that afternoon. We must go to Vine Street. The matter was argued at some length, but my sergeant could make no impression on them, and we walked through Long Acre, Leicester Square and Piccadilly Circus, past the Piccadilly Hotel, and then suddenly up a side turning into the Police Station at Vine Street. Here they consented to take the charge, and a large sheet of yellow paper was produced, my name written upon it and the charge, which was that, being a member of the Special Reserve of His Majesty's Army, I had absented myself when called to the colours for permanent service. What had I to say? I said that I did not admit being under the Military Service Act. Down went this in the official notebook.'

Duckers was then given the choice of appearing at Marlborough Street Court that afternoon or Bow Street the following day. He chose Marlborough Street, and was allowed to telephone his office with this information. When he appeared, after lunching out with the police sergeant, the court precincts contained several of his friends wearing 'Stop the War' badges, but they were not allowed into the hearing.

Conducting his own case, Duckers quoted a Home Office circular of 9 March which recommended that proceedings against COs be taken by way of summons rather than by summary arrest, and wrung from the police sergeant the admission that this procedure had been ruled out in Duckers' case by instruction of the recruiting officer, a Captain Vansattart. This secured from the magistrate a remand on recognisances of £10. A week later he again appeared before the court, where the magistrate declared that he 'could not enter into the defendant's views'. Duckers was found guilty of failing to report, fined £2, and ordered to be handed over to the Army. A crowd of supporters outside, which included J. M. Hogge MP and Lady Clare Annesley, created a disturbance when the verdict was made known to them, and an arrest was made.

Duckers was taken by military escort to the Army-occupied Old Scotland Yard. 'The escort took me across the courtyard into a small office, where I saw a fine, alert, soldierly looking man with a wide stretch of ribbons across his breast. "Well, sir," he said, "you've been through the police court. Now it's my duty to make you a soldier." "And I think it my duty to refuse to be one," I replied. "Oh, we'll see about that," he rejoined pleasantly. "I've had some thousands through my hands, and they've all settled down quietly in the end." '

Duckers refused to supply personal details of full name, age and address. 'Look here, Mr Duckers,' replied the officer, 'I quite understand the way you look at things, but it's no good being awkward now. You've made your protest, you've done all you can, but you're in the Army, and I can tell you it will be very, very unpleasant for you if you make useless trouble. Don't you think you can bring yourself to take things reasonably now? If so, I'm sure you will enjoy the life and get on very well.'

The solicitor deemed to be a soldier still refused to answer questions, and followed by refusing to attest or to undress for a medical examination. 'At this they professed to lose patience with me. In the Army, if a man refused to obey an order, force was employed. They would be sorry to take any drastic measures, but . . .'

Force was not employed in this case, however, and Duckers was eventually hauled before the Commanding Officer, who ordered him to be remanded in a guardroom cell. 'I was taken away,' Duckers' account continues, 'down the stairs, across the courtyard to the guardroom, where I gave up my umbrella but was not searched.' Still wearing his silk hat and black coat, he was then removed to a cell 30 feet long, 15 feet wide and 12 feet high, which already housed five prisoners. 'It was an abominable, disgraceful place, unfit for occupation by any human soul . . . Along one wall were ranged four folding plank beds (one so much broken as to be quite useless) and a filthy, corroded bucket three parts full of urine. This was the only convenience in the place, and the floor round about it was in a very objectional condition. The bucket was not in the far corner, but in between the beds on the one hand and the door on the other, and could be watched through a hole in which the guard peeped at us when necessary and our food was passed in.

The whole place smelt abominably, and the floor was used as a general spittoon.'

After one night in the cell, Duckers was told that despite his refusal to submit to medical examination he was 'deemed to be fit for general service', and was to be sent to Winchester for enrolment in the Rifle Brigade. At Winchester he continued his refusal to obey orders. At first the Army seemed reluctant to bring him before a District Court Martial, but after three weeks, on 11 May, he was formally charged with refusing to put on uniform. The court-martial sentenced him to twelve months' hard labour, subsequently commuted to ninety-eight days' detention. But his refusal to accept military discipline was continued and on 29 August he was court-martialled a second time and sentenced to twelve months' hard labour. During sentence he continued to resist and a third court-martial in January 1917 sentenced him, for 'wilful defiance of military authority', to two years' hard labour. In a written statement to the court Duckers said:

> As this is my third trial by court-martial I presume that by now you know something of my views. Though not adopted since the commencement, or merely for the duration, of the present war, they have certainly been strengthened by the experiences I have gone through. The more I see of the Army the less I like it, and the greater is my determination to show that the punishments by which you are accustomed to subdue the spirits of soldiers are quite ineffective against anyone who knows his own mind and will continue steadfast. Whatever happens to me personally, I know that I have done something to maintain those principles of freedom which can only be preserved by individuals, and which will, perhaps more quickly than you think, successfully reassert themselves against all the muddle, waste, mismanagement and blundering incompetence of modern militarism, which these ridiculous trials help to illustrate.

★ ★ ★

Scott Duckers was more fortunate than many. He doubtless had more than his fair share of the Army's 'mismanagement and blundering incompetence', but he escaped as many of his fellow objectors did not, its deliberate and calculated brutality. The Army was organised to prevail by force and was unfamiliar with any other language. If the Tribunals had little understanding of the psychology of conscientious objectors, the military had much less.

On 13 April 1916 the N-CF received a letter signed by seven members of its Kingston branch, all of them in Hounslow barracks after having gone through similar procedures to those described in the case of Scott Duckers. The letter said:

We, seven conscientious objectors, would like you to know our present condition. In all cases the Tribunals have refused exemption from military service. We have been arrested by the police, imprisoned in the cells, brought before courts, and handed over to the military. We have, as politely as possible, refused to obey all military orders, but they have forced us into solitary confinement, dragged us to be forcibly examined by the doctor. Today our clothes have been wrenched off our bodies and a uniform forced on. When we removed it on principle, they took us from the cells to the detention room, and left us with only an undershirt for four and a half hours, with no heating. We were made to stand thus naked before officers in front of the door, and in view from the public highway, while certain particulars were taken for a court-martial to be held, probably on Friday at 11 am. We demanded counsel, but Mr Larkman, to arrange for it, was obliged to cross barrack yard with only a blanket.—(Signed) Templeman, Larkman, Jones, Jones, Ebeling, Forrester, Moat.[1]

Another objector, F. Beaumont, wrote from the guardroom, Pontefract barracks:

Dear Comrades,—Still alive and fighting. Have been forcibly examined, but have refused any payment or to sign any papers, and have refused to don the uniform about half a dozen times. Consequently I am still in civilian's; but they are going to use force in the end. They have tried all means to induce me to wear the uniform, threats, demands, requests, entreaties, and worst of all, have impressed upon me the absolute insignificance of one individual in a modern army. The officers told me that having been handed over by the country to the army authorities, they could do just as they liked with me. It is not until then that one realises the worst of conscription. When I refused to be examined, they told me it would be of no avail, since they could tame lions in the army. I replied that they could perhaps make lions tame, but they could never make lambs fierce! They have offered to forgive my past offences if I will start and be a soldier from this moment, and thus save themselves a great deal of trouble and myself a good deal of suffering, they say. I expect I shall get about two years in a military prison, probably as an example . . . Numerous kindly-intentioned officers have endeavoured to persuade me to accept the inevitable, and give up 'acting the goat'. But when a man is prepared to give his life for his ideals, surely veiled threats or suffering will not alter his decision.—Yours for the Cause, F. Beaumont.

Another letter, from Shoreham-by-Sea camp, to Will Chamberlain, honorary organiser of the N-CF and editor of *The Tribunal*, read:

Dear Comrade,—Just a line from another happy man who has been sentenced to two years' detention by DCM for remaining true to his principles of International Socialism. I feel the time I have spent amongst the soldiers has not been in vain, as I have preached the Gospel of Brotherhood and Internationalism, from the workers' point of view, to them whenever possible. On every occasion they have listened attentively to me, have asked me many questions which troubled them, and at the conclusion have almost invariably said, 'You are quite right, it would be a happier world if it could come about.' The pathetic way in which this has been said to me, both by young boys and men, has helped to make me more determined and resolute to suffer and save the curse of militarism from being shackled on the workers of this country. I go, therefore, to my confinement with a light heart and a smiling face, feeling that those who are persecuting us now will, in the near future, be dethroned and that that feeling of International Brotherhood will one day triumph and a permanent peace be secured. I will now bid goodbye to all my comrades in case we do not meet again.—Yours for freedom, K. Otley.

The opportunity to preach peace and socialism among the soldiers was taken by many other objectors. Fifteen N-CF members wrote to Chamberlain from the Guardroom, Drill Hall, Cardiff:

Hope to smuggle you just a word. Escorted to Roller Rink, Cardiff, on Monday evening. No supper. No beds. Slept on floor. Tuesday morning, no breakfast. Taken before Major and asked to sign rations form. Refused. Asked to see doctor and sign papers. Refused. Threat by Major of death penalty, or anything less court-martial should determine. All orders disobeyed. Still no food. After 24 hours fast asked again to sign rations form or send out for food. Refused to do either. Victory at last! Bread and cheese for supper. Delicious beyond words! Blankets!! Salmon for breakfast!!! Wild excitement. Flag flying cheerfully. Concerts on guardroom floor a speciality. Soldiers learning the *Red Flag*. Whatever lies before us we can face it. On behalf of the Guardroom Branch N-CF, Fraternally Yours, George Dardis (chairman), Dorian Herbert (vice-chairman), T. C. Griffiths (secretary), J. Shepherd (treasurer). Committee: E. B. James, R. T. James, C. G. James, T. Shepherd, A. Rudall, N. Hewinson, C. Faithfull, B. Dacres, J. H. Davies, P. Pope, P. R. Bainton.

And a letter from A. E. Daniell in Reading Barracks reported:

There are seven of us since Monday. We have formed a branch of the N-CF! We have refused all orders and are awaiting court-martial . . . We went to the CO's office (Conscientious Objector's office, we call it!) and were there told we should be court-martialled . . . We have made many converts here. Have now been removed to separate cells.

The Tribunal of 4 May 1916 reported that 102 N-CF members were, on the eve of May Day, in the hands of the military. Only two had 'given in, as a result of pressure brought to bear upon them'.

'Pressure' was an inadequate word for it. A group of Lancashire men at Preston Barracks were forcibly stripped and marched round the barracks square, partly or wholly naked. In this condition the men were then 'frog-marched', the right arm and left leg being raised above the head and held in position while the prisoner was forced to move on his left arm and right leg. Philip Snowden, describing this 'pressure' in the House of Commons on 17 May 1916, declared that the men were indecently assaulted, beaten with sticks and kicked across the square. Similar treatment was accorded three men at Bettisfield Camp, who were paraded naked after being emptied out of their civilian clothing. One man, D. S. Parkes, was told to prepare for death and then forced to watch while a rifle was loaded, pointed at his chest, and lowered only after a bogus order to fire was given. Another man was handcuffed to a bar with his arms above his head for forty minutes, 'standing on tiptoe to relieve the pressure on my wrists'.

More horrifying still was the treatment meted out to James Brightmore, a young solicitor's clerk from Manchester. After serving eight months of a twelve-month sentence of detention, Brightmore was given twenty-eight days' solitary confinement for continuing his refusal to obey orders. The Commanding Officer of Shore Camp, Cleethorpes, where the young man was stationed, finding no guardroom cell available, ordered that a pit be dug on open ground outside the guardroom. According to Brightmore's own account:

> A hole was in course of construction which was already about four feet deep . . . For four days intermittently the pit was deepened a little at a time, from seven feet on Monday night to ten before the week was out. On the Tuesday water was struck, but instructions were given that the hole must go deeper still. For four days I was up to the ankles in mud and water, but on the Friday two strips of wood were let into the wall of the pit for me to stand on. They were not more than three inches wide and 10 or 11 inches apart. One of them, owing to the clay giving way, sank into the water after 24 hours.

Brightmore was told by an officer who visited the mouth of the pit that his five friends and fellow-objectors had been shipped to France, where they had been executed. This was a lie, but Brightmore had no means of knowing that. He was told that he was receiving favoured treatment, but that he too would be sent to France and shot if he continued to resist.

One day it rained heavily and the pit became waterlogged. A group of soldiers removed Brightmore to a marquee, where he slept the night. The following day the soldiers concerned were reprimanded for putting him under cover, and he was removed from the marquee to spend the night on the sodden ground, without blankets. He was then returned to the pit.

After a week of this punishment Brightmore won the sympathy of a soldier who, at considerable risk to himself, managed to pass down into the pit a cigarette packet and a pencil. On the cigarette packet, ripped open to form a single sheet of card, Brightmore wrote the following letter to his family:

My dear ones,—This is the best stuff I can find to write what may be my last letter. Everything has been taken off me, and I should not have this pencil but for chance. I was bullied horribly when I was tried, and sentenced to 28 days' detention in military confinement— to be given raw rations and to cook food for myself. This does not sound bad, but I have found the confinement was in a pit which started at the surface at three feet by two, and tapered off to two feet six inches by 15 inches. Water was struck, but they continued until it was 10 feet deep. The bottom is full of water, and I have to stand on two strips of wood all day long just above the water line. There is no room to walk about, and sitting is impossible. The sun beats down, and through the long day there are only the walls of clay to look at. Already I am half mad.

I have not heard from you since I came out of prison, but I know there are many letters waiting for me. I cannot, therefore, tell what may happen when I get to France, whether the death sentence is being exacted . . . I hunger-struck for two days in the hole here, but found I was getting too weak to resist, and my brain, too, seemed to be giving under the strain.

I wish I could see your letters. I could be reassured or know your wishes. As it is, I feel sentenced to death, knowing that within a few days I shall be in France and shot. The fact that men are being sent to France at all is proof positive to me that the military authorities have captured the machine, and are able to do as they like with us.

What have our friends been doing? It is nothing but cold-blooded murder to send men out into the trenches to be shot like dogs for disobedience. I am not afraid to die, but this suspense, this ignorance linked up with the torture of this pit, have plunged me into misery, despair, madness, almost insanity . . . The hardest thing is leaving you three dearest ones behind, and the suffering and anxiety I am bringing upon you. All these weary months of imprisonment we have lived on hopefully. Now the cup is being dashed from our hands, and in liberty's name! . . . Goodbye.

The soldier who had supplied the pencil and cigarette packet sent the letter to Brightmore's family, who sent it on to the *Manchester Guardian*. On the eleventh day of Brightmore's confinement in the pit, the newspaper published a comment on the story. Forty minutes after the paper arrived at the camp Brightmore was removed from the pit and orders were given that it be filled in immediately. But the scandal was not to be so easily hidden. The soldier who had helped Brightmore testified against his officers. On 18 and 23 July, questions were asked about the case in the Commons. A public enquiry followed, which resulted in the dismissal of the two responsible officers.

Brightmore's was one of two cases of brutal persecution which shocked liberal opinion in the summer of 1917—more than a year after the first intake of conscientious objectors, and nine months after publication of a War Office circular (quoted later in this chapter) warning camp commanders against ill-treating objectors. The other was the case of nineteen-year-old Jack Gray at Hornsea Camp, whose story was told by a fellow-objector, James Crawshaw, in a letter dated 23 June 1917. Crawshaw wrote to the N-CF.

On the Monday morning, 7 May 1917, the breaking-in processes were begun on Gray by the bombing officer, who used his powers of persuasion by means of more or less gentle ankle-tapping to bring him to attention. Then, on Gray's refusal to salute, he foamed at the mouth and gave vent to terrible language. Subsequently he threw a live Mills bomb at his feet, after removing the pin and failing to persuade Gray to throw it when ordered. Gray stood perfectly calm and still when the bomb was hissing at his feet, and the officer who threw it had to run for cover. The officer then wanted to shake hands with Gray, saying, 'Your —— guts are in the right place, anyhow,' but Gray declined.

After dinner there was a repetition. Tuesday morning, May 8th, Gray was introduced to the physical training staff and Lieutenant ——. Here abuse and persuasion were blended, and on Gray's refusing to obey, his tunic was removed, shirt neck opened, puttee tied round his waist in lieu of a belt. Orders were then given, all of which he refused to obey, and was knocked into the various positions each time. The sergeant burst his mouth with a heavy blow. He was threatened with a ducking in the pond. Next day there was a repetition, and he had to endure a very long stand in the position referred to, facing a bitterly cold wind (the camp is a very exposed one), interlarded with threats hurled at him by the company sergeant-major, who had a valise filled with stones, which Gray was to be made to carry as a pack under forced marching. Under these accumulated threats Gray broke down for the first time, the ordeal being beyond physical endurance. Many other and varied acts of brutality were committed which can all be proved by eye witnesses, such as the use of soft soap rubbed over the head and face by NCOs, and others, who manifested unmitigated delight in exercising their brutality.

One day his arms were trussed up his back by force, he was tied in that position with a rope, and a man then pulled him round the field by the rope, walking, running, etc., alternately. On another day he was strippped naked, a rope tightly fastened round his abdomen, and he was then pushed forcibly and entirely immersed in a filthy pond in the camp grounds eight or nine times in succession and dragged out each time by the rope. The pond contained sewage. He says the effect of the tightening of the rope after the second immersion cannot be described, and was still more intolerable when, after the last immersion, they put upon his wet and muddy body a sack with a hole through for the head and one for each arm.

The foregoing is only a part of the illegal and brutal acts perpetrated upon Jack Gray, in such a manner that eight of the men ordered to carry out orders refused to do so, and thereby rendered themselves open to a most serious charge.

Gray gave in, and the Army won a famous victory. But Crawshaw's letter provoked demands for an enquiry, to which the War Office eventually acceded. The officers concerned were censured and Gray transferred to another unit.

The Tribunal of 19 July 1917 carried a letter from a serving soldier protesting bitterly at the treatment accorded to Brightmore and Gray. 'Although I do not agree with "COs" in the slightest degree', he wrote, 'it makes me utterly disgusted to hear that such a thing could be practised in England of all places . . . After many months in the trenches, I am going out again now, ostensibly to carry on the fight for freedom. It seems to me that our services are largely wasted if such frightful tyranny has become possible at home.' Paradoxically, the same issue of *The Tribunal* carried a letter from a CO deprecating the publicity given by the N-CF to the Brightmore case. 'The deliberate spreading of atrocity stories, however authentic, incites to bitterness, hatred and revenge . . . These trials are sent us that we may witness to a better way than retaliation, hate and enmity, viz., the spirit of loving-forgiveness. Christ, "when he was reviled, reviled not again," not even by publishing the truth!' This view was certainly as unrepresentative of the N-CF and conscientious objectors as the soldier's letter was of the Army.

One of the worst of the Army's corps of tormentors was Lieutenant-Colonel Reginald Brooke, Commandant of Wandsworth Military Detention Barracks. Brooke made no secret of his opinion that the Government was both soft and treacherous in permitting conscientious objectors to escape the firing squad, nor of his intention to mete out 'justice' in the Government's place. He declared he cared nothing for Asquith or Parliament, but would 'do just as I like with these men'. He would treat 'his' prisoners in 'his' barracks as he thought fit. 'I do not care an atom', he boasted, 'for public opinion.'

Brooke had the misfortune, however, to meet the stubborn resistance of C. H. Norman, a founder-member of the N-CF, who spent his war first undergoing torture at the hands of the military, then organising work strikes among objectors at Princetown Settlement, and finally suffering solitary confinement in jail. While he was at Wandsworth, Norman became a target of Brooke's sadistic persecutions, but countered by preferring charges which resulted in Brooke being court-martialled and dismissed from his command. Norman gave evidence at the court-martial as follows:

> I was put into a strait-jacket on two occasions for over twenty-four hours, and during that time I became unconscious. I was in hospital for seven days, and was brought out to parade. I declined, and was put on a bread and water diet. Then I made a hunger, thirst and sleep strike for forty-eight hours. For two nights I walked about my cell, and then I found I could not go on. So I went on with the hunger and thirst strike, and was forcibly fed on two occasions.
>
> The process was this. I was laid in a strait-jacket on the bed on the first occasion, with three or four attendants, although I offered no resistance of any sort or kind. A tube was put in my nose, and the food was pumped down through the nose for fifteen minutes. After that I was kept for an hour and a half in a strait-jacket. The Commandant came round and looked at me, and was most abusive and insulting. I noticed that Colonel Brooke was usually most abusive and insulting when I was in a strait-jacket.
>
> I declined any food and the next day there was the same process,

except that it was done through the mouth, and the feed tube which was used was too large for my throat. The result was that I had twenty minutes of the utmost agony, and naturally that had very grave effects upon my general health and nervous condition. In the meantime I had got out of communication with my friends as to what was going on, and I decided that I would not—in fact, I could not—go on, in view of the treatment I was undergoing, with that sort of thing. For several days I was spitting blood, and still had internal pains, as the result of this operation. It was unnecessary to do it this way, because if the food had been administered in the ordinary way I should have taken it. It was done as a punishment. It was a form of torture.

It was perfectly impossible for any man with self-respect, or who calls himself a gentleman, to obey the orders of the Commandant. He called me a swine, a beast and a coward, and I have not uttered a discourteous or uncivil word to anyone, notwithstanding the treatment I have had. I have been spat at by the Commanding Officer three times. The Commandant's excuse for the strait-jacket was that I had threatened suicide. I did not say that. I said I gathered from the treatment that I should be driven to suicide. I was put into a strait-jacket fifteen minutes after I was taken into the place, and it was deliberately done, in my opinion, to break my health. I was only given a bowl of milk to drink, and I fainted during the night. The strait-jacket, which was too small, led to a great increase of the ordinary pain.[2]

The particular occurrence of violence which forced the War Office to make some attempt to curb the zeal of the conscientious objectors' persecutors occurred in August 1916 at the camp of the 3rd Cheshire Regiment, Birkenhead. The victims were George Beardsworth, John Dukes and George Benson. Beardsworth made the following statement, sworn to a Commissioner of Oaths and subsequently published during a public enquiry. It begins with an account of bullying by the military police, and continues:

On Thursday morning, August 31, I was ordered out for parade, and I refused to go. Several soldiers then came in and led me out. I was marched on to the parade ground in Birkenhead Park. I still refused to obey orders. Every time I refused to do something I was forced physically to carry out the action or ill-treated, e.g. on refusing to mark time two soldiers kicked my legs the whole time the men had to mark time. On refusing to turn my eyes right someone punched the side of my head and my head was forcibly twisted in the desired direction. During the morning relays of men (about six at a time) ran me round the field punching me. This happened before breakfast and in public. I am not sure whether there were any officers present on this occasion.

I was taken before the medical officer to be vaccinated, and upon my refusal to be vaccinated I was taken to the park by an escort. On arrival at the park (between 10 and 10.30) I was handed over to a gymnasium instructor. I was taken to the vaulting horse, and refusing to jump was thrown over by several men. I was rushed to the water jump and pushed into the water. This was repeated at the command of Captain Mills and other officers who were standing by, and kept on saying: 'Take him back again.' I cannot remember how many more times this was done, but I should say at least half-a-dozen.

I was then taken to some wooden hoardings, I should say at least eight feet high. Some men got hold of me by the arms and legs and threw me over; I remember this being done twice in succession, but it may have been done more times than that. Then I was allowed a rest with the others. I stood against the hoarding while the gymnasium instructor invited the soldiers to come along and see what kind of a 'b——' I was. Just about then I caught sight of my wife. Then they took me to a wooden inclined plane, put my head between my knees, and rolled me to the top, where I fell off to the ground, a drop of about six feet. After this I cannot remember the order of events, or even all that happened to me. I remember being rushed up some sloping ground, thrown over some railings, run down a slope on the other side, then back again, and thrown over the railings again. This was done over and over again. I had my arms and legs 'drilled' by men, the latter being done while on my back with a man's foot on my stomach. I was rushed about to an accompaniment of kicks and punches, and my ankles and legs were kicked to make me 'mark time'.

At the end of this Major Roddy rode up to me and spoke to me, saying he did not understand my position. I pointed out that I was not in a fit condition to argue or explain. He suggested that I might do physical exercises. I refused, and was thereupon taken back to the Gym. Squad, and put through a treatment similar to that already described. I was taken back to the camp with the other men. Again I did not go to get any dinner because I did not feel that I could eat. After dinner time I was again taken to the park. A lieutenant came up and asked me if I was going to do the drill. I said I was not in a fit physical condition to drill, even if I was willing to do so. He insisted on a reply and I refused to give it. I was then taken to the Gym. Squad again. Captain Mills then sent for me and again asked me if I would drill. I said that for that afternoon I would drill as far as my condition would allow. I drilled during the afternoon.

I was taken back to the barracks for tea, but again I felt no inclination for food, and I did not go to get any. During the evening I asked to be allowed out of barracks, but this was refused. The sergeant-major came and asked me if I was going to drill in the morning. I replied that my conscientious objection had not abated in the slightest degree, and I could give no undertaking.

Dukes told a similar story, and Benson recounted lesser bullying to which he had been subjected. The mistake of the officers at Birkenhead was to mete out this treatment in a public park, in full view of civilians, including Beardsworth's wife. Protests reached the War Office and developed until, after questions had been asked in the Commons, a court of enquiry was directed to look into the charges. The court's work was not made easier by the fact that Dukes and Beardsworth refused to give evidence against the soldiers who had maltreated them, regarding the officers as the real culprits. The officers did not deny the facts in Beardsworth's statement, though they objected to the use of the word 'brutality' to describe their actions and orders. Officers and men involved were subsequently court-martialled and punished.

The Birkenhead case aroused much public resentment and the War Office acted on 19 September by sending a drastic circular to all Commanding Officers. This referred to 'reports which have been received in this Department that in certain instances attempts have been made by Commanding Officers to compel conscientious objectors to perform their military duties by ignoring acts of grave insubordination and ensuring compliance by physical means'. The correct procedure, continued the letter, was for objectors to 'immediately be placed in arrest and remanded for trial by court-martial, unless a minor punishment is awarded or the soldier concerned elects to accept the award of his Commanding Officer'. Where Commanding Officers were awarding sentences of detention without troubling about court-martial proceedings, 'the Army Council will seriously consider whether the officer concerned, who has been guilty of a grave dereliction of duty and disregard of the law, can be permitted to retain his command'. In a parting paragraph, the letter reminded Commanding Officers that conscientious objectors were to be treated exactly like 'other soldiers guilty of acts of insubordination', and that 'any special treatment in the way of coercion other than by the methods of punishment laid down in the Army Act and King's Regulations is strictly prohibited, and that very serious notice will be taken of any irregularities in this respect which may come to light'.

But even this stern warning had little effect in preventing outbreaks of what the War Office chose to call 'special treatment in the way of coercion'. The Brightmore and Gray cases quoted above post-dated the circular by nearly a year, and other brutalities were committed within days of the letter's dispatch. At the end of September an objector named A. Robinson, at Lancaster Barracks, was frogmarched to parade with his equipment on his back. When he refused to work he had a pick and shovel tied round his neck. Still refusing, he was handcuffed and his feet were tied together. A cord was tied from his ankles to his hands, and pulled tight to double him up. He was left like this for two hours. Next morning he was beaten 'black and blue' by military policemen armed with sticks. One knocked him down and sat on his chest, and others then stood on his chest. When he refused to work with an oat-crushing machine his hands were tied to the handle, which was then turned by one soldier while another rapped his knuckles at every rotation until they swelled and so tightened the pressure of the ropes.

At Gosport barracks a soldier who had enlisted under family pressure and against his convictions decided to join the objectors. Another, in identical circumstances, made the same decision at Hereford Camp. James Devlin, at Gosport, was given fourteen weeks solitary confinement, with only half-an-hour's exercise each week and a daily diet of bread and water, prescribed for that period by the camp doctor despite a rule that punishment diets of this kind should run for no more than three days. Devlin's health was broken. Maurice Andrews, at Hereford, was stripped of his civilian clothes and left for eight days in his vest and underpants. For four hours a day his hands were either strapped or handcuffed behind his back. A guard explained that Army discipline could only be maintained by making detention so terrible that a man would do anything rather than endure it.

Non-Combatant Corps objectors overseas, refusing orders which they took to serve a combatant purpose or which otherwise offended their consciences, suffered scandalous treatment not at all mitigated by the fact that distance from public opinion at home tended to release the inhibitions of their superiors. W. G. Tyrell was tied to a stake every day for a month at Bapaume, often within the range of shell fire which drove his guard a hundred yards away for safety. A group of fourteen Seventh-Day Adventists doing non-combatant work in France refused to work on their Sabbath, which ran from dusk on Friday to dusk on Saturday. They were sentenced to six months' hard labour. Twelve of them wrote an account of their experiences for *The Tribunal* of 4 April 1918:

> We were interviewed by the Prison Governor who told us that we should be compelled to work Saturdays, as they were authorised to employ physical means in order to secure their object. On leaving the Governor we were set to work on the parade ground with some other prisoners who were working there. This was at three o'clock on Friday afternoon, one hour before our observance of the Sabbath Day commenced. We had plainly stated that we could not consistently continue work beyond four o'clock. By that time five or six sergeants, each armed with stick and revolver, had collected near the working party. As soon as we ceased work, with one accord these men rushed at us and knocked us down in turn with their fists. As each man rose from the ground this treatment was repeated. We still refused to work and the attack was renewed with sticks. In several instances we were kicked brutally whilst on the ground. Two of the sergeants became so infuriated that they now drew their revolvers, but were prevented from levelling them by the intervention of their fellow NCOs. In no case was the slightest resistance offered by us.
>
> We were then rushed to the punishment cells, the sticks being freely used on the way, and several sergeants ran in amongst us deliberately tripping us, thus bringing us heavily to the ground on the square. On reaching the cells were were placed in irons—called

'figures of eight' on account of their shape—which are made in various sizes to grip the wrists securely, one above the other, behind the back. In some cases the irons were too small, and caused the most excruciating pain on being screwed up. In this helpless condition we were again punched severely about the face and body, after which we were isolated, each man in a small cell about seven feet by four-and-a-half feet, having a concrete floor and iron walls. The extreme cold was very trying in this condition.

At this point one of the fourteen was selected to be made an example. He continues the story—anonymously:

In the cell passage the sergeants agreed that I was the ringleader, probably because I was the tallest. The smallest pair of 'figure eights' was brought and screwed down upon my wrists. So small was the pair that to get them on my flesh was ripped and cut in several places. The circulation was practically cut off, leaving my hands dead. I was then pushed into a cell, and pinned against the wall by one sergeant, whilst the others in a most passionate rage struck me continually about the head and in the stomach. Then one burly NCO lifted me up bodily, and with his knee threw me backwards to the other side. The contact with the iron wall caused the irons to cut more, and sent acute pain to all my nerves. This kind of treatment continued until I dropped to the floor. I was picked up, but collapsed again, whereupon I was kicked several times in the middle of the back. Finally I became unconscious. I had made no opposition by force, or even uttered a word which could have given the slightest offence.

The next morning a staff sergeant and a sergeant visited me, and again violently knocked me about until I fell to the ground winded by a sharp punch. I felt pains and bruises everywhere; my eyes were blackened, and one was completely closed; my jaw seemed locked on one side, and my nerves were out of control. Towards 9 a.m. a corporal opened the cell door and ordered me to work. To my reply 'I cannot,' he seized me and threw me against the wall. He repeated the order, and receiving the same reply, drew his revolver, placing the barrel to my forehead, threatening to shoot me if I again objected. He reminded me that 'Dead men tell no tales.' He meant that his word (stating that his action was necessary in self-defence) would not be disputed. Seeing that I remained quite calm, and did not reply, he put up the revolver and left me with a curse.

About 10 a.m. I was taken out of my cell, and two cement blocks weighing about 35 lb each were roped round my neck, one hanging upon my chest, the other upon my back. With my wrists still in irons behind my back I was made to pace the passage at a quick march. At last, from exhaustion, I sank beneath the strain, and remained in a fit about an hour. When I came to, I was placed in the cell again till the afternoon, when the Governor visited me and gave permission for me to have my blankets. At 4 p.m., I was given six ounces of bread—the first food for twenty-four hours. At 3.40, my companions were sent back to their sections, but I was too ill to go, and remained the night and next day in the cell without further medical attention until 12 a.m. The food given for this day was two rations (6 oz) of bread. The next morning I was taken before the doctor, and a sergeant in a misleading way stated what had happened. In a casual way the doctor examined me, and gave me 'Light Duty', stating that I had palpitations of the heart, and that the occurrence was unfortunate. With this I was promptly dismissed to my section.

The same account goes on to give a revealing picture of life in a military prison in the field:

Apart from our own experiences we heard and saw many cases similar to a few we here mention. One poor fellow—an Australian fighting soldier—was continually the sport of the NCOs, who seemed to delight in venting their feelings upon this perhaps somewhat eccentric individual. When they were off duty at night they would come to the cells and torment him by poking him viciously in the ribs, by forcing his arms (which were in irons) into such positions as absolutely to torture him. His groans and shrieks were terrible to hear, and often they would gag him with a bar of soap wrapped in cloth in order that they might continue their sport without his cries being heard outside the prison.

One man—a little, shrivelled physical wreck—was tortured most frightfully because he would not admit himself to be a deserter. He was punished, kicked, and bullied very cruelly. On several occasions the sergeant-major came and interjected much questioning of a bullying nature, with vicious slashes from a steel-lined riding stock he always carried.

In one cell was an old man who was very simple-minded, and who, in addition, had a weak bladder. One bitterly cold day in December this old fellow was taken, on account of his uncleanliness, and forced under a cold spray in the bath house. He was then scrubbed with a stiff yard brush until his flesh was raw in places; on returning to his cell he could not speak. The Governor made his daily inspection shortly after, and found the old man in such a terrible state that he was removed from the cells at once, and food had to be given him.

As to the general conditions under which the prisoners live much could be written that would never be believed, and much could not be described in words. We were huddled fourteen men in each tent. Owing to shocking sanitary conditions, and the fact that it is impossible to wash in the two minutes allowed in the wash-house twice daily, the vilest diseases are prevalent. We were sleeping next to men suffering from venereal disease. In the sections where the men sleep there is provided one open bucket for the use of about sixty men, and latrine paper is almost impossible to obtain; the stench from these buckets is vile.

Each man has several rusty implements to clean in his section after 5 p.m. and for this he is supposed to use a piece of sacking and water. Frequently the water bucket is dry, and the men have to use the urine pail for this purpose. If they did not do this the task would be unfinished, and they would be severely punished next morning. Many of the cases of skin disease must be much aggravated by the blunt and dirty razors and brushes which have to be used by the men in turn.

The combined effect of those conditions is to make the men very quarrelsome even among themselves. Fighting, stealing each other's food, etc. being daily occurrences. After two years of this life they leave the prison vowing vengeance on their tormentors, declaring that they will never play the man again. In fact, they, in many cases, are turned out finished criminals, though they have been sent to prison for some trivial thing which might be more appropriately termed a misfortune than a crime. So desperate do men become under these conditions that they will gladly do anything to contract a disease that will necessitate their removal to hospital. Thus, one fellow actually took venereal germs and rubbed them into his eyes, of which eventually he lost the sight.

Many men are covered with bad sores—the result of being unable to wash themselves properly. In wet weather the men's blankets are often wet through on account of the bad condition of the tents.

The ill-treatment which we received, and which is common throughout the prison, appeared to be administered, in the first instance, apart from the Governor's authority. He could not, however, have been totally ignorant of subsequent abuses. A chaplain from a neighbouring camp was passing the prison one day, and hearing shrieks from the cells he entered the prison and asked to see us (he knew we were in the prison). He was not permitted to see us, nor was he allowed inside the prison again, in spite of the fact that he held a service there once a week. Not once were we visited by the prison chaplain, nor were we allowed to have Bibles—our own were demanded from us on entering the prison.

We certainly think that the authorities at home cannot be cognisant of the terrible conditions existing in our military prisons in the Field. The men absolutely hate their own country, so embittered does the life make them. It is common to hear men say that they will never fight again for their country, so emaciated and reduced were we by our stay of one month in prison that it was difficult for us at first to recognise several of our comrades.

We should emphasise the fact that throughout our whole experience we remained quite passive. No resistance of any kind was offered at any time.

We have seen the treatment of prisoners from other prisons whilst the men were out in working parties, and know the conditions in each case to be much the same. Indeed, it is the subject of much scandal and bad feeling among the British troops in the bases where the prisons are located.

Other examples of brutal treatment of COs were reported from Alexandria, Egypt. One concerned an objector from Halesworth, Suffolk, named J. B. Saunders, who was arrested in May 1916 and persuaded against his convictions to enlist. After enlistment his convictions reasserted themselves and he went absent without leave. Court-martialled, he was given a year's detention. After three months in Britain he was secretly shipped to France under a false name and regiment, court-martialled again for refusing to carry his equipment, and after seven days' detention sent to Alexandria on 14 April 1917. Again he was court-martialled for disobedience and sentenced to six months' hard labour in Gabarree prison. In August he wrote to his wife from Mustapha Camp, Alexandria:

You remember I said I would face the music. You may believe what I say that I am not afraid of anything the military can do. I have been in chains and handcuffs, crucified to a tree in this broiling sun nearly every morning and evening, for five months have had bread and water and solitary confinement. I refused to do any work whatever, so I leave you to guess what five months alone in a cell, doing nothing, is like. Seven times I went down with dysentery, and seven times I managed to get on my feet and face the music. I fainted, and had to be driven away in a barrow. This tropical sun and chaining up nearly drove me mad. I stuck it, and got finally bowled out, and was sent to 19th General Schools Hospital for seventeen days. I was offered RAMC work. I refused it, and asked to be sent back to prison to do full six months. I left hospital next day, and was doing seven days' No. 1 Punishment diet, chained up in the sun, etc., when suddenly I had the chains taken off and I was released. They have discovered at last that they cannot break me. They failed at Barlinnie, and I intend them to fail here. I am determined to sacrifice all rather than give in. Many times I thought I should hang in the sun and die. I pleaded with the sentry to shoot me. I cannot tell you the misery of it . . . I'll die fifty times rather than endorse the wicked thing. I have several friends here. If I am to be flattened out, they can do it in jail. They can have my body; my mind I will destroy rather than allow the military cult to take it. I was flooded for weeks in my cell with water, two buckets of creosol were thrown in, and I was gassed. I was naked for several days and nights in chains. I had to lie on the concrete floor. However, I believe the doctor stopped these horrible proceedings. To chain a man up in the tropical sun is illegal . . . If my letters suddenly cease, I shall be in prison in Gabarree. Don't misunderstand me. I am determined to do nothing out here.

Other cases at Alexandria concerned NCC men who resisted a compulsory but illegal transfer to combatant work. In the summer of 1917 several hundred such transfers were made, until the resultant agitation forced the military authorities to transfer the men back to non-combatant work. But in the summer of 1918 about fifty objectors in the Royal Army Medical Corps at Alexandria were put on combatant duties, on refusing which they were thrown into Gabarree prison with sentences of two years hard labour. Only thirteen of the fifty were recorded as returning to Britain in May 1919 to complete their sentences in civil prisons. One of the remaining thirty-seven, Norman Stafford, contracted first bronchial pneumonia and then malaria in prison, and secured a release on health grounds. The others served their full sentences at Gabarree.

★   ★   ★

I have left to the end of this grim catalogue the most remarkable of all these scandals although in point of time it occurred almost immediately the Army began to get its hands on conscientious objectors, in the early summer of 1916.

During the passage of the first Military Service Act Snowden and others had pressed, as we have seen, for assurances that conscientious objectors would not be subject to the death penalty. These assurances were duly given, but Snowden sought to point out an alarming loophole. What was the position, he asked, concerning men who had been rejected by the Tribunals and handed over to the Army as insincere in their conscientious objection? They remained *de facto* objectors, but was their objection legally recognised? If it was so recognised, they should not be in the Army; and if it was not, they were subject to Army regulations, which prescribed death by shooting as the punishment for disobedience on active service.

Clear-cut assurances on this point were never forthcoming. The loophole stayed open. The Army, therefore, bewildered and enfuriated both by the numbers of persistent objectors who passed into their hands, and by the unnerving persistence of their uncompromising resistance, reached for the ultimate deterrent, sentence of death. In their determination to make the deterrent credible, military authority challenged civil authority in one of the most extraordinary and bizarre episodes in the history of modern British government.

In April a squad of hard-core objectors were confined in irons at Landguard Fort, Harwich, a circular redoubt built by French prisoners in the Napoleonic wars. They were kept in darkness on a diet of bread and water. All had been forcibly attached to the Eastern Non-Combatant Corps, despite their objection to both combatant and non-combatant service.

The men refused the work given them, carting stones from the beach, because they believed the stones were to be used for building an access road to a military camp. They were threatened by a sergeant that continuing disobedience would entail dire consequences. On 6 May they were visited by an officer who told them they would leave for France the following day, where disobedience would be met with the death sentence. 'Once you are across the channel', said the officer, 'your friends in Parliament and elsewhere won't be able to do anything for you.' The men were then told that an immediate undertaking to obey orders would save them from 'certain death'. All refused.

On 7 May, in the early hours of the morning while it was still dark, a batch of seventeen were released from their irons and packed into a train for Southampton with several hundred NCC men. As the train passed slowly through the London suburbs one of the NCC men scribbled a note and tossed it through the window on to a station platform. Astonishingly, it was picked up and reached its destination—the No-Conscription Fellowship. N-CF officials had already been alerted by NCC men at Harwich and had sent a representative hurrying to Landguard Fort. Arriving on the afternoon of the 7th, he was told that the train-load had already left for France.

These facts, scanty as they were, were put before the N-CF's friends in Parliament. On 9 May Arnold Rowntree confronted Asquith with the Fellowship's charges. Asquith replied that he had no knowledge of the situation. To further questioning from Philip Snowden he declared that if the men had been sent to France the Army did not have the authority to shoot them.

The following day Professor Gilbert Murray returned from France to find in London a telegram from the parents of one of the seventeen objectors, Rendel Wyatt. It stated that their son was one of a group sent to France to be shot. Could Murray help? Inclined not to believe the rumour, but anxious to set the parents' minds at rest, Murray went to the Commons and saw his brother-in-law, Geoffrey Howard, a pro-war, pro-conscriptionist MP who was nevertheless critical of army brutalities. Howard recommended an interview with Lord Derby, then director of recruiting. Derby gave Murray the impression that he knew all about the affair and maintained that the Army had every right to send whom it liked to

France. 'If they disobey orders,' he asserted, 'of course they will be shot, and quite right too!'

Now thoroughly alarmed, Murray insisted on seeing Asquith. Pressed by Howard, the Prime Minister granted a five-minute interview. Murray told of his conversation with Derby, and Asquith became increasingly angry. Muttering 'Abominable! Abominable!' he promised to despatch an immediate message to the front, forbidding any executions without the knowledge of the Cabinet. The message reached Haig the following day. But Asquith was no longer riding the tiger.

On 15 May Philip Morrell asked in the Commons for confirmation that the seventeen had been sent to France to be shot. Sir George Cave, the Solicitor-General, replied ambiguously to the effect that as conscientious objectors they were not subject to the death penalty but as 'men drafted into the Army' they were. Snowden demanded: 'What is the Government going to do? Are they going to have these lads shot in France? If they are, all I can say is that throughout the length and breadth of this land a wave of public indignation will be aroused against the treatment of these men.' *Hansard* records at this point the eloquent comment: 'HON MEMBERS —"NO!" '

But there was indeed some public reaction by now, if not of tidal wave proportions. Eminent churchmen were signing round-robins of protest to the press, and the small liberal newspapers were getting agitated. The War Office reacted by inviting a party of journalists to visit the non-combatant men in France. A series of white-washing stories appeared in the press, praising the beautiful surroundings and idyllic circumstances of the NCC men, the implication being that these were the seventeen about whom all the fuss was being made. So successful was this device for damping down public disquiet that the Under-Secretary for War, Harold Tennant, parried further Parliamentary questions from Snowden on 24 May by irrelevant allusions to the same Non-Combatant Corps.

Indeed, disquiet was so successfully allayed that barely three weeks after the dispatch of the Harwich men the army felt free to brandish its ultimate deterrent again. On 28 May, sixteen objectors at Richmond, Yorkshire, were attached to a unit leaving for France. On 29 May, eight men at Kinmel Park, Abergele, were sent to France via Southampton. And on 30 May a group of nine military prisoners at Seaford, Sussex, some but not all of whom were conscientious objectors, were despatched by the same route in handcuffs.

While the Seaford men travelled under escort to Southampton a group of anti-conscriptionist MPs were being assured by Mr Tennant in a private interview that there was no intention on the part of the Government to send objectors to France, either to be shot or to be forced to fight. The MPs, armed with details of the latest despatches provided by the diligent N-CF, refused to accept Tennant's assurances. The following day Arnold Rowntree pressed the matter on the floor of the House. The unfortunate Mr Tennant had to admit that the men had been sent after all. He read out telegrams sent the previous day to the commanding officers at Kinmel Park, Seaford and Richmond: 'Take steps to ensure that they do not go to France, but remain to undergo sentence . . . If they have already gone, take steps to recall if still in this country or state whereabouts as far as is known.'

Tennant went on to reveal the extent to which the elected civil authority had lost control of its military arm. After admitting that the telegrams had arrived too late to be effective he told the House: 'It is not easy to rescue them, though it is very desirable.' As if to underline its independence of meddling civilian control, the Army proceeded to send yet another batch from Kinmel Park the following day. The men were told they were being sent to France to be shot for disobedience. As they were taken through the gates of the camp a military band played the 'Dead March' for them.

Meanwhile, in France, the seventeen men from the Landguard Fort had arrived at Le Havre on 8 May. On arrival at camp they were told they were 'no longer prisoners but soldiers of the King'. Their past disobediences were to be forgiven and forgotten.

Free to move about the camp as they pleased, they were also free to plan a strategy of resistance. The first stage of the strategy was simple and dramatic. On the afternoon of 10 May they paraded with the British Expeditionary Forces. The order was given: 'Right turn! Quick March!' The company moved briskly off—but dotted on the parade ground were seventeen conscientious objectors, standing rigidly in their original positions.

The infuriated NCOs ordered that they be locked up and 'treated as prisoners of war'. Physical ill-treatment, bullying and threats of execution followed. The men were split up. Some were sent to Harfleur and put to work in a quarry. They refused to handle the tools. In desperation, the authorities prescribed the punishment already referred to as 'crucifixion'.

'Crucifixion'—which the army abandoned a few months later, largely as a result of the publicity its application to conscientious objectors received—was listed officially as 'Field Punishment No. 1'. It allowed for a man to be kept in handcuffs or fetters or both, and secured to a fixed object to prevent escape. The 'fixed object' was generally a wheel or gun carriage, a horizontal rope, a tree or a tent pole. There were many refinements to this torture.

One of the men who suffered crucifixion in France was Cornelius Barritt, who described the experience later for the N-CF. 'The Quartermaster Sergeant had us each handcuffed to a tent with our hands round the pole behind us, which made the shoulders ache to a quite excruciating degree. A young Canadian, who had been most hostile the previous evening, came up. He broke into a torrent of curses at the authorities who imposed such penalties. After three hours, one of the handcuffs was unlocked to enable me to feed myself, after which the punishment was again inflicted.'

The treatment, applied to a dozen men beside Barritt, was then intensified.

> Each of us was placed with our backs to the framework, consisting of uprights at intervals of four or five yards, and cross-beams at a height of about five feet from the ground. Our ankles were tied together and our arms then tied tightly at the wrists to the cross-beams; and we prepared to remain in this position for the next two hours.

The following evening 'we were placed with our faces to the barbed wire of the inner fence. As the ropes with which we were tied fastened round the barbed wire instead of the usual thick wooden post, it was possible to tie them much more tightly, and I found myself drawn so closely to the fence that when I wished to turn my head I had to do so very cautiously to avoid my face being torn by the barbs. To make matters less comfortable, it came on to rain and the cold wind blew straight across the top of the hill.'

Still the men refused to budge, and they were told that arrangements would be made to send them to Boulogne and on to the front line. At this point, however, their spirits were revived by a telegram of encouragement from the Friends Service Committee, addressed to Rendel Wyatt. When, a day or two later, they set out under escort for Boulogne, they had the knowledge that friends at home were at least partially aware of their danger.

Arriving at Boulogne, the men were despatched to a disused fish market on the quay, newly equipped as a Field Punishment Barracks. Refusal to work led to further crucifixion in crowded, windowless punishment cells, on a bread and water diet.

We were placed in handcuffs [wrote one prisoner, Howard Marten, in his diary] and locked in the cells and tied up for two hours in the afternoon. We were tied up by the wrists to horizontal ropes about five feet from the ground, with our arms outstretched and feet tied together. Our cells were roughly constructed from planks of wood, the wall of the prison forming the back. Then we were confined to cells for three days on 'punishment diet' (four biscuits a day, and water). We were also handcuffed with our arms behind us and then placed in the cells, to the recesses of which little daylight penetrated.

In these conditions, communicating only through knot holes in the walls, some of the men held a Quaker meeting. At other times they sang. Sometimes it was *The Red Flag*, sometimes *Simply Trusting*—

> *Trusting Him while life shall last,*
> *Trusting Him till death is past,*
> *Till within the jasper wall,*
> *Trusting Jesus, that is all.*

And when they were tired of singing they held debates and discussions—'varying from the existence of a personal Devil', wrote Marten, 'to one on the merits of Esperanto, from the doctrines of Marx and the Tolstoyan philosophy to vaccination.'

Back in England, the families and friends of the COs in France still had no official news of their whereabouts. The Landguard group were understood to be at Boulogne, but there was no news whatever of the Richmond, Seaford and Kinmel Park parties. Tennant continued to deny that anything was amiss. A group of Free Church ministers obtained a meeting with Kitchener on the eve of his fatal visit to Russia, but he knew or would tell nothing. The Joint

Advisory Council of the No-Conscription Fellowship, the Friends Service Committee and the Fellowship of Reconciliation decided in desperation to send its own representative to France. They approached T. Edmund Harvey, a pacifist Liberal MP, but he could not undertake the journey. He suggested that the Council should approach a non-pacifist but sympathetic Churchman, whose report might carry more weight with the press. The Council approached Dr F. B. Meyer, a distinguished liberal Free Churchman, who agreed to go and invited Hubert Peet, the organising secretary of the Friends Service Committee, to accompany him as secretary.

The War Office vouchsafed no information whatever on the whereabouts of the missing men. Probably it had none. But a singular stroke of fortune attended the efforts of the pacifist bodies. On 4 June a strange postcard arrived at the N-CF office. It was an official War Office card, issued to all men posted overseas. Designed to lighten the work of the army censors, it carried half a dozen stereotyped printed messages.

The card which dropped on the N-CF's doormat was sent by J. H. Brocklesby, one of the sixteen men in the missing Richmond contingent. All but two of the stereotyped messages were scored through, and the two remaining sentences read: 'I am being sent to base', and 'I have not heard from you for a long time'. But individual letters and words in these two sentences had also been struck through. 'I crossed off the last three letters of "base",' wrote Brocklesby in his (unpublished) diary, 'and everything in the second but the second and third letters of "you" and the word 'long''. I made my cancellings look as haphazard as possible, but thought it looked blatantly clear. Yet it evaded an overworked censor and told the folks at home: "I am being sent to b . . . ou . . . long".' Brocklesby and the Richmond, Seaford and Kinmel Park parties were all, in fact, at Henriville Camp, just outside Boulogne. The War Office was enlightened as to the whereabouts of its prisoners (though not as to the source of the N-CF's information), and Meyer and Peet were granted passports. They crossed to Boulogne on 7 June.

Even while they were crossing, another note was smuggled out of Henriville Camp. It was from one of the Seaford party, Stuart Beavis, and it told his mother:

We have been warned today that we are now within the war zone, and the military authorities have absolute power, and disobedience may be followed by very severe penalties, and very possibly the death penalty . . . Do not be downhearted if the worst comes to the worst; many have died cheerfully before for a worse cause.

For circulating copies of this letter in an attempt to rouse public opinion to the dangers of the COs in France, an Enfield N-CF member, H. Runham Brown, was prosecuted under the Defence of the Realm Act and 'deemed to be fined £50 or imprisoned for two months'.

Dr Meyer and Hubert Peet were shepherded about by the War Office. 'We were only able to see what the authorities wanted us to see', wrote Peet in an account published by the N-CF at the end of the war, 'and there was the additional difficulty that I was looked upon as a suspicious person, my name having been noticed in some of the letters sent to the men. I was allowed no communication with the men, although after pressing Col Wilberforce, the Base Commandant, I was allowed to shake hands with four I knew personally. Dr Meyer was allowed to speak briefly to the prisoners in the presence of the Commandant and an imposing and impatient staff.'

The prisoners were brought out in groups to meet Dr Meyer, who was refused permission to visit their cells at the Boulogne punishment barracks. Small wonder: 'Rats were not infrequent visitors', wrote Cornelius Barritt in his diary. 'They would sit on the edge of a fire bucket to drink the water and occasionally run up one's back during a meal . . . There were now eleven of us in the one cell (for a time there had been twelve, till Evans was sent to hospital with dysentery) and the adjoining cell was occupied by twelve more COs who had been sent down from the guardroom at the Henriville Camp nearby. The conditions of living twelve in a cell can be better imagined than described. We could just lie six a side with our feet almost touching; but it was a problem to find room for the bucket placed in the cell for "sanitary" purposes. The cells measured 11 feet 9 inches by 11 feet 3 inches.'

Meyer and Peet were depressed at their own apparent inability to do anything for the prisoners. But the COs themselves drew some strength from the certain knowledge that they were being supported at home. The military authorities, too, were made aware of the impossibility of carrying their plan through to the bitter end without publicity. Meyer's brief appearance at Boulogne was undoubtedly one of the factors which, while not deterring the army from its determined intention of securing the pronouncement of death sentences, nevertheless succeeded in forcing some kind of compromise.

Four men selected by the authorities as ringleaders—Cornelius Barritt of Pinner, J. Foister of Cambridge, J. R. Ring of Kilburn, and H. W. Scullard of Sutton—had already been court-martialled for disobedience before Meyer's arrival. They were first arraigned on 2 June, Barritt having been refused the Base Commandant's permission to wire to London for legal aid, but the trial was abandoned on a technicality. After prolonged crucifixion, the four men were again court-martialled on 7 June and pronounced guilty.

On 15 June they were taken from the punishment barracks to Henriville to be 'read out', or sentenced. This is how one of the four, quoted by Hubert Peet but unfortunately unnamed, described what followed.

> We found an escort awaiting us in the courtyard below . . . We turned towards the outskirts of the town, and climbed one of the hills overlooking it which afford a wide view of the Channel. I cast many a glance in the direction of the white cliffs of Dover, for this might be our last opportunity. We turned into the midst of a huge military camp and many curious eyes, evidently puzzled by our cheerful demeanour under such circumstances, followed us as we made our way to a large open space in the middle, 150 yards or more square, and evidently used as a parade ground . . . After a wait of perhaps three-quarters of an hour, the various groups of soldiers began to form themselves into three sides of a huge square until several thousands were present . . . When an appropriate hush had been arranged, the Adjutant, who was to read out the sentence, took charge . . . 'Private ————, No. ————, of the 2nd Eastern Company Non-Combatant Corps, tried by Field Court-Martial for disobedience whilst undergoing field punishment. Sentenced to death by being shot.'—(Here a pause). 'Confirmed by General Sir Douglas Haig'—(a longer pause)—'and commuted to ten years' penal servitude' . . . I was number three on the list, and as I stepped forward I caught a

glimpse of my paper as it was handed to the Adjutant. Printed at the top in large red letters, and doubly underlined, was the word 'Death'.

I can hardly analyse the feelings that flashed through my mind as I caught sight of the word. They could certainly not be described as an emotion. I had faced the possibility of a death sentence before, and now accepted the fact almost without concern, whilst my mind was occupied mechanically and dispassionately with considering the immediate practical effects. It would be a great trial for mother. My sister would have to leave school. People in England would make a great fuss. The thought of why I should receive a different sentence from the others did not occur to me. I simply accepted it as a fact . . .

'And commuted to ten years' penal servitude.' So it was not so after all!

But as I stood listening to the sentences of the rest of our party, the feeling of joy and triumph surged up within me, and I felt proud to have the privilege of being one of that small company of COs testifying to a truth which the world as yet had not grasped, but which it would one day treasure as a most precious inheritance.

Barritt, Foister, Ring and Scullard were the first to be subjected to this ghoulish treatment. They were not the last. During the ten days that followed there were almost daily repeat performances. Altogether in June 1916 thirty-four men received the death sentenced, commuted to ten years' penal servitude, and another seven received lesser sentences. 'The Captain was very considerate', wrote Brocklesby in his diary, after hearing his own death sentence on 24 June. 'He admitted that he thought we were very brave men. It is, I think, a long-standing tradition in the army to acknowledge the courage of the enemy.'

The orgy of death sentencing and commuting went on at Henriville while in London the War Office continued to pooh-pooh the suggestion that COs in France were in danger. A full week after the first sentences, 22 June, George Barnes, the pro-war Labour MP for the Blackfriars division of Glasgow and later a member of the War Council, raised the question in the Commons. Emphasising that he had given prior notice of the question, Barnes asked the Under-Secretary for War, Mr Tennant, about 'a report current in the lobbies tonight that four [sic] men in France have been sentenced to death. These men,' he went on, 'are stated to be conscientious objectors, and there is a very general feeling of resentment or alarm that after the many statements which have been made about them being turned over to the civil power by the military, and the assurances that these men should not be sent to France at all, it is somewhat alarming that a report of this sort should be current. I cannot believe it is true, and I merely raise the question now to give the right hon. gentleman an opportunity of assuring the House that this particular report is not true.'

The unfortunate Mr Tennant, perversely briefed by his department, replied that the great majority of rumours about the treatment of conscientious objectors were untrue, and this, he assumed, was just one more such unfounded rumour. He promised an investigation and a full report to the House. 'There is no intention of dealing with them in any way harshly', he promised, 'and there will be no question of their being sentenced to death.'

Four days later the helpless Minister was forced to tell the House that sentence of death had, after all, been pronounced, not on four but on thirty-four objectors. Tennant seems, in fact, to have believed that the sentences might have been carried out already, for he declared himself ignorant of whether they had been commuted and then proceeded to defend the sentences on the ground that 'wilful disobedience of orders, though not in face of the enemy, is punishable by death'.

Asquith himself, accused of misleading the House, promised a statement later in the week. On 29 June he pledged that it would never happen again.

The incident did much to bring home to the public the fact that many who called themselves conscientious objectors were genuine in their profession, willing as they evidently were to face even death for conscience's sake. 'The final test of sincerity is the willingness to face consequences, and the supreme test the perserverance to death,' commented the *Manchester Guardian*. '. . . We hope that people will now be satisfied that the conscientious objector may at least be what he professes to be, and is not necessarily a mere coward masquerading under a fine pretence.' The *Daily News* was shocked by the civil authority's ignorance of the doings of its military arm, and asked: 'Where are we drifting? . . .''

At the end of June the War Office succeeded in bringing home the

COs at Boulogne. After sentence their ill-treatment had ceased and they had been allowed two or three visitors, including Quaker 'chaplain' J. Rowntree Gillet. French soldiers hissed them as they embarked at Rouen and a British crowd pelted them with eggs and tomatoes when they arrived at Southampton, where they were split up and sent to various civil jails.

That should have been the end of the 'COs to France' affair. But it was not. Nearly two years later, in March 1917, three more were despatched across the channel. The N-CF's Parliamentary Secretary, C. G. Ammon, wrote immediately to General Childs at the War Office, who successfully ordered that the men be sent back. Three months later five objectors were sent from the Manchester Regiment, but were brought back when Charles Trevelyan brought their case before Parliament. Two men from Hackney were also sent, one of them, Ernest V. Millwood, an only son—a category exempted from service by Asquith. Millwood was sent to Courcelles, on the fighting line, where he was sentenced to five years penal servitude. He didn't return to England until April 1919. In December another objector, A. Catherall, was sent to France. A barrage of Parliamentary questions secured a Government admission that he had been sent, in defiance of Asquith's pledge of 29 June 1916, and eventually secured his committal to a civil prison in England in February 1918. But during the two months he was in France he was confined in an iron-sheeted, concrete-floored cell, four yards by two, in irons, on a biscuits-and-water diet. The biscuits were so hard that he broke a tooth. When this treatment failed to make a soldier of him he was ordered to be roped as tightly as possible to a post, still in irons. There followed further disobedience, further punishment and hard labour. Once he was removed to another room to hear the death sentence pronounced on a soldier convicted of disobedience—'just to show me what the Army can do'.

This recurring military defiance of Government pledges meant that every young man who went before a Tribunal to testify to a conscientious objection to war knew that he might be called upon to die for that testimony. It enabled the Tribunals to threaten death, and to go on threatening it in the face of Government denials that such a thing was possible. When the news of the first death sentences came through in June 1915 there were already some 1,200 objectors in military guardrooms. It required either high courage or rare obstinacy—or the two combined—to stand firm in such circumstances.

REFERENCES

1 COs' letters in this chapter are quoted either from *The Tribunal* or from unpublished papers made available to me by the writers' families.
2 John W. Graham, *op cit*

Chapter VII

Dissension

DURING those spring and summer months of 1916 when the military strove to cope with an unprecedented situation entirely beyond the range of its own comprehension, the No-Conscription Fellowship, brought by adversity and political defeat to the peak of its strength, fashioned itself into the most efficient instrument the British peace movement ever had, before or since.

From its tiny offices just off Fleet Street, the Fellowship ran an intelligence service which astonished its own members, embarrassed the War Office and enfuriated the police. Every known objector—and few were unknown to the N-CF—had his own record card, which was regularly marked up with his movements and events of importance in his army or prison career. Every card was duplicated in case the first set should be taken by the police or otherwise lost, and the duplicate set was arranged as a geographical index, showing at a glance the day-by-day movements of every member. A daily court-martial list was compiled, showing the number of first, second, third and further courts-martial. The department issued a daily bulletin, showing the exact number of men arrested, with full information on their whereabouts and category. By this means the N-CF was able to keep friends and relatives in touch with men who were temporarily unable to communicate themselves. On one occasion, after the War Office had admitted to having lost track of a CO whose family were trying to trace him, the N-CF sent a special messenger to the War Office giving the whereabouts of the missing man, plus a detailed account of his movements during the previous three months. The War Office replied with a courteous note of thanks.

The Fellowship's progressive encyclopaedia of information was also used to publicise illegalities and brutalities. In guardrooms and prisons news travelled fast, and much of it filtered through the stone walls and iron bars by means of the N-CF's network of prison visitors. To the bewilderment of the authorities, the friends of the enlisted or imprisoned objectors knew more about them than their jailors did. From the data supplied by the intelligence arm—known more prosaically as the Record Department—numerous pamphlets and articles were written, and briefings for Parliamentary speeches and questions prepared.

The Record Department was established by a militant suffragette named Catherine Marshall who had attended the first convention of the Fellowship in 1915 as a delegate of the Women's International League and had been captivated in more or less equal measure by both Clifford Allen and his cause. She quickly became a full-time unpaid worker at head office, and later honorary secretary. 'She came,' recalled John Graham in *Conscription and Conscience*, 'with a wide and varied political experience, and a knowledge of people and affairs acquired during her great work for the suffrage movement. In the important negotiations with those in authority which became inevitable she was indispensable. Being possessed of a passionate belief in the righteousness of the cause, and being a firm absolutist, she was doubly armed in her contact with authority; and this, added to an amazing ingenuity and great political wisdom, produced a combination which was of the highest value to the movement, whilst her instinct of tolerance made her the friend of all sections, sensitive as they were.' Her devotion to Allen personally was shown most vividly after the war when he came out of prison in broken health and close to death. She nursed him back to strength and travelled abroad with him extensively.

Records was only one of several departments into which the N-CF divided. A Visitation Department organised a network of prison visitors and camp and guardroom contacts. Most courts-martial were attended by an N-CF representative, and at Wormwood Scrubs—described by Barratt Brown as 'the spiritual headquarters of the Fellowship'—an effective system of picketing was set up, to be duplicated later at other prisons with large CO intakes. Ways were found of communicating with the men inside, and of smuggling in newspapers and periodicals. Important policy decisions were conveyed to them, and the results of referenda and discussion inside were conveyed to the National Committee.

A Press Department supplied the newspapers with a steady

stream of information both on the work of the Fellowship and on the treatment of its members in the army or in prison. A Literature Department published more than a million copies of leaflets and pamphlets, and from March 1916 onwards brought out the weekly *Tribunal*. A Maintenance Organisation championed the dependents of COs, and a Central Fund Committee to which Ramsay MacDonald lent his name as chairman raised more than £20,000 to alleviate this kind of hardship.

A Campaign Department led the agitation for release of COs and organised release petitions signed by distinguished, and often non-pacifist, men and women in all walks of life. Finally there was a Political Department, organised both to express the Fellowship's attitude towards the series of proposals put forward in Parliament for dealing with COs, and to keep MPs—particularly the Parliamentary 'peace party'—acquainted with the facts as to the treatment of prisoners. The Political Department drafted questions to Ministers and briefed Philip Snowden to put them. It organised innumerable public lobbies and private deputations to Government departments.

The Fellowship was in ceaseless conflict with the authorities. Its offices were constantly raided by the police, and its branch meetings broken up. Papers and books were indiscriminately seized and often never returned. When police raids became almost daily occurrences the Fellowship met the challenge by virtually going underground. A skeleton staff continued to man the office. Inessential and sometimes quite irrelevant documents were laid out on the shelves for the police to seize. But the real work of the Fellowship was delegated to the departments, which were made autonomous to safeguard them in the event of the Fellowship itself being suppressed. The departments were provided with shadow leaders, and at one time their activities were being directed from six different centres in London. The vital Record Department was separated altogether from the vulnerable head office, and re-formed as a nominally independent 'Conscientious Objectors' Information Bureau'.

From 9 March 1916, the Fellowship published its own newspaper every week. It was called, ironically, *The Tribunal*, and carried under its masthead the definition: 'Tribunal. A Court of Justice—Webster's Dictionary.' A four-page sheet of the cheapest newsprint, printed in tiny, close-packed type and selling first at a half-penny and later one penny, *The Tribunal* quickly became a

jewel in the crown of dissenting journalism. Its fiery advocacy and
racy panache brought it a circulation of 100,000 at its peak, and
attracted the angry attention of the Government and its agencies in
almost every issue. For its first four months it was edited by the
N-CF's honorary organiser, Will Chamberlain. When he went to
prison, in circumstances shortly to be told, the editorship was taken
over by Bernard Boothroyd. Clifford Allen contributed a regular
inspirational message until his imprisonment, and Fenner Brockway and Bertrand Russell were constant contributors.

But the first prosecutions of N-CF members involved branch
officials, not National Committee members or head office staff.
During April members of the Fellowship's branches in Penrith,
Liverpool, Merthyr and Abercynon were fined or imprisoned for
distributing leaflets 'calculated to prejudice recruiting'. Before the
National Committee had time to mount an effective protest it found
itself collectively arraigned on a similar charge. The full committee,
with the strange exception of the chairman, Clifford Allen, and of
C. H. Norman, who had already been 'handed over' to the army,
was summoned under the Defence of the Realm Act for publishing
a leaflet on conscription called *Repeal the Act*. Some such action
against the national leadership was widely expected. On 10 May, in
reply to a demand from Conservative backbenchers that the Home
Secretary 'take steps to suppress the N-CF, the Union of Democratic Control and any other association the effect of whose operations is to assist the enemy by weakening the national effort and
determination to win the war', Home Secretary Herbert Samuel had
declared himself powerless to suppress but eager to prosecute illegal
action. The choice of this particular leaflet, however, was clumsy
and curious. The Government professed to make a distinction
between agitation for the repeal of conscription and plain obstructionism. The Home Office itself had assured a private deputation of
the N-CF that public advocacy of repeal was perfectly legal. Much
of the Fellowship's literature, to be sure, went much further than
this by way of direct incitement to defy the Acts, and it was widely
assumed that such legal action as the authorities chose to take would
be on the ground of incitement. But the Director of Public Prosecutions chose to pick on *Repeal the Act*, maintaining that it was calculated to 'prejudice recruiting, training, discipline or administration
of His Majesty's forces'.

The eight National Committee members were charged at the Mansion House, London, on Wednesday, 17 May. They asserted their right to publicise the Fellowship's pacifist views. The prosecution counter-asserted that the contents of the offending leaflet prejudiced the war effort. The eight were convicted and fined £100 each. *The Tribunal* made its own characteristic comment by publishing part of the Sermon on the Mount—'Love your enemies, bless them that curse you, do good to them that hate you'—and adding: 'We should esteem it a favour if the Director of Public Prosecutions and Lord Derby would kindly inform us whether in their considered judgment the above quotations are calculated to "prejudice recruiting, training, discipline or administration of any of His Majesty's forces".' The paper also noted with wry satisfaction that as a result of the prosecution the contents of *Repeal the Act* 'have been made known through the columns of the press in every home in the country and to every soldier who reads a daily paper'. Indeed, the *Manchester Guardian* quoted the entire text without suffering any legal action.

The N-CF conviction was unsuccessfully appealed. In a special emergency session the National Committee debated whether or not to pay the fines. A majority were for refusal, knowing that this would force the hands of the authorities and help publicise the Fellowship's stand; but it was felt that the translation to jail of the entire committee would disrupt the administration of the organisation at a crucial moment in its history, particularly since Clifford Allen's own call-up was known to be imminent. It was therefore agreed that five members—Fenner Brockway, Will Chamberlain, Walter Ayles, A. Barratt Brown and John Fletcher—should refuse the fine and take the consequences. On 17 July they surrendered to the police at the Mansion House, accompanied by a large crowd of well-wishers and the curious. 'After friendly leave-taking with the detectives and police who have been responsible for the carrying out of the Government instructions in this matter,' reported *The Tribunal* on 20 July, 'they were driven off to Pentonville Prison to serve their term of imprisonment of 61 days.' Catherine Marshall was appointed to take over from Fenner Brockway as honorary secretary of the Fellowship, and B. J. Boothroyd took over editorship of *The Tribunal* from Will Chamberlain.

In the time that elapsed between the original hearing of the case against the National Committee and their imprisonment, the N-CF became involved in other major prosecutions brought under DORA. The most important was that known as 'the Everett case'.

Ernest Everett was a young Lancashire school teacher who objected on Socialist grounds. He made no secret of his radical and republican politics when he appeared before the St Helens Tribunal. He was refused exemption, and appealed to the Liverpool Appeal Tribunal. Appearing before them, he was astonished to hear the following letter read out, addressed to the chairman of the Appeal Tribunal from the chairman of the Tribunal at St Helens:

> This man belongs to a group who are coaching men of military age to object to service. He has no religious convictions, and would see his sisters ravished or the war lost rather than do anything to help. He is willing to take Government money. He considers himself first and only.

The Appeal Tribunal refused Everett permission to call witnesses to testify to his character, and dismissed his appeal. The chairman described him as a 'selfish coward', and subsequently wrote to his employers, the St Helens Education Authority, suggesting he be dismissed. Everett was handed over to the army. On 10 April, at Kinmel Park, Abergele, he was court-martialled for disobedience and given the savage—and at that time unprecedented—sentence of two years' hard labour, subsequently commuted to 112 days' detention.

The N-CF produced a leaflet giving a factual account of the case. It was widely distributed, and its anonymous authorship provoked speculation. By the end of May six N-CF members in different parts of the country had been prosecuted for distributing it. At Cefn, two young objectors who had distributed the leaflet were hauled before the self-same magistrate who a day or two earlier had appeared at their Tribunal hearings as Military Representative, deputed to oppose their applications. He fined them each £10 and for good measure sentenced them to one month's hard labour.

In these circumstances, the writer of the leaflet decided to come into the open and take all responsibility. In a letter to *The Times*, Bertrand Russell declared himself the unrepentant author of the offending publication. The case, he argued, was a simple one. Was a factual pamphlet which assisted the supremacy of conscience contrary to the Defence of the Realm Act?

Russell was prosecuted and brought before the Mansion House court on 5 June. He conducted his own defence. No reasonable interpretation of the Act, he argued, would bring the leaflet within its scope. It could not be construed as prejudicial to service discipline since it was addressed to the civil population to explain to them the persecution going on. As such it came within the admitted right of political agitation—a right repeatedly assured by Parliament, even in war time. Its effect was to inform civilians that if they chose to become conscientious objectors they would get two years' hard labour. The court could hardly object to the dissemination of such information, which would discourage those tempted to feign an objection, and further discourage soldiers to resist discipline. If the knowledge of such punishments undermined discipline, as the prosecution appeared to be arguing, why were they inflicted? The leaflet had criticised the sentence as savage. The Army Council appeared to be of the same opinion in commuting it to 112 days. So why all the fuss?

The broader intention of the leaflet, as of the No-Conscription Fellowship [declared Russell] is to secure the rights of conscience. There are some men in the community who will not fight, not from any self-regarding motive, but because they consider it wrong to fight. We wish to secure recognition of the fact that such men cannot be forced to fight, that the attempt to force them is useless from the point of view of obtaining soldiers, and that the State ought to recognise their right to their principles. The struggle to secure liberty for those who think it wrong to fight is now at its height. All who know the history of human freedom can recognise in this contest all the familiar features of the old struggles for liberty by which intolerance has been defeated in the past.

He concluded:

Whether I personally am acquitted or condemned is a matter of no great importance. But it is not only I that am in the dock; it is the whole tradition of British liberty which our forefathers built up with great trouble and with great sacrifice. Other nations may excel us in some respects, but the tradition of liberty has been the supreme good that we in this country have cultivated. We have preserved, more than any other Power, respect for the individual conscience. It is for that I stand. I think that under the stress of fear the authorities have somewhat forgotten that ancient tradition, and I think the fear is unworthy, and the tyranny which is resulting will be disastrous if it is not resisted. I would say to them. 'You cannot defeat such men—'.

At this point the Lord Mayor, presiding over the bench of magistrates, interrupted to say that he could not allow a political speech. Russell had planned to end his defence with the following words, later published by the N-CF in a penny pamphlet on the case:

> The persecution which conscientious objectors have endured has enormously increased their moral weight. It illustrates the invincible power of that better way of passive resistance, which pacifists believe to be stronger than all the armies and navies in the world. Men inspired by faith and freed from the dominion of fear are unconquerable. The noblest thing in a man is the spiritual force which enables him to stand firm against the whole world in obedience to his sense of right; and I will never acquiesce in silence while men in whom spiritual force is strong are treated as a danger to the community rather than as its most precious heritage. I would say to the persecutors, 'You cannot defeat such men; you cannot make their testimony of no avail. For every one whom you silence by force a hundred will be moved to carry on his work, until at last you yourselves will be won over, and will recognise, with a sense of liberation from bondage, that all the material force the world contains is powerless against the spirit of indomitable love.'

Russell was sentenced to a fine of £100 with £10 costs, or sixty-one days' imprisonment. When he refused to pay, his goods at Trinity College, Cambridge, were distrained upon. Cambridge was outraged, and Russell was temporarily deprived of his Fellowship. The Government refused him a passport to travel to the United States, where he had been invited to lecture on mathematics at Harvard, and subsequently debarred him from lecturing in certain parts of England and Scotland—the 'prohibited areas' round the coast where, perhaps, it was thought Russell might signal to enemy ships from the cliff-tops! So rigidly was this prohibition enforced that on one occasion Russell found himself prevented from delivering in coastal Glasgow a lecture on the philosophical principles of politics which he had successfully delivered the night before in inland Manchester. Instead, a learned speech was delivered by the miners' leader Robert Smillie, who afterwards informed his delighted audience that he had read the banned Russell lecture.

The National Committee and Russell cases were only two of a spate of prosecutions under DORA that spring and summer. Some 150 N-CF branch officials had their homes raided, and many were arrested for possessing subversive pacifist literature. A South Wales member, T. Mainwaring, was prosecuted for a speech describing the treatment of 'political prisoners'; and H. Runham Brown, chairman of the Enfield branch, was given a fine of £30 or two months' imprisonment for circulating to MPs and assorted clergymen three hundred copies of a letter written from France by Stuart Beavis, one of the thirty-four men sentenced to death.

In all the London prosecutions under DORA the Crown Advocate was Mr (later Sir) Archibald Bodkin. In the course of putting his case Mr Bodkin remarked that 'war would become impossible if all men were to have the view that war was wrong'. The N-CF offered its gratitude for so neat and concise a statement of its own case, and proceeded to issue posters containing Bodkin's words, prominently credited to their author. This enraged the authorities, who added farce to comedy by prosecuting the poster. Bodkin himself prosecuted. The defendant unsuccessfully demanded the arrest of the prosecutor, as author of the subversive words. *The Tribunal* suggested it was his patriotic duty to prosecute himself, and magnanimously offered to maintain his wife and children in the event of his prosecution being successful.

★   ★   ★

Anxious to avoid repetition of the public scandals and brutalities to which many of the first batch of COs had been subjected after being handed over to the army, the authorities decreed in Army Order X on 25 May that 'a soldier who is sentenced to imprisonment for an offence against discipline, which was represented by the soldier at his trial to have been the result of a conscientious objection to military service, will be committed to the nearest public civil prison'. Despite the fact that the decision was not retroactive, and therefore left several hundred objectors in military prisons and guardrooms, the intention to hand over future COs to the civil powers was welcomed by *The Tribunal* as 'the first Government move in the right direction, and, incidentally, a tribute to the work of the N-CF', which had been pressing hard for such a change.

But in the same issue—25 May—Clifford Allen also warned of 'proposals constantly mooted from different quarters to involve the Fellowship in some "arrangement" for settling the problem of the conscientious objector'. A problem it was. First the guardrooms and now the civil prisons were becoming inconveniently crowded. On 28 June Prime Minister Asquith explained the 'arrangement' he had in mind. Every CO imprisoned since Army Order X was to have his case reviewed; either a War Office committee would examine his Tribunal records or special sub-committees of the Central Appeal Tribunal would reinterrogate him to determine whether or not his conscientious objection was genuine. Those held to be genuine would be released from prison 'on their undertaking to perform work of national importance under civil control'. A Home Office committee under W. Brace MP would organise this work. Conscientious objectors accepting the scheme would be transferred to Section W of the Army Reserve and cease to be subject to military discipline or the Army Act so long as they continued to carry out satisfactorily the 'duties imposed on them'.

Asquith had two comments on the plan. 'The first is that all men whose objections to military service are founded on honest convictions ought to be able, and will be able, to avail themselves of the exemption which Parliament has provided; and, in the second place, it is necessary that men who put forward objections of this kind as a pretext and cloak to cover their indifferences to the national call, and who are therefore guilty of the double offence of cowardice and hypocrisy, should be treated, as they ought to be treated, with the utmost vigour.'

Lloyd George, now Secretary for War, was even more explicit. 'With that kind of man,' he told the Commons on 26 July, speaking of those who refused alternative service and the Home Office scheme, 'I, personally, have no sympathy whatsoever. I do not think that they deserve the slightest consideration. With regard to those who object to shedding blood, it is the traditional policy of this country to respect that view, and we do not propose to depart from it; but in the other case I shall only consider the best means of making the path of that class as hard as possible.'

So was buried the clause about absolute exemption, affirmed in the Military Service Acts and regularly but unavailingly reaffirmed by Government spokesmen, including the Prime Minister himself.

The Home Office scheme provoked a bitter division within the ranks of the N-CF and its associated bodies. The accusation was commonly made that the real object of the scheme was to split the CO movement, and it looked for a time as if, whether or not this was the intention, it would be the effect.

An anguished debate about 'alternative service' and 'work of national importance' had been a permanent feature of the Fellowship almost from its foundation. Following Allen's lead, the National Committee had set itself resolutely against the Non-Combatant Corps, and this stand was endorsed and followed by an overwhelming part of the Fellowship. The formation in March 1916 of the Pelham Committee to advise Tribunals on 'work of national importance' had provoked deeper divisions, but a major quarrel at this point was averted by the Fellowship's adoption of a verbal formula which left it to individual conscience to determine each member's stand.

While using such formulae to prevent splits, Allen and the National Committee nevertheless made abundantly clear their own rejection of what they saw as unacceptable compromise with the Military Service Acts. The refusal of many Tribunals to have any dealings with the Pelham Committee, and the widespread tendency to prescribe the kind of 'work of national importance' clearly designed to punish the applicant served to justify the National Committee's uncompromising stand for 'absolutism'. But the announcement of the Home Office scheme brought new hope to hundreds who had experienced army brutality and the rigours of prison. They were ready to welcome any plan which promised to make them constructive members of society without demanding unacceptable compromises of principle.

The N-CF leadership reacted to the scheme by pouring ice-cold water on it. *The Tribunal* of 29 June, the day following Asquith's announcement to the Commons, published Allen's detailed condemnation of it:

The Government's new proposal for dealing with conscientious objectors results from an entire misconception of our views and the character of our protest . . . There can be little doubt that the new scheme will give rise to anger and resentment in the minds of many who deplore persecution but had withheld their protest in the hope that some way out would be discovered by Mr Asquith. As it is, the persecution will be intensified, and brutality officially encouraged as the result of a proposal which disregards the stand already made by those who have been sentenced to death, penal servitude or other penalties. One might almost describe as ludicrous the proposal to institute a further enquiry into the genuineness of such conscientious objectors through the medium of the War Office, which is the last body in the world that can or ought to deal with such matters. Months will slip by whilst thousands of cases are being investigated, and for a while men will linger in prison and penal servitude.

The Army Order which transferred men to the civil power was welcomed on all sides by those who believed the Government had a genuine desire to solve the problem. Their confidence must have been rudely shattered by the complete reversal of policy initiated by the new scheme, which allows the Army Council to commit such men as they fail to certify as conscientious objectors to military detention, to be treated with the 'utmost rigour' . . . There is every reason to hope that our friends and critics in Parliament are nettled by the way the Government is trifling with the matter, and that the Free Churches and many other sections of the public will not tolerate this new attempt of the Army authorities to crush a movement which menaces their authority and contests their domination over civil rights and religious freedom . . .

It only remains for us to make clear why we believe the Government must always fail to settle this problem, unless they extend to conscientious objectors the right to absolute exemption allowed under the Military Service Act. The crux of the position lies here: conscription cannot be justly administered.

Let it not be supposed for a moment that the offer of civil work to the men whose consciences are recognised by the War Office is likely to ease the situation. Without doubt many of our members will, in all sincerity, undertake that work, but it is interesting to speculate how many of them, when they are in possession of the facts, will reject the conditions that will probably govern their status, or will agree to becoming a means of exploiting the trade union movement, or consent to abstain from giving expression to their pacifist views.

It is only natural that the final struggle will centre round the men who decline to enter into such a bargain with the Military Service Act, and who are entirely disregarded by the Government proposal. None of us can yet estimate what measure the Government will adopt to break the spirit of these men, but all of us realise that the future of Militarism in this country will be decided by the conscientious objector, and we take courage when we hear how gladly our men are accepting the penalties imposed upon them, and how eager we are that they should maintain our uncompromising policy. Indeed, the Fellowship is unaffected by the repeated attempts of the Government to avoid doing the right thing.

That fierce argument was raging throughout the movement is apparent from Allen's final paragraph. Referring to the imminent imprisonment of the National Committee, following the *Repeal the Act* prosecution, and his own equally imminent call-up, he writes:

It is possible that this week many of those hitherto entrusted with the work of the Fellowship will cease their present work, and change the character of their service. We know now that nothing can happen in our absence to deflect the Fellowship from its true purpose. We have been urged to rest content with the witness the Fellowship has so far made. May those who remain to carry on the work have a like experience to our own and return the same answer we have believed it right to give. Our strength must still rest in a full understanding of each other's point of view, but we cannot compromise if we hope to render effective service.

Specific points of objection to the Home Office scheme were listed in a statement signed by Allen and Brockway for the N-CF, Robert Mennell and Hubert Peet for the FSC and H. T. Hodgkin and Richard Roberts for the FoR. They pointed out that

1. Those sentenced before the passing of Army Order X on 25 May, and consequently still in military custody, were not covered;
2. Inquisition by Tribunals having failed, there was little hope for a further sifting, particularly by the War Office;

3. Since official reports had not been made of most Tribunal proceedings, the sifters would have to rely on such unofficial and unreliable reports as those contained in the newspapers;

4. The questions likely to be put would be unfairly difficult for uneducated men;

5. The testimony of ministers of religion, which would be invited under the new sifting arrangements, would be of no assistance to Socialist objectors outside the Churches;

6. The whole process would inevitably lead to even harsher treatment of those not passed as genuine conscientious objectors;

7. The formal transfer to Army Reserve W meant that they were still a part of the military machine and liable to recall;

8. No amount of tinkering with the scheme would make it acceptable to the convinced 'absolutist', who would inevitably refuse to make the bargain suggested.

This uncompromising hostility to the scheme, the full details of which were still to be finalised and presented to the public, was by no means shared by all rank-and-file members and branch officials. The quarrel became more embittered when some professed to see it as a case of a free leadership urging extremes of sacrifice on men already suffering the deprivations of imprisonment.

On 17 July—the day Brockway and his four National Committee colleagues surrendered themselves to the police at the Mansion House—the new honorary secretary, Catherine Marshall, received a letter from T. Edmund Harvey, Quaker MP and chairman of the Pelham Committee advising the Tribunals on 'work of national importance'. The letter pleaded with the new National Committee to think again about alternative service and the Home Office scheme.

Those of us [it said] who think that it is right to undertake, at the demand of the community, work which is not directed to the prosecution of the war, but yet can be realised by our fellow-countrymen as of service to the national life, do not believe that such work is called for with any sinister purpose of dividing the ranks of pacifists; conscientious objectors are neither numerous enough, nor important enough, in the eyes of statesmen, to be treated by such subtle methods.

Over and above the natural wish of all Ministers and officials that

the machinery of government should run smoothly, there is a real
desire, even among statesmen and politicians, to get rid of persecution and to find some way of utilising the help of men who cannot
fight without doing wrong to their conscience. Other ways there are
by which the true interests of the nation may be served; but I believe
that for most of us who are debarred by our deepest convictions from
undertaking military service, the way by which we can interpret the
spirit of citizenship most effectively is by accepting without complaint the humbler tasks which the community now offers to many
who would help it in an hour of great need.

Harvey's letter enclosed another from Professor Gilbert Murray,
making the same appeal. Murray's letter was addressed specifically
to the men in prison, and expressed the earnest hope that, when
offered work of national importance, provided it was in no way
connected with warfare or the army, they would not refuse it.

They have made their protest [declared the Professor]. They have
vindicated their courage. They have established the rights of conscience. The State no longer demands that they should do anything
to which, before the present crisis, they had expressed any objection.
All that the State now asks is that they should be willing in some way
to work for the good of their fellow citizens in a time of extreme need.

Some of them argue: 'The State is absorbed in war, which is a
great crime; to give any help to the State is indirectly to help the
crime.'

'I will not pause to consider to what strange results this argument
would lead us, if logically pursued. But I would appeal to every man
of ordinary feeling to recognise the utter falsity of saying that we, his
average fellow-citizens, whom he regards as engaged in crime, are
entirely absorbed in our criminality, and have no life outside it. Even
the hardest fighter in the trenches is not always fighting. He is sometimes writing home, planting flower beds, playing with children,
reading, sleeping, eating and doing all the ordinary things of which
the life of a human being is composed. Granted that the objectors are
early Christians, and the rest of us Pagans, the early Christians did
not as a rule refuse all help to Pagans in distress. They did not say:
'If we save the life of this Pagan child it will merely encourage
idolatry.'

Why do I plead in this way or care so much what the objectors do? Not because of the actual amount of help they can bring to the country; but for two reasons. First I respect and value these people with extra sensitive consciences and imperious ideals; I am on their side as against those who decide against them. And therefore I cannot bear to see them behave in a manner which savours less of brotherly love than of insatiable pugnacity, and tends to bring idealism itself into disrepute. And secondly, like most Englishmen, I hate to see decent people punished like felons, and other decent people forced into so punishing them.

If the COs will be content with what they have won, and face the problem before them in a spirit of love and not of strife, they may make a positive contribution to our national life which will have a permanent effect also in the wider world of international relationships.

B. J. Boothroyd, editing his first issue of *The Tribunal* after Chamberlain's imprisonment, published both letters on 27 July together with an unsigned reply putting the National Committee's case. The reply after thanking Harvey for his 'unsparing labour for us and our cause', proceeded:

Mr Harvey goes straight to the root of the matter when he implies an objection to the word 'alternative'. It is mainly because such work is forced upon men as an alternative to military service, that we object to it. If this is not so why is it that if a man does not accept it, or says he cannot find it, he is forced into the army? Conversely, why is it that, with negligible exceptions, a man is only exempted from the army on condition that he does this work? Why is it, also, that even if he is already doing such work, and has been granted a conscience by a tribunal, he is given only a conditional exemption, or even taken away from the work he is doing, and sent to do similar work in another place? We submit that this is done merely because the authorities mean to make it clear that the alternative to his doing such work is military service. We further submit that all these orders and restrictions regarding those who are either doing, or ordered to do, such work, are imposed because such work is compulsory, and is compulsory because it is part of a Compulsion Act, passed solely for military purposes.

Mr Murray says we have made our protest. Yes, but we feel it our duty to go on protesting until the evil stops, and not merely protest

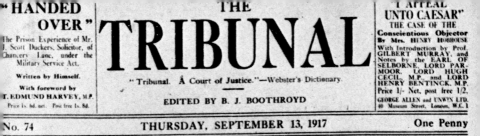

"HANDED OVER"

The Prison Experience of Mr. J. Scott Duckers, Solicitor, of Chancery Lane, under the Military Service Act.

Written by Himself.

With foreword by T. EDMUND HARVEY, M.P.

Price 1s. 6d. net.   Post free 1s. 8d.

THE TRIBUNAL

"Tribunal. A Court of Justice."—Webster's Dictionary.

EDITED BY B. J. BOOTHROYD

"I APPEAL UNTO CAESAR"
THE CASE OF THE Conscientious Objector
By Mrs. HENRY HOBHOUSE
With Introduction by Prof. GILBERT MURRAY. and Notes by the EARL OF SELBORNE, LORD PARMOOR, LORD HUGH CECIL, M.P., and LORD HENRY BENTINCK, M.P.

Price 1/- Net, post free 1/2.

GEORGE ALLEN and UNWIN LTD.
40 Museum Street, London, W.C.1

No. 74   THURSDAY, SEPTEMBER 13, 1917   One Penny

THE FIGHT FOR RIGHT

For the third time Fenner Brockway and J. H. Hudson, members of the National Committee of the No-Conscription Fellowship, have been court-martialled for refusing to obey military commands. They are but two among many, but we print extracts from their court-martial statements as an expression of the undaunted faith of those who are bearing aloft the banner of peace and freedom in guard-room and prison.

A. FENNER BROCKWAY

At Chester, Wednesday, September 5th, 1917.

When the present war broke out I seriously considered what my duty was as a citizen of this country. I saw that the war could be concluded by one of two ways—the Militarist way of victory by human slaughter, the Pacifist way of reconciliation by human sympathy. . . .

I saw the Pacifist way leading to a peace based not on force, but on goodwill. I saw that the Pacifist way must be the education of the peoples of every country, to a realisation that they have no cause for quarrel, that the conflict is the result of the Imperialist policy pursued by all the Governments involved and of the machinations of interested financiers and capitalists, that the masses have no reason to desire territorial conquest from each other, that they have, indeed, every reason to desire freedom and justice for all nations, and that the democracies of the world, whatever the military situation, must take common action to secure a settlement by agreement based on principles of liberty and co-operation. I saw that a permanent peace depends not on the position of armies, but on the mind of the peoples, and consequently, from the first day of the war, I did what I could to influence my fellow-citizens towards that broader attitude of mind from which alone reconciliation can come.

All that has since occurred has deepened my conviction of the wrongfulness and futility of war and strengthened my faith that the Pacifist way is the only way leading to a permanent peace. Six months ago, when I was last tried by court-martial, my hope that the war would be concluded by the common action of the democracies of the belligerent nations seemed impractical and visionary; to-day, despite the postponement of the Stockholm Conference, it seems not only possible of realisation, but probable. In every country the International Socialists are leading a larger and still larger section of the public, and I believe that the time will come, before many months have passed, when the forces of organised Labour in all lands will rally in support of a common peace programme. When that day dawns, if the Governments do not listen to the demands of the workers, I hope we may see the soldiers of all lands laying down their arms, declaring a general strike against war, and entrusting the settlement of peace to representatives of the people, not to the ambassadors of the ruling classes. If my attitude and actions during the war have hastened by one hour the coming of such a time I can never feel it has been in vain.

J. H. HUDSON

At Oswestry, Wednesday, September 5th, 1917.

No national boundaries can divide the truths for which we stand. Wherever men and women are struggling towards freedom, our duty in the conflict is with them, never against them. Had I been a German, I should have worked with Karl Liebknecht for the defeat of Kaiserdom. If Ireland had been my native land, in the pacifist faith of the murdered Skeffington, there, too, would I have fought Kaiserdom. In Russia I would have organised revolution against Czardom; or have worked with the anti-war Socialists of France or Italy. A Colonial in Australia, I would not have failed to be a supporter of those who successfully defeated Conscription there; and an opponent to tyrants and deporters of free labour in South Africa. Gladly had I given my allegiance to the Hindoo, seeking salvation from the degrading rule of the sword in a free, democratic and independent India; to the Arab, breaking the yoke of the Turk; to the Persian Constitutionalist undermining Shahism, and the infamous support of Shahism by the diplomacy of the Czar and the British. Perhaps the hardest lot had been to witness, as a Belgian, the shameful invasion of my country by Germany. Yet even then, like Camille Huysmans, the greatest of the Belgian Socialists, I had stained neither sword nor honour in the torrents of blood with which the Great Powers were deluging my country. My best for Belgium would have been, with Huysmans, to gather together the scattered International until I saw it, as all men are now seeing it, the real menace and foe of Capitalism and Militarism. . . .

The banner of light and reason goes forward, and Englishmen are in the van. I must go with them.

The State took from me my loved ones, my livelihood, my purse. Unlike the capitalists, I asked no five or six per cent. to be ground from the bones and sucked from the blood of generations of workers, but gave myself to the gaoler. But when the State, with a lie as its standard, says "Follow me; submit your conception of the truth to my keeping, conscript your soul and your private judgment under my ensign of falsity"; then, with Carlyle, I reply, "No; by God's help, no! you may take my purse; but I cannot have my moral self annihilated. The purse is any highwayman's who might meet me with a loaded pistol; but the self is mine and God my maker's; it is not yours; and I will resist you to the death; and revolt against you, and front all manner of extremities, accusations and confusions in defence of that."

The Tribunal, weekly organ of the No-Conscription Fellowship.

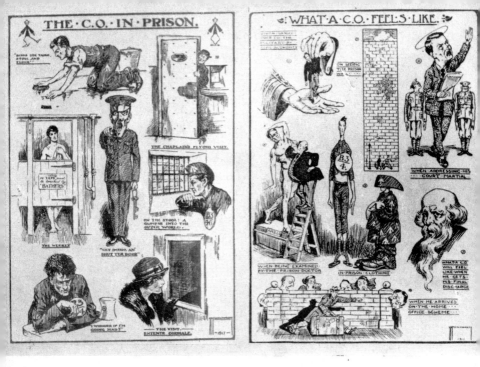

Above: A CO's view of prison life. *Below:* A CO work party at the Dartmoor Work Centre, Princetown.

once and then shut our mouths and acquiesce in it. He says we have
vindicated our courage; this is unimportant, the soldiers have shown
more. He says we have established the rights of conscience. We reply
that the Tribunals, the Houses of Parliament, the Churches, the
newspapers, the Universities, and the general public daily show by
their actions and words that they do not yet begin to understand the
word as it applies to us. To the vast majority of the nation a conscientious objector is either one who doesn't like fighting because he
is a coward, or else one who, owing to a kind of malicious insanity,
refuses to help his country in the only way open to able-bodied men.

He says all the State asks is that we should help our fellow-citizens
in time of need. We reply that, by refusing to allow men to be free to
continue useful work even after they have shown that they are nothing but impediments when forced into the army, the State has shown
that it is not our service that it wants, but our subservience to the
military law. We deny, emphatically, that we are refusing to help the
community or even the State (Mr Harvey and Mr Murray seem to
forget the great difference between the two) merely because the
latter happens to be engaged in a war. We are, on the contrary, willing to help the nation; but not in a manner which would imply
acquiescence in what we consider immoral.

He says that our argument, if logically pursued, would lead an
early Christian to refuse to help a Pagan child. That is the reverse of
logical. Logically pursued, our argument would merely lead an early
Christian to refuse to be ordered to take care of a Pagan child in order
that its father might be free to go out and kill somebody. And such an
order would be all the more impossible to obey if accompanied by a
strict injunction not to try and persuade the father to stop killing.

All that, however, is merely the negative side of our argument. We
cannot repeat too often or too emphatically that our action is not
negative, but positive and definite. Professor Murray is incorrect in
describing our argument as a refusal to help the State in doing what
we think wrong. That is like describing a sprinter as a man who
refuses to stand still. If our action was merely a refusal to help our
fellows because we were asked to do so by a Government with which
we disagree, it would be harder to defend. But it is nothing of the
sort; it is an active protest against what we consider the greatest evil
in the world, and our method of protesting is to refuse to acquiesce
by a single act or deed in a system which is indescribably evil, both in

origin and purpose. By doing this—by making this protest—we believe we are doing more for the community than by doing safe civil jobs as plain-clothes conscripts.

We are accused of insatiable pugnacity, and asked to show a spirit of love. If it is 'pugnacity' to refuse to compromise with a vile thing then we hope we are pugnacious. As for a spirit of love, we have no love to show for militarism—nothing but hatred; on the contrary, it is our love which dictates our attitude—our love for freedom. And freedom is a greater need for a nation than the temporary convenience of its Government, and freedom will never come to any land so long as men meet the commands of a military law with anything less than uncompromising hostility.

During the first week in August batches of prisoners were sent under escort to Wormwood Scrubs, where they were each interviewed in turn by the Central Tribunal under Lord Salisbury. The proceedings were perfunctory in the extreme, seldom lasting more than three minutes. Most men were formally passed as genuine and sent back to their prisons to await an offer of employment under the newly appointed Committee for the Employment of Conscientious Objectors—the Brace Committee. Several hundred prisoners were released altogether on temporary furlough awaiting the hearing of their case.

In these circumstances, the widening division within the Fellowship continued, and when on 6 August the National Committee sent a reasoned statement of the Fellowship's position to the Prime Minister, three wings of the movement were delineated:

(1). Those who, whilst recognising their obligation to the community, cannot admit obligations imposed as part of the Military Service Act, and therefore cannot accept any form of service as an alternative to military duties.

(2). Those who cannot refuse work under civil control on grounds of conscience, however much they may desire to do so on grounds of policy.

(3). Those who feel it their duty to undertake civil work of national importance even when imposed under the Military Service Act.

The greater part of the long letter that followed was given over to demands made on behalf of those who, despite the reservations of the

N-CF leadership, were inclined to accept alternative service, under the new scheme. The work, the letter demanded, must be such as to satisfy the conscientious objector that he is 'rendering service of real value to the community'. It must not become a means of 'inflicting some disability in the name of what is called "equality of sacrifice" '; if it were imposed as a penalty rather than permitted as a service it would be refused by many who would otherwise undertake it. COs must not be transferred from work for which they had been trained to work for which they were untrained and unsuited. They must not be allotted to 'work even indirectly associated with the war or its non-combatant organisation'. They must not be so placed as to release others for the army. They must not be 'organised in a way so as to be used as "blackleg" labour, or to form a reserve in case of labour disputes'. They must not be so paid as to 'perpetuate sweated trades, or to undercut trade union standards or conditions, or to enable employers to reduce their wages bill'. They must be paid rates broadly equivalent to those of soldiers and their dependants. They must not be deprived of the right to express pacifist, religious or political views, or to engage in peace propaganda.

Thus the new National Committee was forced by the large numbers of Fellowship members favouring the scheme to abandon its all-out opposition, at least temporarily. It is not often that a radical leadership is subjected in such a way to the moderating pressures of its rank-and-file; the reverse is the more usual process on the Left. But this is not to say that the N-CF leaders abandoned their advocacy of absolutism and defence of those absolutists who were refusing the scheme. The letter to Asquith ended:

Whilst desiring justice for those of our members who will accept civil work, and offering our criticism upon the method so far adopted for imposing this work, we desire to stress in the strongest possible terms the inevitable disaster that must follow any further refusal on the part of the Government to grant absolute exemption to the men who cannot accept any service imposed by a *Military* Service Act. These include many Quakers, and some of those who have already faced the death sentence in France and are now undergoing periods of ten years' penal servitude. To them it is not the character or the conditions of the service offered that affects their decision. It is not killing only to which they object; it is war and therefore militarism.

They believe it wrong to accept conditional exemption because they hold it to be a bargain with a *Military* Service Act, which to them is the most complete expression of militarism yet admitted in this country. They welcome the obligation of every man to serve the community, but believe that their refusal to be a party to this Act is the highest form of service they can render.

It is these men of whom Mr Lloyd George stated: 'I shall only consider the best means of making the path of that class a very hard one.' Thus, for the very reason that they cannot waive their conviction, they are to be subjected to prolonged persecution, expressly authorised by the Government with a view to breaking their determination to be loyal to their sense of right and wrong.

On 21 August the Home Office published the conditions on which men would be accepted for alternative service at special Home Office centres and work camps. None of the N-CF's demands were met. Men judged by the Central Tribunal and the War Office to be genuine conscientious objectors were required, as a condition of joining the scheme, to sign the following undertaking:

I promise for so long as I am allowed to be free from military control and military duties:

(1). To serve the Committee for the Employment of Conscientious Objectors (hereinafter called the Committee), their Agents or Representatives, with diligence and fidelity on such work of National Importance as the Committee may prescribe for me.

(2). To reside at such place as the Committee, their Agents or Representatives, may from time to time determine.

(3). To conform to such regulations with regard to conduct, and to such as are framed to secure the well-being of men working under similar conditions to myself as may be made by the Committee, or by the Agents, or the Representatives of the Committee, or as may be made by duly appointed Representatives of the men so working and approved by the Committee.

I understand that if and when I cease to carry out any of the foregoing conditions I shall be liable to complete the term of my sentence, and subsequently to be recalled to military service.

Peace propaganda and all such activity was forbidden. As the Prime Minister had intimated, prisoners under the scheme were to be transferred to Section W of the Army Reserve. Those given outdoor work—timber cutting, road making, quarrying, railway maintenance and agriculture—were to be housed under canvas or in huts. Those on indoor work—mailbag, brush and basket making—were to be housed in prisons, workhouses and asylums. All were subject to police surveillance and paid through the police. In short, they were to continue to be treated as political prisoners, with work imposed as a punishment rather than for its 'national importance' or opportunities for service.

When we contemplate the difference between alternative service as it was presented to us by its inventors and apologists, and its actual realisation as witnessed this week [commented *The Tribunal* bitterly on 24 August] we realise the futility, not only of expecting a War Government to use justice and sense in civil affairs, but also of attempting to compromise with such a thing as a Conscription Act . . . Not only do we hope that none of our members will defend such a system, but also that very few men will acquiesce in it.

Fenner Brockway went further. Of the undertaking demanded of prisoners as their passport to the scheme he wrote: 'I have no hesitation in describing it as one of the most monstrous contracts into which a human being was ever asked to enter. It represents indentured labour at its worst . . . To term work under such conditions "service" is ludicrous. It is slavery'[1].

Referring to the Fellowship's three categories of attitude to alternative service, Brockway continued: 'By its policy the Government has alienated all three.' The two groups of 'alternativists' would see the scheme in its final form as having been 'denuded of the very thing—the sense of service—by which its champions justified it . . . They will see in the scheme the menace of industrial conscription. They will see that its effect is to fight by proxy since it releases other men to do the fighting which they themselves will not undertake.'

Temporarily the Government may get men to accept alternative service even under such conditions. But as the men released from prison regain their physical strength and their full powers of judgment we are convinced that large numbers of them will decline to proceed with the work. They will prefer to go back to prison to throw in their lot with the 'absolutists', despite all the dangers which they now know such a course involves.[2]

The argument raged at every local branch meeting. The Mill Hill Guard Room branch resolved that 'the scheme is in spirit and effect subversive of all freedom and justice in that (a) it perpetuates a form of punishment beyond the term of imprisonment, and (b) it fixes a rate of remuneration and existence which are best expressed as a condition of slavery, and (c) that it is in essence a bargain with the Government to facilitate the working of the Conscription Acts'. But from the Croydon branch came an opposite point of view. 'It is contended by some that this work is alternative to military service; by others that it is a penalty. We regard it as both, and accept it as such. We feel that the real victory against military service has been won; that it was won when Army Order X was secured, providing civil imprisonment after court-martial in lieu of military detention . . . It seems to us that COs have in fact got complete exemption, and we do not trouble our heads whether complete exemption is "total exemption" within the meaning of the Acts. We are not concerned with legal technicalities but with facts . . . Some COs regard the Home Office scheme as slavery. But our present struggle is against military service. We can fight such questions as slavery later on, if need be.'

The weight of opinion, measured in terms of resolutions from the branches, seems to have been with the majority of the National Committee against the scheme. But it soon became clear that large numbers of COs in prison were prepared to sign the undertaking and accept work under the Brace Committee, despite the tough line of their leaders. These included thirty of the thirty-four who had received death sentences in France (though some were soon to revolt against the scheme and rejoin the 'absolutists' in prison). They also included C. H. Norman, one of the original members of the National Committee and a fierce individualist who could be guaranteed to be somewhere near the centre of any row among the leadership.

On 2 September, while Norman was between prison spells, he attended a National Committee meeting and pressed for a definite statement of its attitude towards the scheme. The National Committee produced a critical resolution which Norman interpreted as a direct vote of censure on those, like himself, who were prepared to sign the undertaking. In a letter to *The Tribunal* on 28 September, written from the Home Office centre at Kedington, Suffolk, where he had been placed in a group of COs on road-making, he wrote bitterly of the National Committee's 'armchair critics, some of whom are anonymous, and most of whom are ridiculous in their language of exaggeration'. Brockway's description of the scheme's contract of employment as a slavery agreement Norman dismissed as 'unbalanced'.

Meanwhile, complications were arising which were both to exacerbate the quarrel and at the same time test the Home Office's sincerity and goodwill in the administration of the scheme. The work at Kedington was in gravel pits providing material for a road from Bury to Haverhill. COs working in the pits and on the road itself became concerned when they heard local people describe it as 'the new military road'. 'All those here,' wrote Norman, 'were assured by the Deputy Governor of Wormwood Scrubs that the work would be civil work under civil control, and would have nothing to do with the war or the War Department. Unfortunately, evidence is accumulating that the Road Board has been set up as a kind of screen to the War Office, and Brigadier-General Child and Mr Lloyd George are under the suspicion of trying to manipulate the genuine conscientious objector into a position in which, though nominally under civil control, he is really acting as a workman for the War Department . . . Should it turn out that there has been trickery, most of the COs will not continue the work . . . Delightful though it is to be free after three months of gross maltreatment, there will be no surrender of principle. Should it be necessary to go back to prison, back one will go.'

Norman called a meeting in the Common Room at Risbridge House, Kedington, where the men were boarded. They agreed to send a letter to the Government enquiring about the purpose of the road and stating that they would refuse to continue work if it were being built for military purposes. 'To go back to chokee for a long period will about send me off my rocker,' wrote one of the men present, reporting the meeting to the N-CF head office, 'but if it comes to it we are all going to march back to Wormwood Scrubs.'

Head Office, diligent in its search for evidence which would dis-
credit the Home Office scheme, turned up an account in the *Poor
Law Officers' Journal* for 11 August of a meeting at which the local
Poor Law Guardians had been requested by the Government to
find accommodation for COs who were to be brought in 'for the
construction of a military road'. An account was also found, in the
South-West Suffolk Echo of 12 August, of the Local Tribunal's
refusal to exempt three gravel diggers who claimed to be engaged in
essential services in that they were employed in 'providing material
for the Bury to Haverhill military road'. Finally, a poster was found
which until a few weeks earlier had been displayed just outside
Kedington. It read:

WEST SUFFOLK COUNTY COUNCIL
Improvement of roads for military purposes

> This road is now undergoing
> extensive repair. Motorists
> and others are advised to
> take an alternative route.

Armed with this evidence, the National Committee proceeded to
make out its case against the scheme and those of its members who
were accepting it. But at the same time Norman and the men at
Kedington received a firm assurance, which was repeated publicly
in the House of Commons, that the road was not being built for
military purposes or at the request of the War Office. The improve-
ments, they were told, had in fact been scheduled ten years earlier.

After some debate and recriminations, Norman and the Kedington group accepted the assurances and continued work. The
National Committee did not disguise its feeling that Norman had
let the Fellowship down, and continued to uphold the uncompromising 'absolutists' as the real cream of the movement.

★ ★ ★

Among these absolutists now was Clifford Allen himself. His
handing over had been delayed nearly five months by his remarkable advocacy before the Tribunals. 'His clever brain devised a
legal loophole through which the proceedings could be quashed
and postponed for several months', Corder Catchpool subsequently
recalled, adding wryly: 'Intellectual brilliance seemed a doubtful

element in a stand for conscience.' But Allen's legalistic delaying tactics had a double purpose. He wanted to be free for as long as possible during the most crucial phase of the Fellowship's struggle, to lead and shape it; and he wanted to use the Tribunal system's appeal procedure to expose the 'fraud' of alternative service.

He appeared before his Local Tribunal at Battersea on 14 March. Several hundred people turned up to hear the case and most were unable to obtain admission. He made his claim for absolute exemption on the ground of his Socialism—

> I am a Socialist, and so hold in all sincerity that the life and personality of every man is sacred, and that there is something of divinity in every human being, irrespective of the nation to which he belongs. I cannot betray my belief in the brotherhood of all men. To me, war is murder and will only become impossible when an increasing number of those who share this conviction remain true to their beliefs and refuse to take part in warfare, whatever be the pretext for which it is waged. I never have and never will shirk my bounden duty to serve my fellow men. At present I believe I can best render such a service by striving to advance the cause of peace. I have set out my claim for absolute exemption from the provisions of the Act, and explained my unalterable determination to refuse non-combatant or any conditional services, since all of these must contribute, directly or indirectly, to the prosecution or organisation of war. In case the Tribunal decides that I have no conscientious objection, I feel it only honourable that I should make it quite clear that, even then, I must remain resolute in my decision. I am not afraid to undergo any hardship or penalty, even death itself, and shall be proud to bear witness to my faith through suffering.

The chairman pointed out that many Socialists had gone to war. 'Yes,' replied Allen, 'but I am justified in interpreting my Socialist faith according to my own judgment. There is an increasing number of Socialists who are opposing all war, and I count myself amongst that number.' Asked if he considered it right on moral grounds to allow a foreign foe to invade Britain, he replied: 'I do not desire to see this country occupied by the Germans, but so far as I am concerned, I could take no part in bearing arms, or in any way assisting in warfare, even if this country was invaded. If everyone shared my views there would be no invasion. No civilised country would think of attacking another country unless that country was a source of danger owing to its being armed.'

Allen was then asked about his occupation. He was still working as appointed liquidator of the defunct *Daily Citizen*. The following exchange enabled him to make a further statement of his attitude to alternative service.

Member of Tribunal: 'Do you consider your work as liquidator of a derelict company as work of national importance. Would you not be better engaged in defending your country?'

Allen: 'You are aware, sir, that I am not claiming exemption in respect of my occupation. I consider I can best work for my country by striving in every possible way after peace. The best service I can render is to use all my strength and energy in advocating peace.'

Member of Tribunal: 'Would you take part in work of a non-combatant nature?'

Allen: 'I cannot engage in either form of activity. There is really no distinction, for a man who believes war is wrong, between fighting and non-combatant service. I am not prepared to become part of the machine of war. If I had wished to assist I would have assisted directly, not indirectly.'

Member of Tribunal: 'Do you smoke?'

Allen: 'Yes.'

Member of Tribunal: 'Do you realise that by continuing to smoke you are voluntarily assisting the country by the provision of revenue for the war. If you hold that your conscience is supreme you should be prepared to forego these various indulgencies such as smoking.'

Allen: 'The question of smoking has little to do with taking up of arms. It is impossible to do anything at the present moment without assisting in the war. If I eat I help the revenue. If I travel by train or bus I help the revenue. If I forgo smoking and left my money in the bank in current or deposit account, it would be used to assist the country. The only alternative is to leave the country, but that the Government will not permit. Therefore I can only go on following my normal habit of life, but always using my energy and doing everything possible to bring about peace.'

The Chairman: 'The Tribunal disallows your claim.'

Allen: 'Can you give me any reason for your decision?'

The Chairman: 'Your application is disallowed.'

Allen: 'Can you give me any reason for the purpose of my appeal?'
The Chairman: 'We consider that you have not made out your case.'[3]

As Allen left, there was a burst of cheering from the gallery. The chairman ordered it to be cleared. 'A bit of a hero, isn't he?' the chairman enquired ruefully of a member of the Tribunal. 'He is the leader of the gang,' the member replied.

The press reported Allen's 'failure' with obvious satisfaction. 'The ineffable Clifford Allen,' gloated the *Daily Sketch*, 'who has been busy perverting the minds of the weak and uninstructed since the outbreak of war, has been collared. He will serve, no doubt, in the Non-Combatant Corps, and contribute to the gaiety of nations with five-minute disputations with his sergeant.'

But Allen was not collared yet. On 17 March he wrote to the County of London Appeal Tribunal, appealing against the Battersea Tribunal's award of conditional exemption and alternative service: 'I desire to re-emphasise my very definite objections to non-combatant or conditional service as set out in my first claim. My conviction is deep and sincere, and I am prepared to submit to any further cross-examination as evidence of my belief; but I will suffer any penalty rather than take part in the organisation of the country for the conduct of war.'

The Appeal Tribunal confirmed the Battersea Tribunal's judgment and required Allen to report within fourteen days what kind of 'work of national importance' he was proposing to adopt. He replied on 11 May in a letter to the chairman. He was working, he explained, without pay, as chairman of the No-Conscription Fellowship, the Joint Advisory Council and 'a number of committees set up to deal with the industrial and social problems which must confront the nation when the war is over'. This, he submitted, was 'work of real national importance'. 'This work, in which I feel it my duty to continue, is of value to the nation. I am confident I can best serve my fellow-men by doing everything in my power to secure that the spirit of peace shall be fostered, and that public opinion shall be stirred to demand a just and lasting peace at the earliest possible moment. This can only be achieved if there are some persons giving thought to the problem of peace whilst others are waging war.'

The statement proceeded to explain 'why I could not permit my occupation to be changed by a Government carrying on war':

I believe that such a transfer would have the effect of assisting the more thorough organisation of the national resources of the country for motives which I believe to be wrong. It is not the nature of the occupation about which I am especially concerned. Agriculture is in itself a harmless occupation, but to me it becomes harmful by virtue of the fact that if I accepted it I should be making it easier for the Government to remove other men from agriculture to do the fighting which I cannot undertake myself. The same argument must apply to all occupations which are only imposed to make the nation more efficient for prosecuting war. I repeat, I cannot consent to be transferred from my present work on behalf of peace to an occupation, however harmless, which will assist national organisation for the prosecution of war.

I venture, however, to point out that throughout my life I have believed it to be the duty of every citizen to serve his fellow men. I have no objection to compulsion as such. I have always tried, and at present am attempting, to render service of value to the community; indeed, such service has been the inspiration of my life hitherto. I have never feared sacrifice, and merely as evidence of this reveal the present condition under which I am working whilst others are suffering in war. I have not cared to make financial profit out of my work, and have therefore refused to take any remuneration in respect of my efforts on behalf of peace and conscientious objectors, though it has been offered many times. I prefer to consume the small amount of money I have saved rather than take any pay for my present work, and only when this is exhausted will it be necessary for me to find some way of providing a livelihood.

Allen did not expect to win his point. As *The Tribunal* had explained on the occasion of his appearance at Battersea, 'It was not Allen's business to get exemption. He had to bear in mind the morale of the Fellowship.' His plea that his pacifist work be accepted as alternative service of national importance may have looked naïve or impudent to members of the County of London Appeal Tribunal, but the whole exercise was in fact directed at his colleagues in the Fellowship, particularly those who were favourably disposed toward alternative service. His object was to prove to them that 'work of national importance' meant to the authorities 'work useful for the prosecution of the war'.

His appeal was rejected, but the Appeal Tribunal did alter his certificate. The exemption conditional on acceptance of work of national importance was changed to exemption from combatant duties only, thus rendering Allen liable to immediate call-up in the Non-Combatant Corps. It is hard to account for the alteration in any terms other than those of pure spite. Allen was able to show, subsequently, that the alteration was illegal, since the second Military Service Act permitted such variations only on the application of either the objector or the military representative. But by the time this admission had been wrung from the clerk of the Tribunal Allen was in military custody and beyond redress.

He was arrested on 6 August, brought before the magistrates at the Mansion House, and handed over to a military escort. His relations with the police were very friendly, and one officer shook him by the hand and said he looked forward to meeting him in heaven. The escort took him to Warley Barracks, where he was forcibly dressed in khaki and placed in a guardroom cell. On 18 August he appeared before his first court-martial, charged with disobeying an order to clean out his cell. 'The detention room and the cell in which I have been confined for twelve days,' he told the court, 'are the necessary basis upon which your discipline depends. I shall never submit to it, and am proud to have joined with so many others in resisting it. So long as my strength remains I will maintain my resistance to non-combatant service to which I have proved my objection, for to me it is but sharpening the sword for another to use. Again I repeat, as I have before every Tribunal, that I will never seek to evade military service by accepting the degrading slavery of civil tasks imposed by a Military Service Act. I desire to serve my country and my fellow men in all nations by striving to preserve the tradition of liberty in a nation fighting for freedom.'

Allen continued to defend himself and with astonishing ingenuity. He maintained that the Battersea Tribunal's award of conditional exemption, while unacceptable, nevertheless implied the Tribunal's acceptance of him as a genuine conscientious objector. As such, he argued, he was not a soldier and the court-martial could therefore have no jurisdiction over him. He slipped at one point, when he

referred to 'my Commanding Officer'. 'There!' shouted the President of the Court triumphantly, 'you admit you have a Commanding Officer, so you must admit to being a soldier!' It was a frail
triumph. Allen succeeded in forcing an adjournment to give him
time to call his own witnesses. They included Philip Snowden,
Bertrand Russell and the clerks of the Battersea Tribunal and the
County of London Appeal Tribunal. On 23 August his case was
concluded and he was sentenced to ninety days' imprisonment with
hard labour.

Reviewing the case in *The Tribunal* of 17 August, while Allen
was awaiting sentence, Bertrand Russell recalled Lloyd George's
promise to 'consider the best means of making the path of that
class a very hard one', adding acidly:

There is a manly note of primitive ferocity about these words.
They show the odd misconception of the nature of conscience which
has been common to almost all our politicians, who may, for aught I
know, have made a careful study of the subject in dictionaries and
histories, but have evidently been denied by nature the opportunity
to learn about it by looking within. Mr Lloyd George seems to think
that conscience can only *forbid* things: the kind that *enjoins* things is
apparently unknown to him. Does he think that St Paul would have
been satisfied with a certificate excusing him from preaching paganism? Does he think that Luther would have acquiesced in a dispensation from maintaining the doctrine of indulgencies, on condition that
he should preserve silence as to his objections to the doctrine? Does
he think that Joan of Arc would have accepted civil alternative
service? Would he himself have been willing to spend his time during
the Boer War in growing cabbages?

All these parallels, and especially the last, are applicable to the case
of Mr Clifford Allen, and, in varying degrees, to the cases of other
men who will not accept alternative service . . . The Government
cannot break the movement which has been led by Clifford Allen,
but they can advertise to the world his sincerity and courage, and
their incapacity to understand the nature of a conscience which does
not consist in isolated prohibitions but in a determination to serve
mankind in every possible way. This is the kind of conscience by
which Clifford Allen is actuated. As one who is bound to him by
strong ties of friendship and affection, I suffer in the thought of the

torture to which he is to be subjected; but as a lover of peace and an opponent of the Government, I rejoice that they have had the folly to subject him and those who think as he does to a special rigour which draws attention to their exceptional merit.

Awaiting transfer to Wormwood Scrubs, Allen's mind continued to be occupied with the problems of the Fellowship from which he had been forcibly separated. Fenner Brockway had taken over as acting chairman, being bought out of jail for that purpose by the National Committee, which paid his £100 fine. Allen remained deeply anxious that the great majority of the Fellowship would back his stand against alternative service and the Home Office Scheme, and follow the same path. In a note to the National Committee, smuggled out of Warley immediately after his sentence, he wrote of those who were taking the Scheme: 'Can you make them see that if they do work which has always been part of prison penalties and refuse any arrangement which Government approve just because it binds the victim, they will remain free and testimony will be effective. If they take work outside which is not part of ordinary prison routine and pretend to call it punishment they are no longer free—they are slaves playing with liberty, and cease to count in struggle for liberty, and thus in efforts now making to prevent future war.'

* * *

Other schisms were racking the Fellowship. The debate about the Home Office Scheme was provoking an almost equally intense argument among the absolutists on whether ordinary prison work should be accepted with resignation or met with organised work striking. Religious members of the Fellowship were angry at the title of a new N-CF pamphlet by Laurence Housman—*Christianity: a Danger to the State*. Barratt Brown resigned from the National Committee because it would not accept his view that the N-CF was concerned only to propagate pacifism and had no business wasting its substance in agitation for the release of prisoners. Schism bred schism, and political divisions which had previously assumed little importance now began to threaten the Fellowship's unity.

The National Committee's answer was to organise a series of divisional conventions throughout October and November.

National speakers addressed meetings in London, Manchester, Leeds, Glasgow, Birmingham, Bristol and Cardiff. Fenner Brockway was arrested on arrival in Glasgow for the Scottish convention, but managed to secure his release in time to get to the meeting at the Central Hall, where he delivered an impassioned call for an immediate peace, to be followed by the 'voluntary disbandment of the Army and the sinking of the Navy'.

Clifford Allen, from his solitary confinement in Wormwood Scrubs, managed to get a message to the conventions. His appeal was addressed to absolutists and alternativists alike. He was becoming aware of the threatening possibility of a split between the two sections, and his message was carefully conciliatory.

> Tell those outside [he wrote] that the success of the stand we are making does not depend on whether we do or refuse to do this thing or that thing, but on whether we are true through everything to the spirit of the Fellowship, making that spirit felt in barracks, in prison and wherever we may be, and using this time as a test and training for the work of the future. Let us do nothing, inside or outside prison, that may divide us from one another, or that we shall have any reason to look back on with regret.

One N-CF member contrived from his guardroom to arrange for a telegram to be sent to the Manchester convention, reading: 'The comrades must unite for peace.' Another member told Brockway after the same meeting: 'I wish we could have more of this spirit in our branch meetings. Absolutists and alternativists were united tonight in acclaiming our message of anti-militarism and peace. If we could more often live as a fellowship in the atmosphere of the great fundamental things that join us, and less often in the atmosphere of the small, personal things that divide us, how much more effective our work might be!'

Bertrand Russell made much the same appeal in *The Tribunal* on 12 October:

> I think that, if we are more filled with the good at which we aim than with the evils against which we fight, some of the domestic questions that distract us will seem less momentous than at times they appear to be. Some men reject alternative service, some accept it; some hold that acceptance is treachery, others that rejection is

mere politics. 'He that eateth, eateth unto the Lord, and he that eateth not, unto the Lord he eateth not,' said St Paul in a very similar controversy. It matters nothing now which of the early disciples ate unclean meats and which did not; what matters still in the world is the positive testimony they gave unitedly to the law of love. If you disbelieve in alternative service, stand out against it, no matter what the Government may do to you; if you believe in it, take it, no matter what the absolutist may say to you. It matters little, in the long run, which way men decide, provided they decide earnestly and sincerely, in the light of their hopes for the world, and not of personal fear or pride.

Let us remember that the goal at which we aim is not some outward result, some admirable mechanical arrangement, but a change of heart and soul in the world. There is some danger of losing sight of the end in the means. But a prolonged resistance, such as has been forced on the N-CF, cannot be carried out in a true pacifist spirit except by constantly remembering the end at which we aim; not only the destruction of militarism (though that might seem a great enough object), but the creation of a free, happier, nobler life for every man and woman in the world. In essentials, each one of us can live this life here and now: Clifford Allen is living it, in spite of prison and illness. It is a life full of joy—a greater joy than any that the militarist can know. For his sake, if we could, we would share our joy with him; we would persuade him, rather than drive him to a puzzled admission that we are invincible.

Throughout the controversies that inevitably must arise, let us remember on both sides the fundamental unity of the Fellowship, and the greatness of the ideal for which it stands. Let us never forget that we are the guardians of a great ideal, and that the first test of our beliefs is our way of dealing with our own internal questions. So long as the spirit of our actions is that for which the Fellowship stands, our loyalty is unimpaired whatever outward form our actions may take. But no outward form will preserve true loyalty if the inward spirit has been lost.

The conventions succeeded in restoring the Fellowship's morale, but also tended to side-step the divisive issue of alternative service by declaring that the Fellowship should concern itself solely with pacifist propaganda, adopting no official attitude at all towards the Home Office scheme and work under the Pelham Committee. This was the view of the conventions at Birmingham (27 votes to 21), Bristol (42 to 1) and Leeds (majority on a show of hands). Glasgow was divided 59-59. The Welsh convention declined to vote on the ground that the issue had not been sufficiently discussed, and the London convention did not discuss alternative service at all. Manchester, by 22 votes to 14, urged the National Committee to demand that the work of alternativists should be honourable rather than penal.

No mechanical system of democracy could have created unity out of such diversity; and, when all was said and done, the conventions were representative only of unconscripted members and associates of the Fellowship. The backbone of the movement, those to whom its decisions were in a special sense immediate and vital, were behind bars—with the exception of the minority on furlough, between prison sentences. If the Fellowship emerged from its conventions more united than it was when it went into them this was due less to the mystical and therapeutic qualities of democratic discussion than to the fact that the leadership was itself learning tolerance. After all, it had little choice: large numbers were accepting the Home Office scheme. Thus Fenner Brockway, who a few weeks earlier had denounced the scheme as 'slavery', was by the end of October writing of those who had accepted it: 'What an opportunity is theirs! What an opportunity of learning the points of view of one's fellow comrades in the fight, what an opportunity of widening one's conception of truth by frank and friendly discussion! . . . I would urge our comrades at Dyce and Kedington, at Warwick and Wakefield and the other settlements and camps to keep their eyes upon the future and to prepare themselves for the life-long service which must be ours.' Alternativists and absolutists were friends again, and the No-Conscription Fellowship was an umbrella organisation for both.

REFERENCES

1 *The Tribunal*, 17 August 1916
2 *The Tribunal*, 24 August 1916
3 *The Tribunal*, 23 March 1916

Chapter VIII

Political Prisoners

On a bleak hillside just outside the remote Aberdeenshire village of Dyce, the Home Office Committee for the Employment of Conscientious Objectors established in August 1916 its first work centre. Some 250 men were transferred there from prison, on accepting the scheme. They were paid eightpence a day for ten hours work in granite quarries, where they were employed in breaking stones for road building. Dyce was a prototype concentration camp.

The prisoners were housed in tents which had been condemned as unfit for soldiers. They were thought good enough for conscientious objectors, even in the wet climate of the north of Scotland. To make matters worse, they were pitched on a slope which proved to be a natural water course. Men who had already been worn down by months of imprisonment and under-feeding were lodged in these conditions, with a sea of mud under their groundsheets and sodden, leaking canvas over their heads.

Early in September the N-CF head office received the following letter from one of its members at Dyce:

> The weather here is wretched. The tents are all leaking . . . Everybody has a lot of wet clothes and no facilities for drying them. Last night, when we got back to camp, our bedding and blankets were all wet . . . Everybody in camp has bad colds . . .
>
> All those men (over one hundred) who are taking up their quarters in a barn were ordered to return to their wet tents. They were also ordered to do ten hours work a day at the heavy quarry work. Many of the chaps are exceedingly weak, not yet having recovered from the effects of ill-treatment. Twenty of the men who were sentenced to death in France are here; also Everett. There are some who are still in a weak condition. The result was a practically unanimous decision

to ignore the order . . . At present our conditions are more like penalisation than exemption . . . We have now got two or three invalids . . . One case is so serious that the doctor says he dare not move the patient.

The serious case was twenty-year-old Walter Roberts of Stockport. He had come to Dyce in a state of exhaustion after four months' hard labour in prison. After a fortnight he collapsed. He wrote to his mother:

As I anticipated, it has only been a question of time for the damp conditions prevailing here to get the better of me. Bartle Wild is now writing to my dictation, as I am too weak to handle a pen myself. I don't want you to worry yourself because doctor says I have only got a severe chill, but it has reduced me very much. All the fellows here are exceedingly kind and are looking after me like bricks, so there is no reason why I should not be strong in a day or two, when I will write personally and more fully.

Two days later Walter Roberts died in his tent. Ironically for those who saw it as a hard-won amelioration, it was the Home Office scheme which provided the N-CF with its first martyr.

Roberts' death stunned the Fellowship and caused panic at the Home Office. An enquiry followed, and the facts that emerged about conditions at Dyce went a long way towards discrediting the scheme. Two illusions were shattered: that service under the Brace Committee offered COs an easy way out of prison, and that its administrators were genuinely concerned to offer objectors socially useful work instead of punishment. At the end of October, barely ten weeks after it had been opened, Dyce camp was closed and the men there dispersed. Some had already chosen to rejoin the absolutists in prison.

Other settlements and centres providing similar work but less harsh conditions were established at Ballachulish, Chelsea, Denton, Grimsby, Hornchurch, Kedington, Loch Awe, Lyme Regis, Lyndhurst, Newhaven, Sunk Island and Sutton. The prisons at Knutsford, Wakefield and Warwick were also transformed into Home Office centres. Locks were removed from cell doors, the warders wore no uniform, and the prisoners were allowed out in the evenings until 9.30. At first the work was the usual prison work on mailbags, mats and baskets. Soon, however, large groups of the men were being hired out to private employers. The Men's Committee at Wakefield protested: 'Men are being sent out to work for private employers, and many here think they are thus being used as direct substitutes to drive men into the army . . . It is feared that this is the beginning of an attempt to use all COs for the purpose of "National Service", and of assisting the prosecution of the war.' About 140 of the 600 men at Wakefield declared themselves so strongly opposed to private employment that they would 'absolutely refuse to co-operate'. Even as the pledges were being collected, forty men were placed under arrest, and seven were returned to prison under military escort.

The greater freedom accorded COs in the work centres, and particularly their freedom to go out in the evenings, brought them into contact with the general public, sometimes with unhappy results. At Knutsford, groups of COs cycled daily from the work centre through the town to a group of farms where they were employed on agricultural labour. They were frequently jeered on their way through the town. One evening, on their return to the centre, a group were pulled off their cycles and punched and kicked. The gang responsible promised to 'do the job properly' the following night. The police were warned, but were nowhere to be seen when the first group of COs cycled into the town. They found the street leading to the work centre blocked by an angry crowd. Their bicycles were seized and they were pulled off. Many were viciously beaten up, and some had their clothes torn off. The cycles were smashed. Fifty men inside the centre heard the disturbance and went to the rescue of their friends, some arming themselves with sticks. Eighteen men were treated that night in hospital.

A police squad arrived at the height of the riot and made ten arrests. When these men were brought before the judge the Superintendent of Police, from the witness box, declared that there was no evidence of the disturbance having been organised. The situation, he suggested, had been exacerbated by the arrival of the fifty rescuers from inside the centre. Their intervention was 'asking for trouble'. The judge remarked that, considering the state of local feeling, the COs were 'literally trailing their coats before the townspeople'. Not to be out-done, the Superintendent added that the 'conchies' were in the habit of jostling wounded soldiers off the footpath, and 'interfering with ladies'. He had once heard of a Mrs Williams being struck on the jaw by a 'conchie' in front of the prison. The judge, suitably appalled, declared that the 'provocative behaviour' of the COs was such that 'it did not require much to put a match to popular opinion'. The ten defendants were bound over to keep the peace for six months.

A similar riot occurred at Wakefield a few days later, when a dozen COs were hurt and the local Quaker meeting house ransacked. Another group, arriving at the Lyndhurst centre, were attacked by soldiers convalescing at a local military hospital. They were dragged from their van and punched and kicked. Their luggage was removed and thrown into a river, followed by two of the COs. Again, a group at Lyme Regis were attacked in a riot incited by women and girls, several of whom joined in what a local newspaper described as 'the entertainment'. One CO was stripped and subjected to crude indignities.

These events lent some support to the claim of Mr Edwin Gilbert, a Quaker warden at Wakefield, that public opinion had become so inflamed against conscientious objectors, that they would be in danger of their lives if allowed to go free. Certainly the public attitude towards COs hardened when the German air attacks were stepped up in 1917. The war was given a terrible immediacy which intensified popular hatred of 'the Hun' and such 'pro-Germans' as the COs were still popularly supposed to be.

In March 1917 several settlements were closed down as part of a plan to rationalise and centralise the scheme. Their occupants were transferred to Dartmoor, near Princetown. The old prison's convict population had been moved out, and the place converted into a work centre. It housed nearly 1,000 men, and was the largest of all the Home Office settlements.

The first arrivals at Dartmoor found it wholly unprepared for them. 'We came to Princetown,' wrote one CO, Ben Hyman, in the COs' own Dartmoor *News Sheet*, 'and found the settlement in a state of chaos; order was unknown, labour was of a desultory character. None cared how the new "shop" of the Government progressed. Topsy-turveydom reigned supreme.'

There was fierce hostility among the local population. On 18 March some marines attacked a party of COs in Tavistock. Five were hurt, and two went to hospital. A few days later another party arriving from Wormwood Scrubs, were attacked at Yelverton station. The Vicar of Walkhampton published in a local newspaper a direct incitement to violence against the unwanted newcomers, and five Anglican COs who attended his evening service the following Sunday were attacked by the congregation when the service was over. The same vicar presided over a meeting of local clergy at which the following resolution was passed:

'This meeting desires to express its gratitude to the editor of the *Western Morning News* for the strong protest that is being made through the medium of his paper against the ridiculously lenient treatment that is accorded at Princetown Prison to so-called conscientious objectors; and guarantees its heartiest support in any steps that may be taken with a view to the introduction and enforcement of stricter methods of dealing with COs generally.'

The enforced idleness of those first few weeks at Dartmoor created unparalleled opportunities for debate, discussion and controversy. The first Men's Committee elected was heavily weighted with militant Socialist objectors who advocated a policy designed to obstruct and wreck an ordered administration of the scheme. As the settlement grew and became more representative of all kinds of CO, the committee was taken over by 'moderates' who toed the more respectable N-CF line. Howard Marten, the committee's secretary, classified the men as follows[1]:

Many of the political and agnostic objectors, together with those belonging to a not inconsiderable 'Artistic' group, were usually arranged in general policy alongside Friends, Tolstoyans and members of the Fellowship of Reconciliation. The so-called 'religious' group included a big section of International Bible Students, Plymouth Brethren and others who, while excellent men individually, took little or no part in the political or social life of the settlement. The most difficult section were those who belonged to the Communist[2] group and who had little real sympathy for the true Pacifist position. In matters of policy these would at times draw to their side many of the 'Fed-ups' and extremists of other political sections.

The N-CF publicly dissociated itself from the militants, and persuaded the Men's Committee at Dartmoor and the other centres to pass resolutions deploring slackness and sabotage. C. H. Norman, transferred from Kedington, again crossed swords with the

National Committee, complaining that it was playing along with the Government and dividing the movement into docile sheep and wild goats.

The Bishop of Exeter, William Gascoyne Cecil, made much of this division. On 8 October 1917 he wrote to *The Times* advocating that religious objectors be set free and political objectors 'be allocated, without money or rations, to that portion of England which is frequently visited by enemy aeroplanes'. The religious objectors he regarded as harmless cranks, their opposition to war being on the same level as the Moslem's opposition to pork and the Hindu's objection to the killing of cows. But the Socialists at Dartmoor, he suggested, were using their time to 'organise resistance, armed or passive, against the existing order of affairs'. He drew a graphic picture of sacks of letters pouring in and out of Dartmoor daily, 'no doubt conveying instructions for those plans of bloodshed which may at some future time bring, according to their view, liberty, and, to our view, ruin, to England'. The political objector was 'an enemy of our commonwealth'. *The Times* headed the letter: 'Anarchic Dartmoor—a Hotbed of Malcontents.'

Work had by now been organised for the new arrivals, much of it identical to that formerly performed by the convicts. Seven hundred men worked on some two thousand acres of land attached to the centre, and most of the rest were engaged on the internal work of the settlement. The men worked 9½ hours a day. In an attempt to perpetuate and formalise the division between 'good conduct' and 'bad conduct' objectors, the authorities proposed to abolish the flat rate of eightpence a day and instead pay the good men one shilling and the trouble-makers only fourpence, at the same time giving the good men foremen's status. The scheme was angrily repudiated. The work itself became progressively more penal and less constructive.

A mounting press campaign, led by the *Daily Mail*, protested that the Dartmoor men were being 'pampered' and 'coddled'. The *Mail* described Dartmoor as 'the COs' Cosy Club'. Sir C. Kinloch-Cooke, MP for the nearby division of Devonport, took up the vindictive campaign in the Commons. This was the signal for a general renewal of persecution—officially described as 'tightening of discipline'—at all Home Office centres. Although William Brace remained nominal chairman of the responsible Home Office committee, it was now dominated by two retired army officers, Major (later Sir) George Terrell and Major George Briscoe. Terrell and Briscoe visited each of the centres in turn and revised the regulations 'to bring them up to army standards'. At Wakefield (where Edwin Gilbert, the Quaker warder, resigned in protest after their visit) the men's allocation of books was cut and they were made to sleep on ground level, their beds having formerly been raised on boxes or blocks to minimise invasion by insects and vermin. At Dartmoor the men were forbidden to enter any town or village except Princetown, their Christmas leave was cancelled and their daily diet, for heavy manual labour, reduced from twenty-two ounces of bread and two pints of porridge to eleven ounces of bread and one and a half of porridge. Finally, men were returned to prison for the slightest indiscipline: one, V. J. Brown, for being ten minutes late for work; another, Ben Hyman, for writing a letter to the *Western Morning News*. Voluntary return to prison to rejoin the absolutists ran at more than one a week.

The men at Dartmoor combated the press charges of idleness by publishing a resolution, passed at a special general meeting of nearly nine hundred men on 17 May 1917. 'This meeting', it read, 'repudiates the charge that the policy of slacking is, or has been, pursued at this Settlement, and declares that the men here are prepared to perform the work provided in a reasonable spirit, but protests against the penal character of the work imposed by the Home Office Committee and demands civil work of real importance with full civil rights.' The campaign for 'civil work of real importance' was taken up by the National Council for Civil Liberties and by organisations outside the pacifist movement. A protest against 'the penal conditions imposed upon conscientious objectors in Home Office Camps', coupled with the demand that the Government 'substitute a scheme of useful social service under honourable conditions' was addressed in July 1917 to all Local Labour Parties and Trades Councils, signed by ten trade union branch secretaries, including Herbert Morrison. More than one hundred Labour organisations endorsed it, and the Scottish Advisory Committee of the Labour Party unanimously passed a resolution based upon it.

But there followed no general amelioration of the scheme. Farms became derelict because farmers were breaking stones at Dartmoor; school classes were amalgamated to unmanageable numbers because teachers were made to sew mail-bags. The scheme which was intended to provide conscientious objectors with socially useful work cost the Home Office more than £1,500 per week.

On 6 February 1918, Henry W. Firth of Norwich died at Dartmoor. He had served nine months at Wormwood Scrubs and Maidstone. In November 1917 he became so ill that he applied for the Home Office scheme. By the time he arrived at Dartmoor, in the new year, he was, in the words of a subsequent report of the Men's Committee, 'a mere bag of bones'. He was nevertheless put to work in the quarry on stone breaking. On his third day, unable to eat, he visited the doctor who told him there was nothing wrong with him and sent him back to work. When he again visited the doctor three days later he was told he was being selfish to be so concerned with his own comfort when thousands were in the trenches. Each day he reported sick, and each day he was rejected for hospital. On 23 January he was put on an all-night white-washing party, and although unable to work was again included in the detail for the following night. On 28 January he resumed work in the quarry. He was finally admitted to the camp hospital on 30 January, where his treatment consisted of a dose of cod-liver oil.

On 4 February a deputation from the Men's Committee interviewed the doctor, with the result that Firth was allowed a milk diet. He also asked for eggs, but was told that eggs were available only for the men in France. On the morning of 6 February one of his friends became so alarmed at his condition that he asked permission to wire Firth's wife. Permission was refused. That afternoon Firth died.

The Men's Committee instructed a solicitor to appear for the widow at the inquest. But the doctor, who declared that the cause of death was diabetes (which he must have had for a considerable time) was exonerated. In protest against the conditions which had led to Firth's death, the committee declared a one-day work and hunger strike. This brought Major Terrell scurrying down from London to inaugurate an enquiry. The committee's secretary, I. P. Hughes, and C. H. Norman were seized upon as the ringleaders, and military escorts removed them from Dartmoor and handed them over to the Army. Both men followed the usual course of disobeying their first order and were then court-martialled and sent to Exeter Prison. Hughes was later allowed a further spell of work under the scheme, but Norman remained in prison until after the end of the war.

On 30 April 1918, Lord Parmoor, who had frequently championed the cause of the COs, initiated a debate in the House of Lords, moving that the work of conscientious objectors should be service of national value and not merely penal. He described the work of two groups of men in Dartmoor, labouring in adjoining courts. One piled up stones and the other cleared the piles: then the groups changed places. 'These men', he declared, of those in work centres and in prison, 'are going downhill on a very steep gradient. The speed is accelerated, health is broken, nerves are unstrung and their mental vision is clouded.' Parmoor was supported by the Bishop of Oxford and Earl Russell—Bertrand Russell's brother. In reply, Viscount Peel for the Government made the most of the Home Office's latest plan, a rehashed scheme for hiring out men to private employers. This 'concession' was refused by many of those to whom it was offered. Since they were not normally allowed to take such employment within twenty-five miles of home they regarded it as still penal; and they were not prepared to undercut prevailing trade union rates.

Altogether, despite the liberal intentions of some of those who planned the Home Office scheme, it proved to be a discreditable shambles. It never came within measuring distance of giving conscientious objectors the 'work of national importance' they were promised. It insisted on punishing men officially declared to be genuine in their conscientious objection. Above all, it went a long way towards justifying its rejection by the absolutists as a diversionary fraud—and towards increasing their numbers.

* * *

Of just over 5,000 objectors interviewed in prison by the Central Tribunal, 3,750 accepted the Home Office scheme. Roughly 1,350 rejected it as absolutists. They remained in prison. With them remained 158 men deemed 'not genuine' by the Central Tribunal, most of whom had refused to recognise the Tribunals or appear before them. Another 127 stayed in prison in consequence either of 'misbehaviour' in the Home Office camps and other venues of approved alternative service, or by reason of a voluntary return to jail from the scheme. Altogether 1,543 objectors served their sentences in civil prisons. These were the incorrigible non-com-promisers, the hard core of resisters of whom Lloyd George had vowed that he would 'only consider the best means of making the path of that class as hard as possible'.

The standard sentence became 112 days' hard labour, reduced from an original sentence of two years. 'Good conduct' could earn remission of up to fourteen days, bringing the sentence actually served to just over three months. But under the 'cat and mouse' procedure originally formulated to deal with suffragette agitation, the end of each sentence became but the prelude to a new one. The released prisoner was again called up, again arrested as a deserter, again handed over to the Army. He again disobeyed orders, was again court-martialled, and after a few days in the guardroom again sent to a civil prison to begin a new sentence. Some objectors served as many as six such consecutive sentences.

During the first month of confinement conditions were doubly hard. Prison work was done in isolation in the cell. The diet was minimal, expressly designed to strip a prisoner of fat and surplus energy resources. The bed consisted of a bare wooden plank, or in some Scottish jails a slab of stone. A mattress was provided after fourteen nights. Not a single visit or letter or any communi-cation from the world outside was allowed during the first two months.

One result of this system was that, under the 'cat and mouse' procedure, conscientious objectors underwent a 'first month' at regular intervals throughout what was in effect a continuous and endless sentence. Further, the more remission they earned by good conduct, the more frequent were their 'first months'. There was thus a positive incentive to COs to disregard the more irksome rules and forego remission. When they eventually appreciated this, the authorities abandoned the 'first month' regulations for second and subsequent terms.

After a year or so, the military courts recognised that 112-day terms were not breaking the conscientious objectors. They accord-ingly ceased the practice of commuting sentences, allowing the full two-year sentences to stand. And still the 'cat and mouse' pro-cedure was followed remorselessly; when one two-year sentence ended, the men were returned to start another.

Two years hard labour was the severest sentence on the statute book, short of hanging and ordinary life imprisonment. It was accepted that a longer sentence carried a serious risk to life or sanity, and where longer terms of imprisonment were prescribed it was always under the much less onerous conditions of penal servitude. Lord Justice Fry and Lord Parmoor, in protesting against the indefinite terms of hard labour meted out to COs by the military courts, declared that they had never given two-year hard labour sentences even to the worst criminals to appear before them. But to the courts-martial these men were hardened shirkers. They had turned down the call to serve King and Country, and no sentence was too harsh for them.

Like other prisoners, COs were confined in cells never more than 14 ft by 7 ft, and often no more than 11 ft by 7 ft. Windows, where the cells were built against external walls, were small and high. The prisoner had to stand on his stool to see through them—and this was forbidden. Often they were of frosted glass. Prisons in areas troubled by Zeppelin raids had their cell windows blacked out with paint. Cells were generally lit by gas lamps in the corridors. Every cell door had an elaborate lock and a warder's peep-hole.

The close confinement of the cell could mean torture in the summer months. One prisoner wrote:

I have seen a man go raving mad in the prison after being shut up in a warm cell from four o'clock in the afternoon until six o'clock next morning. The cells are very badly ventilated; the one I was in had all the windows fastened down so that they were a fixture. Some cells have got two little windows out, but some have not, and it gets very hot in there; especially when the sun is beating in it gets unbearable. I have seen cell doors opened in the morning and the men stretched out on the floor in fits of fainting; and the warders do not take any notice of them, but simply pass on and leave the door open. It really is very brutal. Men in the first stage are kept in the cell and not let out, only for three-quarters of an hour early in the morning, and it is more than you dare ask to go out of your cell for anything for the first month, so you can just tell what it is like to be so closely confined this hot weather.[3]

Cold spells in winter provided the reverse hardship. Heating systems were generally primitive. At Maidstone Jail, where tiled flooring undid the work of the inadequate central heating, treatment for chilblains became part of the daily routine, like breakfast and the emptying of slops. A CO's wife wrote:

> When I met my husband coming out of prison on February 10th last, I was horrified to see how very badly he was suffering from the cold. His face showed this very much, and in addition to this his hands were literally covered with chilblains and the prison doctor had painted them with iodine. I was still more disturbed when he said that was nothing to what they had been. He also told me that for the last few weeks it had been so cold that he had been quite unable to read at all—he could only pace up and down his cell. I might say that normally he does not feel the cold at all, and I have never known him to have a chilblain on his hands before.[4]

Work during the first month of hard labour was carried out in the cell. Subsequently prisoners were permitted to work 'in association', either on their stools in the corridor immediately outside the cell door, or in workshops or out-door working parties. The usual prison work was mailbag sewing, mat-making or stone-breaking. Prisoners were worked ten hours a day. At 5.30 a.m. they were awakened and paraded out to the lavatories to wash and empty their cell pails. Then they scrubbed their cells and furniture—bedboard, stool, table and shelf. Cutlery and pails were cleaned, bedding folded to regulation patterns. At 6 a.m. came breakfast: one pint of porridge, without milk. Then forty-five minutes controlled exercise in the exercise yard. Then work. Then lunch at midday (typical menu: ½ lb potatoes, 6 oz bread, 10 oz haricots, 2 oz crude-fat bacon). Then work again until 4.15 p.m. Then supper: 1 pint porridge, ½ lb bread. Cocoa was at first served to prisoners of four months standing or offered as a reward for good work, but this bonus was withdrawn under war-time economies in 1918. That, with time in the evenings for reading and an outing to the prison service on Sundays, was the routine of prison life.

The food was not only grossly inadequate but of the lowest quality in regard both to nutrition and simple hygiene. One prisoner wrote:

> The rice invariably disclosed the fact that there must be a swarm of mice in the prison kitchen or store. This tended to sicken one, although low feeding made me proof even against this—I had a black

beetle in my mouth one day. This I readily admit was an exception, yet I mentioned it to a warder, and he told me not to say anything about it, because the other prisoners may ask for them too. Yet the mice's dirt was the rule, and never a day passed when we had rice but that I picked out half a dozen or more lumps of evidence.[5]

The most arduous of all prison regulations was the notorious 'silence rule'. Prisoners at that time were not allowed any conversation at all, either among themselves or with warders, except to answer a warder's question or make an official request. Sometimes the rule was not too harshly administered: the real crime was to be *caught* talking. But a few COs, including Ernest Everett, who felt conscientiously bound to obey all regulations, were reduced to months of almost total silence. Prisoners who openly rebelled against the rule, as Fenner Brockway did eventually after several months acquiescence, were dealt with with the utmost rigour. Brockway received eight months solitary confinement and three months bread and water.

After the first two months, prisoners were allowed to write and receive one letter a month, plus one personal visit. Letters in were read by the Governor or chief warder. Correspondents, who had to be either relatives or 'respectable friends', were warned to keep their letters short, to avoid slang, and to make no mention of public affairs. Letters out were not allowed to carry references to prison conditions or other prisoners. These monthly letters and visits were bestowed as privileges which could be, and frequently were, cancelled or postponed in punishment of minor offences. Pencils were issued at letter-writing time, then carefully collected in. The only other writing materials allowed consisted of a slate and crayon.

The Bible and Prayer Book and one 'educational book' were allowed during the first month. Subsequently, the educational book could be changed monthly and a fictional work was also allowed, which could be changed weekly. Prisoners generally had no choice of their first educational work. W. J. Chamberlain was given *The Fifteen Decisive Battles of the World*.

'Chapel' on Sundays was a welcome break in routine. Chamberlain described it in *The Tribunal*, 21 September 1916:

The prisoners seated on the first two forms compose the choir. We are seated at intervals of about 30 inches, and from remarks hurled at us by a warder, we gather that we have to sit quite still, with our eyes looking straight in front; and departure from this instruction would bring dire penalties upon us. We contrive, however, by various devices to take in a general view of our environment.

The chapel is severely plain in every detail, and is rendered more so by the hideous dress of its congregation. The altar has nothing beautiful about it; even the few flowers placed on either side of the crucifix are drooping their heads as if conscious of their incongruity. There is nothing bearing the least resemblance to art in the picture of Christ on the Cross; on the contrary, it is ugly and appears to have been designed as a caricature. The only touch of colour in the building is the blue uniforms and bright buttons of the warders, who are seated on elevated stools at various points. Presently the organ begins to breathe soft, restful music, and we begin to appreciate the service. We stand as the chaplain enters, and everyone then kneels for silent prayer—except the warders, who remain seated . . .

The service continues. The first lesson from the Old Testament is fierce and bloodthirsty, but quite appropriate to the times. We sing a hymn. The second lesson is being read from the New Testament. 'Woe unto you, Scribes and Pharisees, hypocrites! for ye devour widows' houses, and for a pretence make long prayers . . .'

We dig our knees into the back of our comrade in front of us. He nods his head so violently that we begin to tremble for him; but nothing happens.

Another hymn, and at its conclusion we find the chaplain in the pulpit. He is a good-natured, bluff, elderly gentleman, with a very homely style. His sermon is full of simple little stories, inserted by way of illustration. His logic was quite unique at times; but, on the whole, he certainly appealed to a considerable portion of his congregation. We remember one gem, obviously addressed to us: 'Do as Christ bids you: never mind your conscience!' We tried to probe into the depths of this injunction, but had to give it up.

The sermon over, we sing the last hymn. The Benediction is pronounced, and the chaplain leaves the chapel. We remain seated. The Governor mounts the steps of the desk from which the lessons are read, unfolds the *Weekly Dispatch*, and gives a résumé of the previous week's war news. He is thankful to say that the German losses are terrible; our losses are also heavy; we must carry on to the last man —and so on in correct retired-Major style. The chaplain has returned

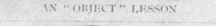

FATHER · BROTHER · MOTHER · SISTER · UNCLE · COUSIN

CONSCIENTIOUS OBJECTOR

Frank Holland

PLATE 9.

—By permission of John Bull

"This little pig stayed at home"

Above: What they thought of the conscientious objector in 1918; from *John Bull.*
Below: The reality: a work-party of CO's in a stone-breaking gang at Dartmoor.

Clifford Allen, aged twenty-nine, on his release from prison in 1918. While in prison he lost nearly three stone in weight.

to listen to the Governor, and nods his head approvingly. The Governor concludes his recital, and we are ordered to stand and sing the National Anthem. We hesitate about standing, but remember that at our own request we have been granted special permission to attend chapel. We stand and fold our arms instead of standing at 'attention', and keep our lips tightly closed, so that we cannot even be suspected of singing! One verse is apparently considered sufficient for the salvation of His Majesty. We resume our seats. The bell twangs to indicate the conclusion of the proceedings. The organ plays a voluntary. The prisoner in the last row leads the way out of the chapel; each row remains seated until the row immediately behind has left. We march out along the corridor, down the stairs, back to our cell, and shut the door. So ends the most remarkable religious service we have ever attended.

Another chaplain argued in one of his sermons that since St Paul was by trade a tent-maker he must have been an army contractor, 'proud to do his bit for his Empire'. Another thundered that those who refused to serve the 'God of War' deserved to be drowned. Another was startled, when he made a ritual reference to the Prince of Peace and the brotherhood of man in a sermon at Wormwood Scrubs, to hear an approving stamping of feet from the COs' quarter, which mounted to a crescendo and forced the sermon to an abrupt conclusion.

Each prison had paid Anglican, Roman Catholic and Nonconformist chaplains. Other denominations provided their own voluntary visiting pastors. The Quakers, too, formed a network of 'Quaker chaplains', despite the Society's lack of a full-time ministry, and these volunteers played an important part in the N-CF's 'intelligence'. Clifford Allen successfully petitioned the Prison Commissioners to allow Socialist objectors of no religion access to the Quaker chaplain. John Graham, Quaker chaplain at Strangeways Jail, Manchester, was allowed to organise Quaker meetings for all COs, religious and political. The Anglican chaplain there made a habit of sending COs back to their cells before giving other prisoners the weekly report on the war. Graham retaliated by giving his own news summary, which included full news of the N-CF and the anti-war movement.

The most treasured ingredient of a good Quaker meeting is

silence, but there was little of it in these jail meetings, which often became animated discussions. Half-an-hour's respite from the silence rule was too valuable to be wasted in mystic meditation or passive endurance of sermonettes.

Innumerable devices were employed for cheating the silence rule. Fenner Brockway describes some of them in the first volume of his autobiography, *Inside the Left*. At his first chapel service at Wormwood Scrubs, the prisoner immediately behind him—A. W. Haycock, subsequently Labour MP for Salford—departed from the set chant, and instead of the words of the Prayer Book Brockway heard:

> *Welcome, Fenner boy!*
> *When did you get here?*
> *How did you like the skilly this morn?*
> *Lord, have mercy upon us!*

Later, at Walton Jail, another prisoner bumped into him in the corridor, and managed without detection to press a sheet of toilet paper into his hand. It contained a 'telephone code', a special prison morse with a pattern of dots and dashes for every letter of the alphabet. The 'telephone' was the hot-water pipe which passed from cell to cell, and the telephone number of each prisoner was his cell number. This became, with practice, a remarkably fast and sophisticated means of communication, almost undetectable since the slightest tap was clearly transmitted through the cells without being heard in the corridors. N-CF news went into the hot-water pipe, and discussions were held which sometimes concluded with resolutions being put and votes being taken. Prisoners also devised a form of 'piped chess'. In Winchester Jail, Clifford Allen played matches with Scott Duckers five cells down the line, and they even organised a tournament in which a score of prisoners participated. The lines must often have been engaged.

Exercise time was fruitful for illicit conversation. The prisoners were marched round in circles in the prison yards, and generally contrived to make enough noise with their boots to cover occasional whispered greetings. But the most daring means of communication was devised by the N-CF head office. Every member awaiting arrest was provided by his branch with a small packet of pencil leads, a piece of sticking plaster, and instructions for smuggling them into his cell. This was far from easy; prisoners were required to strip before changing into prison clothes, so false pockets and the like were out. Moreover, the medical examination on entrance was likely to involve an inspection of the teeth, plus a hunt for piles or signs of venereal disease. One place was left: the arches of the feet. The N-CF recommended COs to place six leads under one arch and seal it with the plaster. Brockway claims that thousands of leads were smuggled through in this way, and the method spread to other prisoners.

It was not without risk. Brockway found to his horror when he stepped into a hot bath after his medical examination that the leads he had been provided with were of the indelible variety which stain water purple. Every time he moved his foot a burst of purple swirled around it. He managed to convince the suspicious warder that it was all due to a surplus of disinfectant in the bath water, and so contrived to keep the precious leads. Towards the end of the war the device was discovered, and thereafter a foot inspection became the rule.

Paper was, if not plentiful, nevertheless obtainable. Coarse, brown-grey toilet sheets were issued to all prisoners in a daily ration. Those who could contrive to miss a day's use could build up a store. Notes could be passed, at exercise or chapel, or while working in association. Brockway tells, again, of a note being tossed through his cell window while he was undergoing solitary confinement on bread and water in Lincoln Jail. It was from Alastar Macaba, one of a group of Sinn Fein prisoners (later to be elected Sinn Fein MP for Sligo while still in prison). It read:

> Dear Brockway—Just heard you are here. What can we do for you? De Valera, Milroy and sixteen other Irish rebels are interned. We are Irishmen and can do anything you want—except get you out. Have your reply ready for 'Trusty' when he calls tomorrow. Cheerio! Alastar Macaba.

Brockway replied that he wanted his wife and friends to know he was keeping well, and that he would appreciate the *Manchester Guardian* every day and the *Labour Leader*, *New Statesman*, *Economist* and *Observer* every weekend! The Irish group were able to smuggle out a letter to Lilla Brockway, and had no difficulty, since they were allowed all the newspapers except the Irish ones, in meeting Brockway's second request. Because of its bulk, the packet of weeklies was hauled up to the cell window on a line. Later, when Brockway was moved to a cell on a higher floor, he found a note telling him that his daily *Manchester Guardian* would be left in the cavity behind a loose brick in the lavatory wall. The Sinn Feiners arranged for a 'trusty' to place it there when cleaning out the place, immediately prior to Brockway's scheduled visits. Fifty years later, at a reunion for 'old lags' of the Great War, Lord Brockway declared that in those eight months of solitary it was the daily *Manchester Guardian* in the lavatory that preserved his sanity.

The smuggled-in pencils were used to good effect in the production of jail journals, written on toilet paper and passed from prisoner to prisoner. Some were produced in astonishingly adverse conditions. Albert Taylor, a former prospective Parliamentary Labour candidate for Rossendale, edited, printed and published a weekly 'newspaper' which was passed from window to window. In Canterbury Jail, Barratt Brown published the *Canterbury Clinker*, which carried verse in English, German and Italian, studies in ethics, philosophy and psychology, and illustrations and cartoons. The *Joyland Journal*, organ of COs at Mountjoy Prison, Dublin, ran a sensational serial story, and was published in cloth covers—made from sackcloth!

Will Chamberlain ran the *Winchester Court Martial*, subtitled 'The Organ of the Absolutely Its'. It ran to four issues before his health broke. Although each page was little bigger than a bus ticket, its microscopic pencilled print was professionally laid out in an excellent imitation of newspaper style.

Literary standards were, to put it kindly, uneven, but the verse was often neat and pointed. Barratt Brown in the *Canterbury Clinker* celebrated the surreptitious communications of the daily exercise periods—

> *Gin a conchy meet a conchy*
> *Comin' through the Clink,*
> *Gin a conchy greet a conchy*
> *Should a conchy wink?*

> *Ilka conchy has a comrade,*
> *Ne'er a one hae I;*
> *But all the comrades smile at me,*
> *Comin' on the sly.*

The *Literary Outlet*, produced first at Birmingham and later Hull, welcomed newcomers thus:

> *Men who hae called Allen head,*
> *Men whom Russell sometime led,*
> *Welcome to your three-plank bed,*
> *With a conscience free!*

Chamberlain's *Winchester Court Martial* carried the following 'News from the Back of the Front':

> Our special correspondent at the back of the front reports that in the early hours of Sunday last the British captured a cow-shed. Our losses were only 10,000. The enemy losses must be at least 100,000.
>
> It is hoped that this splendid victory will stop the cry for peace, which seems to have taken hold of a large section of the British people.
>
> (Later) In the early hours of Monday the enemy made a strong counter-attack and recaptured the above cow-shed. Their losses are estimated at 250,000; our casualties were practically nil.
>
> The cow-shed is of no military value.

The same paper carried mock advertisements, including one for a 'Special War Edition of the New Testament, sanctioned by the Archbishop of Canterbury, in which every reference to peace has been deleted'.

The *Winchester Whisper*, which succeeded the *Court Martial*, carried a hymn beginning 'What a friend we have in Asquith', and an advertisement for prison cocoa: 'One teaspoonful makes a quart of delicious and nourishing food. Invaluable for the Nursery, will not stain the tablecloth.'

Fenner Brockway produced the *Walton Leader* twice weekly. More ambitious than most of its contemporaries, it consisted of as many as forty sheets of toilet paper, and ran to more than a hundred issues. The weekly subscription was one clean sheet, and it was viewed, appropriately enough, in the lavatory. On press days—Tuesdays and Thursdays—there were always queues at the 'reading room'. The medical officer was instructed to enquire into the diet on Mondays and Wednesdays, but before he could prepare his report the newspaper was discovered and its editor sentenced to six days on bread and water. While it ran, the *Walton Leader* carried articles on the Russian revolution, which Brockway applauded, on the abortive Leeds Conference organised to import Socialist revolution to Britain, and on President Wilson's 'Fourteen Points' for peace, about which the editor was sceptical. The paper published at least one scoop: an account of Passchendaele brought in by a CO who had shared a guardroom with a survivor of one of the bloodiest and most senseless battles of the war. At a time when such reports were prohibited in the national newspapers, a tiny prison journal told in graphic terms of the wave upon wave of 'cannon fodder' sent 'over the top' by the generals, suffering decimation for the sake of a few feet of land—or a cow-shed.

At the end of the war the N-CF published a selection from these journals under the title *The COs' Clink Chronicle*, and sold it as a threepenny pamphlet. The edition was quickly exhausted.

For the first few months following their collective rejection of the Home Office scheme, the absolutists accepted prison life quietly. Most of them saw their period of active resistance against militarism as having ended with their transfer to civil prison from the Army. They did not foresee the cat-and-mouse game which would force them to go through the same process of resistance again and again and again.

Prison letters during those first few months indicate a certain proud contentment, and a confidence that all would work out well in the end. 'I am thoroughly well and I am happy,' wrote Fenner Brockway to his wife in February 1917. 'I do not seem to be in prison. You know how contentedly I entered: that feeling has remained all through. I am calmer in spirit than I have been for a really long time, and, possessing that calmness within, the harshness which makes prison prison don't seem to exist . . . I cannot describe to you the wonderful sense of comradeship there is among the COs in prison. We are not allowed to speak to each other but the unity we feel does not need expression in speech. I shall never forget the first day I went on exercise at Scrubs—you cannot conceive the sense of spiritual exultation and expansion received from the sight of those two hundred COs marching in step round the prison yard . . .'

This mood did not last for long. Hard labour was designed to wear a man down by slow degrees, but all it killed in the conscientious objectors was their tendency to passivism. Before long they were provoked to a declaration of active war on the prison system. Martyrs became aggressive rebels, and prison officers were faced with mutinies and work-strikes. Men who thought their period of greatest trial was over found that in reality it was only just beginning.

Nor was it merely the monotony of prison routine against which they rebelled. There was a widespread, growing uneasiness in 1917, and the prison walls, high as they were, couldn't prevent a whiff of it drifting into the cells. The British public were beginning to grow war weary. Civilians were experiencing war at first hand in the new terror of air attacks. Demands for a negotiated peace were ceasing to be the sole prerogative of pacifist groups. The trade union movement was experiencing a fresh rank-and-file militancy which was to give rise to the shop stewards' movement. The Labour Party was painfully rediscovering its pre-war independence and beginning to embarrass other parties to the national Coalition. But over and above these developments, two events in 1917 changed the course of the war. One was the entry of America. The second, and to Labour much the more important, was the Russian Revolution.

REFERENCES

1 Note to John W. Graham, published as a footnote in *Conscription and Conscience*
2 There was as yet no Communist Party in Britain, but several Marxist groups to the Left of the ILP labelled themselves Communist.
3 Quoted by Mrs Henry Hobhouse, *I Appeal Unto Caesar*, 1917
4 Quoted by Mrs Henry Hobhouse, *op cit*
5 Quoted by Mrs Henry Hobhouse, *op cit*

Chapter IX

For a Soviet Britain

'A NEW star of hope has risen over Europe.' Thus George Lansbury's *Herald* welcomed Russia's March revolution—the enforced abdication of the Tsar and his replacement by a Provisional Government. The overthrow of Russian autocracy, so long predicted, had become a reality, and its implications for the Allied war effort opened up entirely new dimensions to the war debate in Britain and the West.

Lloyd George's Government was quick to recognise the new regime in Moscow and offer the hand of friendship. Moreover, though the Government would hardly have endorsed the enthusiastic language of Lansbury, the offer was genuine enough. Liberals, and even some Conservatives, were not altogether sorry to see the back of an autocrat who had always been an embarrassment to them in their defence of the war as a crusade for liberty and democracy. In addition, there was the hope that a reformed administration would boost the sagging morale of the Russian troops and thus strengthen the allies' Eastern front. So Parliament's message to the revolutionary Provisional Government, moved by Bonar Law, offered the Russian people 'heartiest congratulations upon the establishment among them of free institutions in full confidence that they will lead not only to the rapid and happy progress of the Russian nation but to the prosecution with renewed vigour of the war against the stronghold of an autocratic militarism which threatens the liberty of Europe'.

Labour's enthusiasm for the revolution, however, was of a very different kind. In April the *Herald* sponsored a Labour rally in the Royal Albert Hall, London, organised by an *ad hoc* body calling itself the Anglo-Russian Democratic Alliance. Twelve thousand throats roared approval of the revolution, and twelve thousand raised hands approved the dispatch of messages of congratulation and solidarity. But these, and similar messages from other Labour meetings in Manchester and Glasgow, had little in common with the message sent by the British Parliament. A growing part of the Labour movement, extending well beyond the ILP and the hard-core Left, saw the revolution not as a means of putting new life into a flagging war but as the first explosive step in a chain reaction which might force a negotiated peace.

The Provisional Government, anxious to maintain Western support, gave assurances that Republican Russia would make no unilateral peace with Germany. But it was not master in the house it had just taken over. The powerful Petrograd Soviet openly avowed its intention of establishing a working-class dictatorship on the Marxist pattern, which would dispossess the propertied classes and put Russia on the road to Communism. Peace was essential to such a programme, and the Soviets, over the heads of the Provisional Government, were demanding an immediate end to the war, multilateral if possible but unilateral if necessary, on the basis of 'no indemnities and no annexations'. While the Provisional Government looked on helplessly, the Soviets issued a decree virtually abolishing the distinction between the Army's commissioned and non-commissioned officers, and vesting control of military strategy in committees where privates and officers had an equal voice on the basis of one man, one vote.

Throughout April and May, as the struggle between the war and peace parties intensified, the British and French Governments sought assurances from the Provisional Government that it would not give way to Soviet pressure. The Labour Left, on the other hand, threw what weight it had behind the Soviet peace plan. In May, Russia passed through the first of the series of political crises which were soon to put all power in the hands of the Soviets. The Provisional Government was forced to accept direct participation by the Petrograd Soviet, which demanded as the price of participation explicit acceptance of its foreign policy. In no position to argue, the Provisional Government capitulated, and Russia, to the fury of its allies, declared its war aim to be 'the speediest achievement of a general peace . . . without annexations or indemnities, on the basis of self-determination of the peoples'.

The British Labour movement was intoxicated. Before the eyes of the world, a fraternal Socialist movement had forced upon an allied Government an explicit statement of war aims which bore the seeds of a negotiated peace. International socialism, after temporary disarray, was on the march again, and what could be achieved in Moscow was capable of achievement in London, given proper organisation and leadership.

The leadership was provided by another *ad hoc* body calling itself the United Socialist Council. Its first move was to convene a national conference of Labour, Socialist and progressive organisations on Sunday 3 June. The *Herald* backed the conference, and Francis Johnson of the ILP and Albert Inkpin of the BSP were made responsible for the arrangements. After prickly negotiations with a suspicious local authority, Leeds Coliseum was booked to house what was surely the most extraordinary conference ever held by any major part of the British Labour movement.[1]

Had the resolutions which emerged from Leeds reflected the views merely of a few score Marxist or pacifist sectarians the conference would properly rate no more than a footnote. But 1,150 duly appointed delegates responded to the United Socialist Council's invitation to celebrate the Russian revolution and consider how best to emulate it. Labour parties and trades councils sent 209 delegates, trades union organisations 371, ILP branches 294, BSP branches eighty-eight, other Socialist organisations sixteen, women's organisations fifty-four, and miscellaneous bodies such as peace societies and UDC branches 118. On the platform were such national figures as MacDonald, Snowden and W. C. Anderson representing the Parliamentary Left; Robert Smillie, Tom Mann and Ben Tillett representing the trade union establishment; and Robert Williams representing revolutionary Marxism. Among delegates on the floor were Willie Gallacher, Sylvia Pankhurst and Bertrand Russell.

MacDonald moved the first resolution, congratulating the Russian people on their revolution. 'When the war broke out,' he said, 'organised Labour in this country lost the initiative. It became a mere echo of the old governing classes' opinions. Now the Russian revolution has given you the chance to take the initiative yourselves. Let us lay down our terms, make our own proclamations, establish our own diplomacy . . . Let us say to the Russian democracy: "Maintain your revolution, stand by your liberties, put yourselves at the head of the peoples of Europe." '

Snowden followed with a resolution which not only supported the new peace aims forced on the Provisional Government by the Soviets, but swallowed them whole, rhetoric and all, as the revised aims of revolutionary Labour in Britain.

'We pledge ourselves,' ran the resolution, 'to work for an agreement with the international democracies for the re-establishment of a general peace which shall not tend towards either dominion by or over any nation, or the seizure of their national possessions, or the violent usurpations of their territories—a peace without annexations or indemnities and based upon the rights of nations to decide their own affairs; and as a first step towards this aim we call upon the British Government immediately to announce its agreement with the declared foreign policy and war aims of the democratic Government of Russia.'

Snowden's resolution passed with only a handful of dissenters, among them delegates of the Seamen's Union and a dockers' delegate, Ernest Bevin, who wanted to know what would happen if the Petrograd-Leeds policy were forced on the British Government but produced no response in Germany. The Conference then moved on to a third resolution on civil liberties, demanding, among other things, the release of all political and religious prisoners, notably conscientious objectors and prisoners under DORA, thereby placing Britain 'in accord with the democracy of Russia'. Russell, attempting to speak from the floor on behalf of COs, was given a standing ovation and pressed to take a place on the platform.

Conference might have been content to have gone so far, and left it at that. It had congratulated the Russians on their revolution, pledged support for their foreign policy and praised their civil liberties as a model for such less enlightened countries as Britain. But eleven hundred men, many of them veteran Socialists who had given a lifetime's service to the movement, sustained by dreams of a better world to come, were intoxicated by the concept of revolution. The dream had become reality in far-away Russia. Capitalism's Day of Judgment in Britain could not be far behind. In a final resolution moved by W. C. Anderson, the platform called for the formation, on the Soviet model, of Councils of Workers' and Soldiers' Delegates 'in every town, urban and rural district' in the country, 'for initiating and co-ordinating working-class activity in support of the policy set out in the foregoing resolutions, and to work strenuously for a peace made by the peoples of the various countries, and for the complete political and economic emancipation of international labour.' The resolution went on to appoint the conveners of the conference 'a Provisional Committee, whose duty shall be to assist the formation of local Workmen's and Soldiers' Councils.'

Anderson was met with cat-calls from the floor when he blunted the revolutionary edge of the resolution by disavowing any intention of leading the Labour movement to the barricades, or into any kind of unconstitutional action. He defined revolution as 'the conquest of political power by a hitherto disinherited class'. The proposed central Council of Workers' and Soldiers' Delegates would 'not be subversive, nor unconstitutional, unless the authorities cared to make it so.' But Conference appeared to prefer the sentiments of Robert Williams of the Transport Workers' Federation, who declared that if the resolution meant anything at all it was a call for 'the dictatorship of the proletariat'. It was directed not only against 'the most competent, the most capable governing class in the whole world,' but also against constitutionalist Labour leaders who had allowed themselves to be used by that ruling class against Labour. Delegates with cold feet were invited to leave the conference without more ado. The object of the Workers' and Soldiers' Councils was 'to break the influence of the industrial and political Labour machines'. Parliament would do nothing for Labour. 'This conference is perfectly competent to speak in the name of the working class, and damn the Constitution. Had the Russian revolutionaries been concerned with the Constitution of Holy Russia, the Romanoffs would have been on the throne today, and I say to you: Have as little concern for the British Constitution as the Russians you are praising had for the dynasty of the Romanoffs. You have a greater right to speak in the name of our people, civilians and soldiers, than have the gang who are in charge of our political destinies at this moment . . . If you are really sincere in sending greetings to Russia, I say to you: Go thou and do likewise!'

The most ardent revolutionists could hardly follow that. Willie Gallacher boasted that the revolution was already under way on the Clyde, and Sylvia Pankhurst voiced her conviction that the Provisional Committee appointed at Leeds would soon be the Provisional Government of what, in effect, would be a Soviet Britain.

The Conference closed, inevitably, with repeated choruses of the *Red Flag* and *England Arise!*

A central Council of Workers' and Soldiers' Delegates did emerge from Leeds, but it appears to have done little more than publish a report of the conference proceedings. Local councils were organised sporadically, including one in Manchester styling itself the 'Manchester Soviet'. Few lasted very long. Developments in Russian itself, culminating in the Bolshevik seizure of power in November, were too bewildering to allow of any close imitation here. Having collectively voted for a Soviet-style revolution in Britain, eleven hundred Labour delegates carried their euphoria home with them, and there let it evaporate away. The few Workers' Councils that did get off the ground soon merged their identity with the shop stewards' movement, or lost themselves in the fascinating but irrelevant sub-culture of anarcho-syndicalism.

But if a significant part of the Labour movement had roared approval for a revolution it was not prepared to sustain, the gesture was not wholly empty. The raised hands at Leeds marked the rank and file's break with the years of class collaboration imposed by the exigencies of war. From June onwards, official Labour found itself increasingly at odds with the Coalition. Leeds was the movement's declaration of independence.

* * *

Among the peace societies at Leeds, the N-CF was represented in some strength. The Fellowship had been quick off the mark in declaring solidarity with the March revolution. Bertrand Russell, its acting chairman, wrote in *The Tribunal* of 22 March 'There is hope at last of a better Europe; a beginning has been made in the East; it is for us in the West to claim the same rights as are being won by our brave comrades in Russia.' In the same article he noted the struggle between Russia's pro-war 'Liberal' forces and anti-war 'Labour' faction, and expressed the not very confident hope that the latter would win through. On 6 April the N-CF National Committee voted to send the following message to the Provisional Government:

To the Russian Revolutionaries:
To our comrades in Free Russia we send cordial congratulations, as lovers of freedom who honour the heroism of the long struggle, and

feel the world a happier place for your final victory. As believers in the brotherhood of all men, we are filled with the fervent hope that recent events in Russia will lead to a peace founded on goodwill and fraternity between all the nations now at war. Signed on behalf of the No-Conscripton Fellowship, and nearly four thousand British men imprisoned because they believe in International Brotherhood and therefore refuse to participate in war, Bertrand Russell, Acting Chairman.

The Leeds demand for the importation of revolution triggered off an anguished debate in the N-CF. Must revolution necessarily involve violence? Was there such a thing as non-violent coercion? What part, if any, could a pacifist play behind the barricades? And of more immediate practical effect, should N-CF branches co-operate in the formation of Workers' Councils?

The National Committee summoned a special meeting on 13 July to discuss these questions and thrash out a Fellowship line on revolution. It developed into a full-scale conference of the executives of the N-CF, the FSC and the FoR. As a result, branches were recommended to co-operate in the formation of the Workers' Councils, but the recommendation carried a summary of 'the various reasons for and against co-operation which had been taken into consideration'. Russell, in a *Tribunal* article headed 'A Pacifist Revolution?' explained the National Committee's decision thus:

> It was felt that the carrying out of our principles in domestic as well as in international affairs would involve such profound economic changes as would constitute a revolution, though it would be one effected, we hope, without violence, merely by the method of passive resistance . . . It is through the new revolutionary spirit that peace is being brought nearer; and as peace comes nearer it grows more important for those who hate violence to realise what is implied by their principles in the way of economic reconstruction. Our present economic system, for no reason of justice, places a terrible power in the hands of the landowner and the capitalist, and condemns the great majority of the population to a life which has few possibilities of free development. The unjust privileges of the rich are supported by the force of the police and the criminal law; without force they would melt away. They have no justification without custom. To secure their abolition force is not necessary, any more than it is to dethrone the

militarists. All that is necessary is that men should refuse to use force for the carrying out of unjust laws.[2]

The same issue of *The Tribunal* carried 'An Appeal for an Un-armed Revolution' by Barratt Brown:

> It is indeed the unpalatable truth that those whose lives are settled in security and comfort, and who on this account desire no change, whether violent or otherwise, are secured in their privileged position by the fact that they have at their disposal all the forces of the State. By the threat of force they hold their power and property; by the threat of starvation they exact their profits—and our industrial system is largely founded upon force . . . To those who stand today as the defenders of the established order, to those in authority and possession we would say: You have it in your power to prevent the need for violent change, you can abandon your claims to privilege and power, and profit and monopoly. You can co-operate in establishing justice and freedom where today there is inequality and slavery, you can help to prepare a bloodless revolution by not resisting the people's aspirations. And to those who are dispossessed and disinherited, we would say: You have it in your power to right your wrongs without the firing of a single shot. Only unite and organise your fellows, soldiers and workers, and you can achieve a revolution by the irresistible methods of non-resistance.

Thus the N-CF leaders were able to identify themselves with the new revolutionary movement by defining revolution, as W. C. Anderson had done at Leeds, in terms which specifically excluded violent upheaval. It made for an unreal unity. Marxists faced the critical problem of the resistance of the propertied classes by proposing a temporary dictatorship of working-class representatives who would use the enforcible sanctions of the State to dispossess and disarm the enemies of the revolution. Pacifists, having renounced force and the threat of force, could only hope that the propertied classes could be persuaded voluntarily to abandon their power. Both theories were shot through with illusions, but that was not readily apparent in July 1917.

★ ★ ★

The Labour leadership, no less than the factions on its Left, had cause to follow closely the fortunes of the Petrograd Soviet. At its

Annual Conference in January 1917 the Labour Party had rejected participation in a proposed meeting of the International Socialist Congress in Stockholm. But when, in May, the Petrograd Soviet announced its intention of inviting socialists of all nations to meet in Stockholm so that 'the work for peace started by the Russian Revolution might be brought to a conclusion by the efforts of the international proletariat', the Labour Party Executive voted to send delegates to Petrograd to discover the Soviet's intentions. The delegation, representative of all wings of the party, was to consist of George Roberts, William Carter and Ramsay MacDonald.

In the face of intense public criticism the Government agreed to issue passports to Petrograd, but at the last moment the Sailors' and Firemen's Union intervened with a refusal to carry men who were prepared to talk to the hated Germans over a conference table. In the meantime, the Labour Leader, Arthur Henderson, had been despatched to Moscow by Lloyd George on a Government mission. He returned, convinced that the international congress would go ahead with or without British participation, and determined, therefore, to see that the viewpoint of British Labour was properly represented.

With MacDonald and G. J. Wardle, Henderson set off for Paris to join French and Russian groups in preparing the ground for Stockholm. He returned to London to find all sorts of wild rumours circulating as a result of his trip abroad in the company of so notorious a character as MacDonald, and when the War Cabinet met on 1 August, Lloyd George made him leave the room, like a naughty boy, while Liberal and Conservative Ministers discussed his 'disloyalty'.

Henderson resisted the powerful pressures of the Cabinet to disown Stockholm and throw his weight against British participation. For the first time since he had agreed to double the roles of Cabinet Minister and Leader of the Labour Party his intellect and emotions in harmony dictated a primary loyalty to his party. On 10 August, at a Special Labour Party Conference, Henderson spoke out for participation. He had his way. The Conference reversed its decision of the previous January and voted by 1,846,000 to 550,000 to send a delegation. But Henderson's strong line had made inevitable a breach with Lloyd George. On the following day he resigned his Cabinet post and was replaced by the much more inflexibly Right-wing George Barnes. Lloyd George, however, held the trump card. Before the reconvened Special Labour Conference had time to select its delegation the Government made it known that no passports would be issued for Stockholm.

The upheaval in the Labour Party caused first by Leeds and then by the Stockholm agitation was immense. Labour remained in the Coalition, but was no longer its obedient servant. Henderson was left free to concentrate on reconstruction of the party organisation in readiness for the post-war political struggle, a reconstruction which gave Labour its modern structure of Constituency Labour Parties, its basis of individual membership and its Socialist constitution, defining the party's goal as the common ownership and control of the means of production. By January 1918, when the Annual Conference met again in Nottingham, official Labour had joined rebel Labour in demanding a statement of war aims as the basis of a negotiated peace, along with the release of conscientious objectors.

REFERENCES

1 The account that follows is taken from *What Happened at Leeds*, the report published by the Council of Workers' and Soldiers' Delegates, London 1917; and *British Labour and the Russian Revolution*, by Stephen Richard Graubard, Harvard, 1956

2 *The Tribunal*, 19 July, 1917

Chapter X

The Limits of Endurance

Troublesome fancies beset me
Sometimes as I sit in my cell,
That comrades and friends may forget me
And foes may remember too well.

That plans which I thought well digested
May prove to be bubbles of air;
And Hopes, when they come to be tested,
May turn to the seeds of despair . . .

For sickness may wreck a brave spirit
And time wear the brain to a shade;
And dastardly age disinherit
Creations that manhood has made.

The objectors in prison must often have shared the doubts and
'troublesome fancies' which beset the Chartist leader Ernest Jones
when he was held in solitary confinement on a bread and water diet
in 1839. In their first few days and weeks in prison they were borne
up by a sense of elation at their own personal victories over the conscription system. They were conscious of being martyrs to truth
and conscience, front-line troops in the war against militarism and
coercion. But as the first weeks and then the months dragged on,
the tedium of prison routine and the oppressiveness of solitary
confinement and the silence rule began to take effect. Outside,
undeterred by minority resistance, the Government continued to
operate the conscription Acts, even to extend them, in pursuance of
a war in which any kind of peace by negotiation had been contemptuously dismissed in favour of a 'fight to the finish'. The autocratic
Lloyd George had by the end of 1916 ousted Asquith from the

Premiership, and was thus in a supreme position to carry out his threat to make the path of the absolutist as hard as possible. The men in prison, or the more militant among them, began to chafe at their enforced inactivity and to look around for means of actively renewing their resistance, even behind prison bars. The result was a wave of work strikes, hunger strikes and prison revolts throughout 1917 and 1918.

Work striking in prison had been advocated from the beginning by a militant section of the N-CF. Prison labour, it was argued, was itself a form of conscription, and it was inconsistent to refuse Government-directed work outside and then accept it in prison. If 'alternative service' freed other men for the trenches, mailbag-sewing in prison might free other prisoners to make munitions. And to accept such work as part of a punishment was to admit guilt.

The National Committee rejected this view and declared against the policy of the work strike. Only a tiny minority of prisoners adopted it on principle as soon as they started their sentences. But by the summer of 1917, after a year of resistance, this particular expression of militancy was beginning to win converts.

On 31 May 1917, immediately after his third court-martial and a sentence of two years' hard labour, Clifford Allen wrote from the Cells, Parkhurst Camp, Salisbury Plain, to the N-CF National Committee. He told them that 'something more vital is wanted now'. On the same day he sent a long letter to Lloyd George giving notice of his intention to refuse prison work and accepting the consequences. It is worth quoting at length.

Dear Mr Lloyd George,

I have today been paraded before the troops here and received my third successive sentence of imprisonment with hard labour. This time my sentence is for two years.

Before I am removed to prison I think it is right to make known to you that, like other men similarly situated, I have recently felt it my duty to consider carefully whether I ought not for the future to refuse all orders to work during imprisonment. I have decided that it is my duty to take this course. This will mean that I shall be sub-jected to severe additional punishments behind prison doors. Pro-vided I have the courage and health to fulfil this intention, I shall have to spend the whole of my sentence in strict solitary confinement in a cell containing no article of any kind—not even a printed regulation. I shall have to rest content with the floor, the ceiling and the bare walls. I shall have nothing to read, and shall not be allowed to write or receive even the rare letters or visits permitted hitherto, and shall live for long periods on bread and water.

I am anxious that you should understand that I have not arrived at this decision from any lust for martyrdom. Hitherto I have exercised my influence with Conscientious Objectors to persuade them to fulfil all prison obligations, but I feel it would be wrong for me to do so any longer, and I beg you to allow me to tell you why.

You, like so many people, have always looked upon us men as either cowards or stupid enough to have a mania for martyrdom. You consider us cowards in that we are at any rate safer and better off in prison than in the trenches. And yet you are perfectly well aware that our choice has not been, and is not, between prison and the trenches. That is not why we are in prison. Before the Tribunals many of us were offered as a condition of exemption an opportunity of finding ordinary civil work in which we should have been free to live our everyday lives, exempted from every kind of military service. We refused the offer, claiming Absolute Exemption.

Then the Government, which included yourself, punished us for this by arresting us and sending us to be soldiers, although we had already proved to the entire satisfaction of the Tribunals that we had a genuine conscientious objection to *every* kind of military service. Naturally we refused to be soldiers and were then (following in some cases upon a spasm of brutal treatment) packed off to prison for disobedience to military orders.

Next you offered to release us from prison, *not* on condition that we would go to the trenches, but provided we would sign an agreement to engage in safe civil work with other men similarly minded to ourselves. We were to be nominally transferred to Army Reserve W, and, if we misbehaved, we should be sent back to our regiments. A recent stipulation has been that those who accept this work should not engage in the public propaganda of their opinion. Again we refused this ostensibly attractive offer, and chose to remain in prison at Hard Labour.

Then you sent us back to the Army, and we were again Court-Martialled and again imprisoned, and now, like many others, after being returned to the Army, and sentenced again, I am to be sent back to prison with Hard Labour for the third time and so, I suppose, *ad infinitum*.

I think this shows that—mad or sane—we are at least not cowards. It is not the fear of physical death in the trenches that has led to our remaining in prison, but rather of spiritual death which we believe must follow our assent to any Conscription Scheme, military or civil.

If, then, we are not cowards, it is argued that we must like playing the martyr. On the contrary, we have chosen to remain in prison rather than accept all those attractive offers, because we cannot honestly accept anything but *Absolute* exemption from a *Military* Service Act, a form of exemption provided for in the Act and actually granted to some 400 Conscientious Objectors.

When we say we can only accept Absolute Exemption, we mean this. As proved and admitted genuine Conscientious Objectors (which we are by the Statutory Tribunals) we believe War to be wrong. Thus we believe the same of Militarism, and thus we believe the same of Conscription, which is designed to equip the nation in its military and civil spheres for war. And so we say nothing in the world will induce us to accept any compromise or enter into any bargain with a Conscription Act.

Our repeated refusal of all those offers does not, however, signify unwillingness to render life service either to our fellow-countrymen or to our fellowmen in other nations. This duty of citizenship we have always welcomed even before the introduction of the Military Service Acts. As I tried to show in my last defence before Court-Martial, it is not the act of service to which we object, but service imposed in such a way as to make us condone Conscription; and if we were released tomorrow with Absolute Exemption we should feel the obligations of citizenship more insistently than ever before. Incidentally, many of us have hitherto been engaged in occupations deemed by the Government to be of the greatest national importance.

But forced service under Conscription is morally useless. Once allow that the State has the right to interfere in the lives of its members to the extent of demanding the taking or the sacrifice of life against their moral convictions, or the absolute disposal of their service without their consent, and you have embarked upon a system of oppression that a hundred Russian Revolutions or American high-minded interventions will never compensate.

We are then so resolutely opposed to war and militarism, and so conscious of the value of liberty, that we will not condone Conscription in any shape or form. We so prize the right of free service that we will not acquiesce in any variety of State Slavery. That is why we continue to refuse all these offers.

We have persisted and shall persist in this refusal, although we are fully alive to the horror of repeated imprisonment. No man or woman who has not experienced this test of sincerity can be expected to form an estimate of the torment of its silence and loneliness. The only men who seem able to develop a true understanding of its terror are the soldiers who have faced the dangers of the trenches and who shrink from the very thought of the alternative of prison.

We are, then, at least not cowards, and our persistence is based upon something more reasoned than a mania for the torture of prison. We have surely shown unmistakably that we are actuated by motives and opinions, which—however unpopular, entitle us to be no longer classed and treated as the lowest of criminals. Nor has there been *from the first* in the cases I am referring to, any question about the genuineness of our opinions. And yet you are imposing sentence after sentence of imprisonment upon us.

Hitherto you have had quite a plausible argument, which ran as follows:—

> We (the Government) must make the lot of a genuine conscientious objector exceedingly hard or everyone will become a conscientious objector and Conscription will fail. Moreover, you cannot expect the Government to straighten out the admitted confusion in the administration of the Military Service Acts in a day.

Very well. You have made your test, and on your own finding have rejected as frauds less than 100 out of nearly 5,000 of us. And you have had your time, during which we have accepted one, two, three and four sentences of Hard Labour.

Your present course is nothing less than the most deliberate persecution of genuine opinion, which one would have thought quite impossible in this country.

I cannot but think that your continued refusal to grant Absolute Exemption to some thousand men out of the whole nation is really due to your belief that by withholding it you will successfully avoid creating a dangerous precedent which might prove an obstacle to your secret determination to retain some form of Conscription in this country after the War. Meantime you are satisfied that you have succeeded in discovering a way of solving the knotty problem of the Conscientious Objector. That method takes the shape of exacting false Conscription service under different guises from every section of Conscientious Objectors. Some you put to work in the Non-Combatant Corps, some in the Home Office Centres and the rest, who have rejected these Schemes, you are pleased to find will in fact do similar or almost the same work in prison. These, I submit are your real reasons for continuing the policy of persecution; you have, in fact, abandoned your old intention to test genuineness and mark time with a view to doing justice in the end.

It is because of this new motive of yours that I have come to believe that it is my duty to refuse to be involved in any one of these schemes at whatever cost and without regard to the further postpone-ment of my release which might result. Three times you have pun-ished me for the same offence, and I believe it to be my duty now to refuse to do anything in prison which would result in my acquiescing in such injustice.

During the whole time that I have been sharing the responsibility of leadership amongst the Conscientious Objectors I have used every endeavour to prevent any policy even remotely resembling mere obstructionism or having its origin in impatience. I still hold the opinion that this must remain our policy. There is abundant evidence that the longer you apply this test of persecution to us, the more surely you establish us in prison as a centre of resistance to all attempts to encroach upon liberty in this country. You are, in fact, affording us the opportunity of arousing indignation and infusing inspiration into many new groups and old organisations which are far more powerful than we can hope to be for some time yet. That influ-ence will grow, for there never were prisoners more full of hope and overjoyed with the chance of service that has fallen to them. You will never break these men; they are indomitable.

But whilst I—like all the others—am ready and glad to accept this test of endurance, and whilst I am certain that if we become mere obstructionists, we should give you your chance to break us—yet I feel it my duty so to act in prison that you cannot exploit my willing-ness to endure penalties and so succeed in fitting me into your various direct and indirect ways of administering Conscription now and making sure of its establishment for the future. This feeling has been strengthened by Lord Derby's statement in the House of Lords last week.

I believe I should be acting wrongly if I tried to persuade my fellow Conscientious Objectors to follow a similar policy, and I do not propose to do so. A decision involving such consequences must arise from a man's profound conviction that by this means alone can he remain faithful to the spiritual guidance, the possession and expression of which he holds more precious than his own life. He dare not refuse to obey; he dare not urge other men to follow such a policy unless their sense of duty coincides with his own.

I can face this new test with far greater confidence now than had I so acted from the first. Every man you have shut away in prison for remaining true to his sense of right and wrong has gathered a courage and quiet determination far more enduring than any inspiration which guided him when engaging as a free man outside in the struggle against social injustice. He has thrilled with joy in his prison cell at the triumph of Russian democracy; he has gained assurance as he has caught the faintest of rumours of the gathering spirit of revolt in this country against the new despotism with which war is threatening our national life.

Any man in whom personal ambition played any part when you first sent him to prison is out for something far different now. You have given him his chance of realising in his own life the unity of all that makes a man strong and free and sincere, you have made him feel equally the unity of all that is most eternal in the life of the world. You have made him an irresistible force in the gathering struggle to defeat everything that leads away from freedom, whether it be amongst individuals, amongst classes, or amongst nations.

Whatever may be your present opinion of the Conscientious Objector, I am sure nothing but good can result from a genuine attempt to explain to you the motives and reasons which prompt the action of these men.

I am,

Yours faithfully,

Clifford Allen,

Salisbury Plain,

May 31, 1917.

Allen's decision embarrassed the National Committee, which had not only thrown its weight into dissuading its members from work striking but had also just launched a new campaign to secure socially useful work for the Home Office men. Other policy disagreements were still threatening its unity. Barratt Brown was about to announce his resignation and a new controversy centred on whether or not the N-CF should sponsor or support independent peace candidates in Parliamentary by-elections. On work strikes, the National Committee, meeting on 15 June under the chairmanship of Bertrand Russell, reaffimed its earlier refusal to organise or sponsor them. To prevent confusion among the rank and file *The Tribunal* reported: 'Clifford Allen wishes it to be known that though he himself feels bound to refuse henceforth to do prison work whilst in custody under the Military Service Act, he entirely concurs with the view of the National Committee that it would not be right to *organise* a general refusal of work in prison.'[1]

Allen's letter to the Prime Minister was printed in full in *The Tribunal* of 14 June 1917, but the same issue carried a vigorous denunciation of the work strike policy from Dr Alfred Salter. Work, he urged was a necessity of human life and sanity.

> Without occupation of some sort a man becomes a gibbering idiot . . . As a matter of sheer fact and hard experience, we know that practically every CO who has carried out a work strike in prison has become insane . . . According to our statement of principles the N-CF is composed of men who will resist conscription to the uttermost and who are prepared to suffer the full consequences and penalties of such refusal. One of the penalties is confinement in a prison; another is the infliction of hard labour in that prison. In accordance with our statement of faith, we are bound to accept the hard labour as much as the confinement.
>
> Dramatic action, like a work or hunger strike, will achieve nothing for our cause. The most that could be hoped for would be the compassionate release of a few individual men who had been brought near to physical and mental death. Nothing would be accomplished for the movement as a whole. To win through we must succeed in influencing the heart and mind and conscience of the nation and the authorities. We have to *convince* them; we cannot threaten or compel them. Our methods must be those which will stand the test of time—

the methods of all-persuasive reasonableness. Prison or camp strikes are a nine-days' wonder, if as much as that. They may make an impression for the moment on the popular imagination—and then the public mind will require a new and bigger sensation. But quiet reason abides, and the victory of our cause cannot be ushered in, indeed the cause itself would remain for ever condemned if it were ushered in, by an outrage on common sense. Continuous abstinence from all work is an outrage upon common sense, because it implies a voluntary destruction of the participant's sanity—possibly for the rest of his life.

There are other objections of a practical character which I would urge.

(1). Only a few isolated men will take part in a work strike. Large numbers of our absolutists are definitely opposed to such a plan, as I can affirm from first-hand knowledge. Clifford Allen agreed with me that he did not think that any of the Quakers would participate, and the FSC state in a recent pamphlet that out of 252 absolutists whose religious views are known, 106 are Quakers. The only chance that a work strike would achieve anything substantial would be if practically all the men in all the prisons struck. They will not, and the authorities will easily deal with a handful of men.

(2). Even if all, or nearly all, the men were likely to agree to a work strike, there is no chance of simultaneous action unless a movement is dexterously and secretly organised from Headquarters, as the COs are distributed in 39 prisons, ranging from Inverness to Exeter, and from Caernarvon to Ipswich. The National Committee . . . will certainly not attempt such organisation.

(3) Many men who strike will be obliged to give in as they find their reason and their balance deserting them. They will then experience a bitter sense of defeat and humiliation. Some of those who have already tried it have been so broken in morale that they have subsequently joined the Army.

(4). Many who strike will find their nervous vitality used up or destroyed to such a degree that they will be practically valueless to the Pacifist, Socialist, and Anti-Militarist movements when the war is over and when Humanity needs them most.

(5). The work strike is a copying of the WSPU [militant suffragette] method, now thoroughly discredited, and long ago abandoned and condemned by almost everyone holding N-CF views.

I understand that Clifford Allen has sent an Open Letter to Lloyd
George, which is to be printed in this issue of *The Tribunal*. I have
not the letter before me as I write, but I heard it read a few days ago.
I am hurriedly putting down the above thoughts on the whole subject in time for simultaneous publication with Allen's letter, in order
that it may not be believed in the Fellowship that the policy now
advocated by him is the policy of the National Committee. It is a
policy which will be opposed by some of us on the Committee with
all our strength and power.

The controversy continued to dominate the correspondence
columns of *The Tribunal*, and renewed efforts were made to get the
National Committee to organise a national prison strike. They were
not successful. The committee continued to give its chairman loyal
support while dissuading others from following his example.
Religious objectors were also unanimous in their rejection of anything that savoured to them of indiscipline or rebellion, and an
attempt at a work strike made by militant socialist objectors in
Winchester in October 1918 failed when the Quaker minority
declined to co-operate, appealing to the rebels 'not to be carried
away by mere policy and by the fighting spirit'. The National Committee again refused to support a call from James Hindle Hudson
in Manchester Prison for a general prison strike on May Day 1919.
Hudson argued that the Labour movement would better understand an active revolt than apparent acquiescence in the tyranny of
keeping conscientious objectors in prison long after the armistice
had been signed. This latter grievance gave rise to a number of
'unofficial' work strikes by socialist objectors in 1919.

The N-CF sometimes had to exercise a considerable degree of
ingenuity in the means by which it communicated to the rebellious
spirits in prison its opposition to strike action. John Graham[2] tells
the story of a controversy within one prison which was referred to
the National Committee for instructions. This was done by means
of a letter smuggled out with a prisoner ending his sentence. The
letter asked the National Committee to signal its wishes by flying a
flag on the third tree in an avenue outside the prison wall—a red
flag for the strike or a white one against. The flag was to be raised
at 4 p.m. on a date twelve days after the writing of the letter. 'It
took eleven days for the letter to reach Miss Catherine Marshall at

headquarters. She doubted if the tree was climbable by herself or another, feared an intrusive policeman, thought the signal might be hidden in the foliage, and was much puzzled. But she presented white kites to some children, and sent them for a walk with Miss Lydia Smith to fly them; and the children wondered why the kites always stuck in a certain tree. It was just in time, and word went silently round the jail, where talking was, of course, forbidden, that there was to be no revolt.'

Much more extreme than the work strike was the hunger strike. Although again the N-CF deprecated resort to what it saw as a sensational and dangerous method of protest, organised hunger strikes by COs took place early in 1918 in Newcastle, Maidstone, Winchester, Wandsworth, Carlisle, Canterbury and Hull Prisons. In almost all cases they were resorted to in protest against specific brutalities or injustices. Thus a hunger strike at Newcastle in February 1918 was begun 'as a protest against the incompetence and inhumanity of the prison doctor'. Eleven COs took part, and all were forcibly fed. They subsequently complained that the same nasal tube was used to feed all eleven men, despite the fact that one of them was known to be suffering from lung trouble. The tube was not washed or otherwise cleaned between insertions. After vigorous protests, the prisoners succeeded in obtaining a tube each.

As with the militant suffragettes who had pioneered the hunger strike, the forcible feeding of conscientious objectors was often carried out in a rough and brutal fashion. The eleven men at Newcastle complained:

> One comrade had a disease of the nose, and suffered terrible agony through the doctor trying to force the tube up his nostril; another had a tear vein burst through the violence of the operation; all bled profusely from the nose and throat, so roughly were they handled. Moreover, on one occasion the doctor pulled a handful of hair out of a man's head in his anger, and frequently used epithets such as 'dirty, filthy scoundrel' and the like.

Colonel Wedgwood took these allegations to the House of Commons on 10 March, only to have them denied, presumably on the word of the prison doctor.

The first hunger strikers in Wandsworth Prison were victims of a more petty cruelty. The action of forcible feeding produces an intense thirst. The prison doctor nevertheless cut down the hunger strikers' water ration, and ordered that their washing water be supplied already soaped to make it undrinkable. The strikers were permitted milk, but this they regarded as food and so could not touch without breaking their strike. When the vigilant Colonel Wedgwood raised this case in the Commons he succeeded in obtaining a promise that this practice should cease.

Sheer inexpertise in the technique of forcible feeding caused terrible suffering and at least one death. W. E. Burns, a belt weaver from Failsworth, near Manchester, was the first CO to go on hunger strike at Hull Prison. He had been arrested on 1 August 1916, and had accepted the Home Office Scheme at Llandensant. After helping organise a strike he found himself back in the Army, where he disobeyed orders, was court-martialled, and sentenced on 11 November 1917 to two years hard labour at Hull. By January his health was beginning to give way. He was losing weight rapidly and found it hard to stand up and support himself unaided. In February he petitioned to the Home Office to be allowed to return to the Scheme, or failing that to Manchester Prison where his family could visit him. Receiving no reply, he determined to go on hunger strike. He was forcibly fed for three days. On the fourth day the food—cocoa and milk—was inhaled into his lungs as a result of the use of what the prison doctor described at the inquest as too short a tube. Burns choked to death. The inquest jury found that death was due to pneumonia accelerated by forcible feeding. No blame, said the jury—despite the use of an inadequate length of tubing— could be attached to the doctor. *The Tribunal* declared the verdict to be a scandal and commented bitterly: 'We should like to know what the jurymen would have said had it been one of their sons who had died this agonising death.'[3]

Deaths and mental breakdowns among imprisoned objectors were by the end of 1917 reaching proportions which, had the situation been allowed to continue unchecked, would certainly have resulted in grave public scandal. The Government accordingly ordered the temporary release of COs classified as dangerously ill. The order was by no means invariably carried out, and sometimes release came too late to prevent death.[3]

Arthur Butler of Stockport, serving his third sentence at Preston, contracted tuberculosis early in 1917. On 10 November he wrote to his family that he was coughing and spitting blood and suffering chest pains. The prison doctor diagnosed influenza. Butler's family petitioned the Home Office for his release on health grounds, but was told that the prison doctor had found him only 'slightly un-well'. On 11 December an enquirer in Parliament was assured that there was no cause for anxiety. On the same day Butler's friends secured special permission for his mother to visit him. She found him gasping for breath and conscious that he was close to death. The Prison Governor refused her permission to stay beyond the normal visiting time. The following day Butler died. The prison doctor was entrusted with a post mortem, and declared that death was due to pneumonia. An inquest jury exonerated the doctor.

Butler had been given a medical classification of A1 by the Army in July 1916. So had Arthur Horton of Manchester, who became seriously ill at Shrewsbury Prison in December 1917, after fourteen months confinement. Horton complained of under-feeding, and became too weak to tramp around his cell, the only way of keeping warm. He was forbidden to cover himself with rugs during the day-time, and developed pneumonia. The prison doctor prescribed a double dose of cough mixture. He petitioned for release under the Government's new concessions to seriously ill prisoners, but by the time the release order came through, on 5 January, he was too ill to be moved. On 16 January he died. Death was ascribed to 'natural causes following pneumonia', and the inquest jury exonerated the prison doctor.

Ernest England, a Leeds Quaker, was at first rejected by the Army as medically unfit. But during the subsequent re-examination and combing out of men of low medical category he was called up, arrested and court-martialled at York. His mother collapsed and died after attending the court. He was allowed leave-under-escort to attend the funeral and then sent to Wormwood Scrubs to begin a two-year sentence of hard labour. During his first night at the Scrubs, on 17 June 1917, he was taken ill. Repeated requests for a chamber pot were refused, and eventually England made use of the floor. The following morning the warder, with a brutality be-yond either description or comprehension, took England by the scruff of his neck and buried his face in his excrement. For seven-teen weeks he was ill and unable to work. Finally, on the doctor's advice, he accepted the Home Office Scheme and was transferred first to Knutsford, then to Wakefield, and finally to Dartmoor. In January 1919 he was on shovel work in the snow, on a daily after-work diet of one thick slice of bread and margarine and a mug of tea. He was offered outside work with an individual employer, and commented in a letter home: 'Nearly all the chaps that go on the new scheme walk straight into the 'flu; quite a number that I know have died.' In February he contracted influenza himself, and in his weakened condition quickly became seriously ill. On 6 March he died at home.

Walter Bone, of Birkenhead, also died of influenza in Winchester Prison on 23 February 1919. He had been weakened by eighteen months imprisonment, which caused his removal to prison hospital suffering from acute digestive and glandular trouble. After nearly six weeks in hospital he was discharged and allocated a cell just vacated by an influenza patient. With little resistance he fell victim to the epidemic then sweeping the country. The Governor and the prison doctor were criticised by the inquest coroner for their misjudgment in the allocation of the cell.

Paul Leo Gillan, a forty-year-old Sinn Feiner and Roman Catholic, fell ill at Wormwood Scrubs and was persuaded to accept the Home Office Scheme. He was transferred to Warwick, but was so weak when he arrived that he was allowed to sew his mailbags in bed. After being six months under the doctor at Warwick he was transferred to Dartmoor in March 1917. His health did not improve, and one morning he reported for work fifteen minutes late through illness. This was charged as an offence, and Gillan was punished with a fortnight's loss of his eightpence-a-day pay. In reply, he wrote a defiant letter to the Home Office Committee describing Dartmoor as a 'slave market' and military discipline as 'refined ruffianism'. The letter continued:

Your Committee delights in preaching vengeance and has decided to steal two weeks' pay. Accordingly I withdraw two weeks' labour. When in the hands of the military I stoutly refused to be intimidated, cheerfully undergoing privations and indignities. When in gaol I adhered to my peacetime resolutions with unswerving fidelity, and consistently refused to do any kind of work. I again cheerfully accepted the punishment and came out of Wormwood Scrubs more dead than alive. I did not ask for the Scheme, but upon being offered same and told that the work was of a civil nature under civil control, I accepted. But the whole position has since been revolutionised, the military having been introduced in Major Terrell! Talk about agreements and scraps of paper! To submit to military discipline means to me the negation of all that is noble, all that is loving, pure and kind, the negation of all that is divine, in short the negation of all that constitutes a man. I proudly refuse to place my soul in the keeping of any military caste.

For his insolence Gillan was returned to the Army. He disobeyed orders, was court-martialled and sent to Mutley Prison, Plymouth, where he began a work strike. At Plymouth he had no opportunities of attending Mass, and after repeated protests about this he was transferred in February 1918 to Winchester. Being under punishment for his refusal to work he was not allowed any communication with his mother. Early in March, not having heard from him for ten months, she wrote to the Governor enquiring about his health, and on 8 March the Governor replied that he was 'alive and fairly well'. He was becoming progressively weaker, however, and on 16 March Mrs Gillan received a wire telling her that her son was dead. Two days later she received a letter from the Governor, dated 16 March, saying that her son was ill and could be visited. On 18 March the Governor wrote confirming that Gillan had died, adding that death was due to 'heart disease, from which the medical officer reports he has suffered for some time'. Despite this admission of a known history of heart trouble, no recommendation was at any time made for a release on medical grounds.

Gillan was described by a friend and fellow Irish objector as 'a rebel of the first rank', with 'a spirit too strong for his poor, worn body. He was a gallant gentleman. Let his name be inscribed in gold along with those of Emmet and Connolly, and may his spirit live with us and spur us on to greater sacrifice and nobler efforts in the greatest and noblest of fights.'

Alexander Campbell of Glasgow committed suicide in an Army guardroom after holding out for nearly nine months. Arrested in October 1916 at the age of eighteen, he served two prison sentences, the first at Wormwood Scrubs and the second at Barlinnie, Glasgow. 'Prison tried him severely', reported *The Tribunal*, 'and on one occasion he expressed the fear that he would be forced to give up the struggle, as he was feeling too weak to carry it on. His third District Court-Martial took place at Ayr on 9 July, and some of those who were present in the Court say that he seemed to be in a state of nervous collapse. In this pitiable condition, he yielded to the persuasion of the Court and consented to become a soldier.'[4]

Two days later he cut his throat with a razor. 'There is no doubt in the minds of those who knew Alexander Campbell best', continues *The Tribunal* report, 'that full of remorse at having, after all, yielded to the system which he had been combating all these months, he could not resist the sudden temptation of seeing the razor lying before him. Quaker chaplains who visited him in prison speak of the high opinion they formed of him, describing him as a sensible, bright and intelligent young man, the sincerity of whose convictions impressed itself upon them. But the long confinement and meagre diet of the prisons had done their work in reducing his physical powers and mental stamina, and his death is another terrible indictment of our penal system.'

Others—seventy-three in all—died in direct consequence of their resistance and its punishment, some of them in the influenza epidemic of 1919 which they met in what proved to be a fatally weakened condition, brought on by months or years of hard labour on an inadequate diet. Some, like A. Peddieson of Glasgow, died while nursing fellow-prisoners in a local epidemic at Red Roses Camp, Carmarthen, in January 1917, official medical attention being wholly inadequate. Tuberculosis contracted in prison killed several men shortly after their release, including C. J. Cobb of Croydon, a lay preacher who served five prison terms totalling three and a half years, and who died from tuberculosis and curvature of the spine three weeks after obtaining a medical release from Winchester on 17 March 1919. Other victims of tuberculosis include twenty-four-year-old John Evans of Cardiff, certified fit for navvying but later discharged as a chronic consumptive; Albert James of Kingston, who contracted the disease at Wormwood Scrubs and was transferred to Wakefield, where he died on 17 May 1917; and Ernest Crosby of Liverpool, who came out of prison with 'consumption' in 1918 and finally died in hospital in March 1921. Some deaths occurred in mysterious circumstances: military hospitals were not obliged to provide relatives or other enquirers with particulars of the cause of death.

9—OO

Of the total of seventy-three deaths, ten occurred in prison, twenty-four in the Home Office centres, six in military custody and the rest shortly after release.

It is likely that there were other deaths among conscientious objectors which never came to be listed by the Conscientious Objectors' Information Bureau, particularly among NCC and FAU men, those who accepted 'work of national importance', and others standing outside the N-CF, the FSC and the FoR. But the list is impressive enough as it stands. Plans were mooted in the 'twenties for a special 'war memorial' to those seventy-three men. The project came to nothing, though the German peace movement later raised a bronze plaque to them, believed to have been destroyed after the Nazis came to power.

The COIB gave the final number of those who 'lost their reason' as thirty-one, but since names and details were not published it is impossible to verify the figure. Lord Peel, in an official statement on 3 April 1919, admitted that twenty conscientious objectors had been certified insane. It seems likely that the higher figure includes a number who were sent to mental hospitals but never certified. At least one objector died after being driven mad—a twenty-two-year-old Presbyterian named Alfred Eungblut, of North London. 'He was arrested in September 1916', *The Tribunal* reported, 'court-martialled and sent to Wormwood Scrubs, where the separate confinement proved a great torment to his highly-strung temperament, and eventually drove him out of his mind.[5]' He was removed from prison to Epsom Asylum, where he died in June 1917.

In the later part of 1917 and throughout 1918 the health of COs, and particularly of the 'two-year' men, began to cause increasing concern outside. Fenner Brockway wrote from Liverpool jail that one man in three was either in hospital, or under examination for serious loss of weight. A prison chaplain wrote: 'My own experience is that the men generally began to feel their heads fuzzy; they read and read without understanding; their thoughts wandered. Their brains, in fact were starved and becoming inoperative. They sometimes had not strength to walk around the yard for the prescribed time.[6]'

Throughout 1918 the men who had been released under the 'cat and mouse' procedure were constantly returning to begin their round again. More and more of Philip Snowden's unending flow of

Parliamentary questions concerned specific cases of broken or failing health. He pointed out that with so many men now undergoing their second or third year's imprisonment, their weight on starting a new sentence was already reduced to its minimum safe level. But prison routine decreed that it be taken as standard, and not until it had dropped much further would the prison doctor prescribe a special diet. Snowden protested bitterly but unavailingly against the war-time rationing which cut back an already dangerously low and unvaried prison diet. One prison wrote to the COIB:

> The test of the diet does not come until all the resources of the body have been brought down to the irreducible minimum and you must rest entirely upon the nourishment provided . . . The common experience is that a man passes into one or all three of the following stages: (1) Merely very hungry all day. (2) Hunger more acute, with pains in the stomach intermittently. (3) Extreme weakness, nervousness and constant and very acute pain. There is a sharp contraction of the muscles, the face may be seen (or, more bitterly, felt) to twitch with pain, and the face also becomes dark, particularly about the eyes. Some of the men in one or another of these stages, may be sent to hospital; many recover somewhat by lying down every available moment; not that they need rest, but if you lie down you do not feel hungry quite so soon.

The growing death roll and mounting evidence of the failing health of COs began to produce a public unease which led to increasing demands for an end to the persecution. More than a thousand trade union branches, trades councils and local Labour Parties petitioned for their release during 1917. Some 2,500 Free Church ministers and 1,000 Anglican clergymen signed protests. The liberal press, in the form of the *Manchester Guardian* and the *Daily News*, found its traditional voice and publicly questioned the wisdom of Lloyd George and his Government in harrying a 'misguided but sincere' minority. Even Northcliffe's *Times* decided that enough was enough, commenting on 25 October 1917:

> When a man has deliberately refused to avail himself of two alternative ways of escape from prison labour; when he has, more than once, of his own deliberate choice, gone back to gaol; when he shows

himself resolute to go back again and again rather than submit to that military service against which he asserts that his conscience raises for him an insuperable barrier—when he thus proves repeatedly his readiness to suffer for what he proclaims to be his beliefs, is it either justifiable or politic to go on with the punishment?

The Government reacted to the first wave of liberal criticism by publishing in December 1917 a list of concessions to men who had served twelve months or more. They were allowed to talk on exercise, to walk in groups of two or three of their own choice, to have two exercise periods a day and to have their library books sent in four at a time. They were permitted to wear their own clothes, and to hire another prisoner to clean their cells at sixpence a day—a privilege they declined to make use of. But no change was made in the routine of hard labour and prison work, and there was no change in the diet. The concessions, grouped under what was known as Rule 243(a) were a rehash of special regulations originally devised for the militant suffragettes, and with them came the promise, publicly voiced by Lord Curzon, that dangerously ill prisoners would be released. The N-CF derided the concessions as too little, too late. In the event, Rule 243(a) was administered erratically—generously in some prisons, grudgingly in others. More erratic still, as has been noted, was the administration of medical releases.

So 1918 dragged on with little remedy for the men in prison. Frustration increased, and was expressed in numerous small-scale work and hunger strikes. On 11 November war hostilities ceased on the signing of a general armistice. But still the COs remained in prison, and still the re-arrests continued under the 'cat and mouse' procedure. Frustration now reached boiling point, and an unprecedented wave of disobedience and obstruction swept from prison to prison.

In the midst of the disorder—which was roundly condemned by the Friends' Service Committee and more circumspectly reproved by the N-CF National Committee—the Government moved to ameliorate the lot of objectors who had served more than two years hard labour. They were all quietly removed from their various prisons and brought to Wakefield. It was the intention of the Home Office to offer them a new scheme of work in rather better conditions than they had been used to, but for the first few days after their arrival there was considerable confusion. The Governor and his staff at Wakefield were still awaiting clear instructions from the Home Office, and while waiting they thought it best to leave the new prisoners largely to their own devices. The men were not slow to appreciate the situation. Since the cell doors were without locks, a relic of the prison's conversion into a Home Office centre, the men were free to associate at will.

They elected their own Advisory Committee under the chairmanship of Councillor Walter Ayles, a member of the N-CF National Committee, and Scott Duckers was one of its members. In the absence of official control, the Advisory Committee took upon itself the task of organising prison life. A house sub-committee was appointed to organise the domestic duties of cooking and kitchen work. A labour sub-committee organised the cleaning and tidying of cells and public rooms. The bewildered warders were told that they would be 'permitted to help' if they so wished. After several days of this unique experiment in self-government the Governor stepped in and proceeded to allot tasks, but the men decided to follow the roster already prepared by their own committees. The bewildered Governor saw his orders ignored, though the work was carried out with impeccable and irreproachable efficiency. He decided against disciplinary action pending Home Office instructions.

When the Home Office proposals eventually arrived the Governor asked Walter Ayles, as chairman of the now officially recognised Advisory Committee, to put them to the prisoners. Their terms showed the Government to have learnt nothing about the absolutist position. As the *Manchester Guardian* reported, 'The Home Office evidently hopes that the Absolutists, now that they are all together and fortified by each other's companionship, will undertake to do work at Wakefield which they have refused to do for two years past when left to their individual resolutions. The Home Office "terms" are that the Absolutists should work with regularity and diligence, and then, in addition to concessions regarding correspondence and visitors, they will be allowed threepence a day and the opportunity to spend these threepences (but not more) at a prison canteen, which will be sanctioned if they run it themselves. The work expected of them was not specified in the communication.'

To this offer the Advisory Committee replied:

It appears that the Government still misunderstand our principles, in that they take for granted that any safe or easy conditions can meet the imperative demands of our conscience. No offer of schemes or concessions can do this. We stand for the inviolable rights of conscience in the affairs of life. We ask for liberty to serve and if necessary to suffer, for the community and its well-being. As long as the Government deny us this right we can only take with cheerfulness and unmistakable determination whatever penalties are imposed on us. We want no concessions. We desire only the liberty to serve.

This reply, with the signatures of the committee, was put in the hands of the Governor. For good measure a copy was sent to the N-CF national office, which published it as a leaflet. The Home Office abandoned its new scheme, and the 'Wakefield Absolutists' were returned to their old prisons to continue their indefinite sentences.

The continuation of imprisonment after enlistment had ceased, and on beyond the armistice, produced a full-scale rebellion among the Socialist COs in Wandsworth. Twenty of them staged a work strike in October, apparently linked with similar but less well supported demonstrations in Leicester, Leeds, Pentonville, Liverpool, Newcastle and Preston jails. Alternating doses of harsh punishment and offers of concessions failed to break the strike which was led by the flamboyant Marxist Guy Aldred. 'They continued striking', wrote E. H. Ellison, who joined them a few days later, 'and forced an hour's talking exercise, and then two, per day. I arrived at that moment. We then asked for books, letters and visitors (these were all stopped) but were refused. We then refused to come in from exercises. Officers draw batons and get excited. This happens at three exercises; it is then knocked off. We had our little concerts through the window, and a little tin-rattling and doorbanging. On 4 December we were suddenly removed to the basement.'

The basement cells were damp and filthy. They had not been used for many years. The rebellion continued. Speeches were made at exercise time, and COs shouted through their windows to soldiers confined in a neighbouring wing. Prison furniture was smashed to pieces and the glass in the spy holes was broken. Guy Aldred bellowed across to the soldiers a lecture on Marxism. A 'concert' was organised, and its twenty items—mostly revolutionary songs—were heard in the neighbouring houses over the prison wall. The COs sang *The Red Flag* in marching out and *The Internationale* on marching in from their exercise periods. The ringleaders were put on bread and water, which they threw out of their cell window. A deputation went to the Governor and threatened to smash more prison furniture if the punishments were not stopped. Finally, after a week's hunger strike, Aldred and nineteen others were released under the 'cat and mouse' procedure.

The Tribunal reported their hunger strike and subsequent release, but made no comment on the rebellion, which the Quaker objectors had refused to join. The rebels complained somewhat bitterly of the 'lack of support by the respectable element', and challenged the N-CF to organise a discussion on 'militant and positive resistance'. The National Committee turned down the invitation.

But the Wandsworth rebellion had a vicious sequel. One of the COs who had refused to take part was taunted by the chief warder with being willing to accept the privileges won by the strikers although afraid to join them. On returning from dinner to his cell he smashed the windows, furniture, pots and pans and declared himself on hunger-strike. What followed, as told in his anonymous but sworn statement to *The Tribunal*, showed the authorities to have a much surer hand in dealing with individual resisters than they had when faced with organised rebellion by a large body of sometimes desperate men.

Two warders entered the cell and pushed me outside on to the landing rails, where I was seized by about five others. I was then frogmarched along the landing, being kneed in the back at every few steps by an officer named ———, who was also half strangling me, and punched in the back of my head by another named ———. In this manner we arrived at a flight of steps leading on to a lower landing. Here an attempt was made to hurl me headlong, but managing to grasp a rail I averted this. I was then marched as before to the top of steps leading to D1 landing, where a second attempt was made to hurl me headlong. The warder ——— himself sustaining a nasty spill in his endeavour to hurl me down. I was here again able to grasp a rail and so landed at the bottom on my feet. Arriving in punishment cell after having been pushed into many obstructions, I was placed in a body-belt and left till tea time, when one hand was released to enable me to eat my tea. This I refused to do, so the cuff was again locked. At bed-time my bed was made by a convict. I was then left for the night.

About 10 a.m. on Friday 3rd, I was taken before the medical officer, who informed me that I was a lunatic, and that I should be treated as such. I was then taken to the padded room and placed in a strait-jacket. At dinner time my dinner was brought in, together with a convict to feed me. I again refused to take any food, but asked to be allowed to make water, as I had been many hours without having done so. I was told I must wait till after dinner, but it was not till nearly 3 p.m. that an officer brought a convict to me for this purpose. By this time I was experiencing very much pain from the strait-jacket which appeared to me to be strapped much too tight and was cramping my shoulders and preventing me breathing freely. The convict I found was to hold a chamber to me and do those things necessary which, owing to my hands being confined, I was unable to do myself. Under these circumstances I found it impossible to ease myself. I was then left until tea-time, when, having refused to eat, I complained of the pain I was experiencing and asked if the straps could be slackened a little. I was told to ask the doctor if this could be done, when he visited me between 6 and 8. He arrived about 7 p.m., and I at once complained to him and asked could he have the jacket removed or eased a little, as I was in great pain. He replied that I was not responsible for my actions, being a lunatic, and that it was unsafe to allow me out of the jacket. I pointed out to him that there was no question of insanity in this case, that what I had done had been done deliberately and as a protest against an unjust and false statement. Saying that if I acted as a lunatic, I must be treated as one and giving orders that I be given a chance to make water, he left me. Some time later an officer came and asked if I wished to make water, but remembering my previous experience and being in great pain otherwise, I said 'No'. I walked up and down the cell for some time, and finally flung myself on to a mattress which had been placed in a corner, hoping to obtain some relief thereby.

I remained so for some time, when the pain in my shoulder, stomach and back becoming so severe, I sought to regain my feet. After many efforts I was able to do this, and at once felt an urgent desire to visit W.C. I called aloud to the warder for some time and when he at last came to the door, I told him what I required. He replied telling me to shut up and do anything I wanted to do in my clothes as I stood, the same as others had to do. Telling him I was not a beast, how impossible it was to do as he suggested, and appealing to him to be reasonable, I was still unsuccessful in obtaining anything but his absence. I continued to call after him for some time until I began to vomit. After the fit of vomiting, during which I was successful in ejecting a little bile, the desire to visit the W.C. somewhat abated. I once more fell on to the mattress, until the pain and the cold once more forced me to struggle to my feet. In this manner I spent the night, alternately lying and walking, but always in great pain. About 7.15 a.m. I was released from jacket to wash, all my clothes but my shirt and socks being taken from me.

Breakfast and a chamber were then left in the cell with me. I enjoyed about half or three-quarters of an hour's freedom from the jacket, which was again placed upon me, and from which I was finally released about 10.30 a.m. I was in all about twenty hours in the body belt and about twenty-three and a half in the strait-jacket, with only the brief respite at breakfast time mentioned above. I made no complaint to the Governor regarding the above, knowing it to be useless to do so.[7]

This man was released after a hunger strike of seven days, again only under the temporary asylum of the 'cat and mouse' procedure.

The long winter of discontent at Wandsworth resulted in the appointment of a new Governor in February 1919, who tried to stamp out the continuing simmerings of revolt by the imposition of iron discipline. Inevitably, open rebellion continued, and led eventually to a Parliamentary inquiry. Evidence was taken from nearly thirty prisoners and from the Governor and his staff. The inquiry was almost wholly abortive, the bewildered committee, under the chairmanship of Albion Richardson MP contenting itself with some bromide observations on the Governor's evident good intentions and the great difficulty of his task. No suggestion was made that, with the war over and a new Government elected pledged to reconstruction and the building of a 'home fit for heroes', the continuing incarceration of conscientious objectors had become an anomaly and a positive incitement to disorder. Several more months were to pass before Britain's jails were free of political prisoners.[8]

REFERENCES

1 *The Tribunal*, 14 June 1917
2 John W. Graham, *op cit*
3 *The Tribunal*, 4 April 1918. Details of all COs' deaths, such as were available, were compiled by the Conscientious Objectors Information Bureau, from whose records the relevant parts of this chapter are taken.
4 *The Tribunal*, 26 July 1917
5 *The Tribunal*, 28 June 1917
6 John W. Graham, *op cit*
7 *The Tribunal*, 23 January 1919
8 In 1921 the COIB compiled the following list of 73 COs who died as a direct result of the treatment they received in prison or at military hands.

Those starred died in prison, the rest in Home Office Centres, in military custody or shortly after release. Allen, Peter (Nelson); Allen, Tom (Nelson); Allen, Walter G. (New Southgate); Barlow, A. (Mansfield Woodhouse); Battenham, F. (Downham Market); Benyon, H. (Swansea); *Bone, Walter (Birkenhead); Bowden, F. (Oldham); Brentnall, A. G. (London); *Bridle, O. S. (Brighton); Brightman, H. (Camden Town); *Burns, W. E. (Failsworth); *Butler, A. (Stockport); Cainey, Thomas (Manchester); Campbell, N. A. (Glasgow); *Campbell, P. (Isle of Skye); Cobb, C. J. (Croydon); Crosby, Ernest (Liverpool); Dardis, G. H. (Risca); Deller, L. (West Brompton); Dunbery, P. (Blackburn); England, E. (Leeds); Eungblut, A. (London); Evans, J. (Cardiff); Evans, R. G. (Reading); Firth, H. W. (Norwich); *Gillane, P. L. (London); Gouldsborough, H. (Blackburn); Hall, Percy (Old Dalby); Haston, H. (Chesterfield); Henderson, A. (Dundee); Hirst, H. M. (Stalybridge); Hoad, H. (Chard Sutton); Hooper, R. (Bradford); *Horton, A. (Manchester); Hurley, W. (Camberwell); Hurst, A. (Southwark); Hurst, H. (Manchester); Jackson, Theodore; James, A. L. (Kingston); James, H. (Worcester); Linscott, S. (Newton Abbot); Malcolm, W. W. (Glasgow); Marriott-Dodington, S. (Hereford); Martlewe, A. (York); Matchett, T. D. (Bath); May, W. (Edinburgh); Moss (Morley); Mountfield, J. (Manchester); Parkin, W. H. (Sheffield); Parton, F. L. (Chiswick); Peddieson, A. (Glasgow); Phipps, H. (Harringay); Richmond, Royle A. (Brighton); Rigg, J. A. (Barrow-in-Furness); Roberts, W. L. (Stockport); Rudall, A. (Newport); Slater, A. J. (Glasgow); Stafford, N. (Hyde); Stanton, W. (Leicester); Statton (Cardiff); Swettenham, W. (Liverpool); Taylor, J. (Silvertown); Thompson, C. (Norwich); Todd, G. (Willesden); Wallis, B. (Newmarket); Whilmore, P. A. (Coventry); Whinnerah, G. (Barrow-in-Furness); *Wilkinson, F. (Dulwich); *Wilson, A. (Blackburn); *Winter, J. G. (Cornsay); Woodward, E. (Birmingham); Zachnies, C. (Glasgow).

Chapter XI

Release

BY THE beginning of 1918, virtually the entire leadership of the N-CF was in jail, excepting only those few who were over military age. Much of the Fellowship's administrative work had now been taken over by women. Catherine Marshall was the acting honorary secretary, and she attracted to the national office a formidable team of militant pacifist women drawn largely from the dormant suffragette movement. Joan Beauchamp began as an assistant in the Political Department and soon took charge not only of the department itself but also of the editing and publishing of *The Tribunal*. Lydia Smith ran the Press Department, Gladys Rinder the Records Department and Ada Salter the Maintenance Fund. And presiding over what one CO maliciously described as 'the coven' was Bertrand Russell.

On 3 January 1918 Russell published in *The Tribunal* a bitter attack on the Allied Governments' refusal of the Germans' December peace offer. Lenin had offered to conclude a separate peace on the basis of no annexations or indemnities. The German and Austrian Governments had declared their willingness to conclude a peace on these terms provided it was a general peace involving the Western Powers as well as Russia. 'This action', wrote Russell, 'has placed the Governments of the Western Powers in a most cruel dilemma. If they refuse the German offer, they are unmasked before the world and before their own Labour and Socialist Parties: they make it clear to all that they are continuing the war for purposes of territorial aggrandisement. If they accept the offer, they afford a triumph to the hated Bolsheviks and an object lesson to democratic revolutionaries everywhere as to the way to treat with capitalists, Imperialists and war-mongers.'

The Western Powers would therefore turn down the German offer and pursue their fight to the finish. Russell deduced some

267

curious motives for such a decision. 'They know that from the patriotic point of view they cannot hope for a better peace by continuing the war, but from the point of view of preventing liberty and universal peace, there is something to be hoped for from continuation. It is known that unless peace comes soon there will be starvation throughout Europe. Mothers will be maddened by the spectacle of their children dying. Men will fight each other for possession of the bare necessities of life. Under such conditions the sane constructive effort required for a successful revolution will be impossible.'

This was a reversal of the argument commonly advanced from the far Left that the devastation of war would lead to revolution. Russell went on to concede the strength of this argument, and to note that some Socialists were 'not unwilling that the war should continue' and so hasten the revolution. But, he warned, 'the kind of revolution with which we shall in that case be threatened will be far too serious and terrible to be a source of good. It would be a revolution full of violence, hatred and bloodshed, driven by hunger, terror and suspicion—a revolution in which all that is best in Western civilisation is bound to perish.'

But Russell's primary fear was that any such attempt at revolution would be crushed by Britain's new allies, the United States of America. He thought it not outside the bounds of possibility that a British Government which felt itself threatened by internal unrest arising from war-weariness would invite the US Army to come in and help maintain law and order. 'The American Garrison', he wrote, 'which will by that time be occupying England and France, whether or not they will prove efficient against the Germans, will no doubt be capable of intimidating strikers, an occupation to which the American Army is accustomed when at home.'

Such strong words against an ally, even within the context of a warning against reliance upon revolution, were too much for the British authorities. Russell as author and Joan Beauchamp as publisher were prosecuted at Bow Street court on 9 February. The reference to the American Army was declared to have 'a diabolical effect' on British and Allied soldiers, an effect which one would suppose to have been enormously increased by the publicity attending the trial. Russell was sentenced to six months' jail in the 'second division' and Joan Beauchamp to a £60 fine plus fifteen guineas costs. When the appeal was heard, on 2 May, Russell was able to produce official reports from Washington on the successful use of troops in putting down strikes. He also quoted from criticism of the Americans made, without incurring any kind of penalty, by *The Times*. Nevertheless his sentence was confirmed, with the concession that it be served in the 'first division' with special privileges. Joan Beauchamp refused to pay her fine and was sentenced to one month in the first division.

For her, this was but the start of a series of prosecutions which continued throughout 1918. Concurrently with the Russell case, she was prosecuted for publishing in the same issue of *The Tribunal* a letter from a CO just released from Wormwood Scrubs and returned to the Army to await a second prison sentence. The letter painted a picture of army morale which infuriated the authorities:

> At Waterloo Station I was greeted by many soldiers whom I met in camp six months ago—we had not forgotten each other and our greetings were most cordial . . . The fellows here have a great respect for COs who defy the authorities; they trust us a great deal and admire our stand. I have found a marked alteration in their attitude. Not one man has reproached me for being a CO, but all of them do not hide their opposition to the continuance of the war, and feel that the COs are the only persons who are really bringing peace nearer . . . Every evening about a dozen of us sit round the fire and they bombard me with questions. Filled with humane feeling, these men talk of their dead and maimed comrades with tearful eyes, and they share with me the hopes for the future. If the war continues much longer, I believe the authorities will be faced with a serious revolt.

Action against Joan Beauchamp was dropped only when her advocate threatened to produce in her defence not only the writer of the letter but some of the soldiers referred to. Mindful, for once, of the damage such publicity would do, the Crown decided to abandon the charge.

Action of a different and more direct kind was taken against *The Tribunal* in February. The issue of 14 February carried an article by Joan Beauchamp protesting at the opening by the French authorities of licensed brothels for British soldiers. Much of the article, headed 'The Moral Aspect of Conscription', consisted of weighty

denunciations by the Archbishop of Canterbury, the Bishop of
Winchester and *The Times*, but Miss Beauchamp's own contribution was to lump together licensed prostitution and conscription as
twin evils. Her complaint, though couched in more indignant
language, was that the military authorities, having conscripted the
flower of the nation's youth, were now bent on deflowering it.

A morally outraged Home Office ordered a police raid on the
N-CF premises. All copies of the paper were seized, and the
National Labour Press, on which *The Tribunal* and other N-CF
publications were printed, was dismantled.

In anticipation of such a disaster, the N-CF had already made
alternative arrangements, and a week later the 97th edition of *The
Tribunal* appeared over the imprint of 'S. Howells Street, 4 Bleg-
borough Road, Streatham SW'. Street was a sympathiser who ran
his own tiny printing shop. He offered to print the paper until the
N-CF could acquire a hand press of its own. *The Tribunal* continued
to be printed at Streatham until 11 April, when its back page took
the form of a poster boldly headed 'STOP THE WAR!':

> Across the Channel the cannons are booming. Every day thousands
> of lives are cut short; every day thousands of men are maimed for
> life; every day millions of women watch for the post with fear and
> dread of the news it may bring. Men are lying with crushed heads
> and limbless bodies on the battlefield, the shell holes are full of stiff
> corpses, the stretchers cannot carry all the wounded and dying. The
> Armies opposing each other are too evenly matched for a decisive
> victory to be possible. If the war continues, it can only end in the
> utter ruin of the whole world. Armies and Navies cannot end this
> war. Who can end it? Only the people have the power.

And it ended with this appeal:

> In all countries the people must say 'WE WILL NOT GO ON'. The
> supreme need of the world is an immediate peace, on the basis of
> self-determination for the peoples with international disarmament.
> Do not remain silent any longer. COME OUT FOR PEACE!

On 22 April six policemen visited Street's premises and smashed
his machinery, destroying £500 worth of plant and carrying off
books, invoices and all records of work in hand. That same night,

three detectives called on Joan Beauchamp and demanded that she tell them the name of the editor of *The Tribunal*.

Since first Will Chamberlain and then Bernard Boothroyd had been jailed, *The Tribunal* had for obvious reasons been edited anonymously. Briefly in October 1917 Lydia Smith's name appeared as editor, but a scheme was then devised by the N-CF National Committee by which Joan Beauchamp and Lydia Smith would share the work of editing and publishing the paper, but with only one name appearing at any one time in the legally required imprint. The two women agreed between themselves that Joan Beauchamp should appear as publisher, and if necessary go to prison, leaving Lydia Smith free to continue the work. So of course Joan Beauchamp refused to reveal to the three detectives the name of her colleague. Her office was ransacked for evidence. References to both Chamberlain and Boothroyd were eagerly seized upon, and it was some time before Joan Beauchamp could persuade her interrogators that both men were in prison. Then a newspaper cutting was unearthed which wrongly ascribed the editorship to Hubert Peet of the FSC, but he turned out to have been in jail for the better part of two years. Not a single reference was found to Lydia Smith.

For the time being Joan Beauchamp was left free, but she soon became aware that she was under constant watch. The work of producing the paper now necessarily devolved almost entirely on Lydia Smith, although Joan Beauchamp's name continued to appear on the imprint. *The Tribunal* continued to come out regularly each week, printed now on a tiny hand press bought by the N-CF and secretly installed in 'the back room of a house in a back street in London'. Extraordinary ruses had to be resorted to to get copy and paper to the printers, and to collect and distribute each edition. Detectives had established themselves in York Buildings, opposite the publishing office, and were watching everyone who passed in or out. Frequent searches were made, but no *Tribunal* copy was ever found. On at least one occasion, proof sheets were smuggled out of the office in the shawls of a baby, carried by an old woman who had apparently called there for relief. Copies of the printed paper were despatched by post from six different postal districts in succession. The *N-CF Souvenir*, published after the war, tells that 'one day a 15-year-old messenger boy arrived at the office. The *Tribunals* had proved too heavy for him, so he had left them on the Embankment in charge of a policeman!' There was consternation at the office. But '*The Tribunal* was quite safe. The nature of his charge was not suspected by the representative of Law and Order, and the secret press remained undiscovered.'

These cloak and dagger arrangements lasted for nearly a year. The press itself was operated by two young printers who were sometimes forced to spend days at a time without leaving the building. In the early days they frequently ran short of type, and the large capital letters required for the masthead had to be 'borrowed' from fellow printers on—of all papers—Northcliffe's *Daily Mail*. Once a capital R was short, and one of the printers set out for the *Mail* to obtain it. But on his way home in the dark he dropped the precious letter. Groping in the gutter failed to locate it, so the following morning, as soon as it was light, he got up and retraced his steps along the street. The R was found, and that afternoon 2,000 impeccably printed copies of *The Tribunal* tumbled from the press.

Unable to find the editor, locate the press or otherwise suppress the paper, the police again turned their attention to Joan Beauchamp. The imprint now read 'Printed and published by J. Beauchamp, 5 York Buildings, Adelphi, WC2'. But the police maintained she was not in fact the printer and that the paper therefore failed to comply with the legal requirement that printed matter carry the name and address of printer as well as publisher. Joan Beauchamp declared that the imprint was true. She was legal owner of the press, and thus the master printer. This failed to impress the magistrate who heard the case on 19 August 1918, and she was given a fine of two hundred pounds with twenty-five guineas costs, or fifty-one days' imprisonment. At the appeal to Quarter Sessions the following October it was established that a printer defaulting on his imprint could only be fined for 'each such copy so printed by him'. Since it was the prosecution's contention that Joan Beauchamp had printed nothing, the case as at first formulated collapsed. But it was nevertheless held that, with no printer discoverable, responsibility rested with the publisher, and that Joan Beauchamp was publisher both she and the police agreed on. The case dragged on for eighteen months as lawyers sought to unravel the tangle. Not until January 1920 was it concluded, when this remarkable young woman was sentenced to twenty-one days in the 'first division'. She was released after eight. Appropriately enough, the last issue of *The Tribunal*, on

8 January 1920, was able to carry a report of this final round of her long battle.

★ ★ ★

The N-CF was a smaller and weaker organisation in 1918 than it had been in 1916. A large part of its membership were in prison. *The Tribunal*'s circulation dropped from 100,000 to 6,000, and finally, during the secret press period, to 2,000. Some who at the outset had thrown everything into the fight for a negotiated peace were beginning to despair of such an outcome, and wondering if one last all-out military push wasn't after all the fastest and surest way of ending the whole bloody business. Some, as we have seen, with the example of the new Soviet Union before them, looked to revolution to follow war, and thereby ceased to see any good reason for advocating a compromise peace. And others, encouraged by the new militancy of the Labour movement and its leadership, found the ILP and the new Constituency Labour Parties more rewarding to work with than a reviled and persecuted organisation which had virtually been driven underground.

But there was still more than enough work for the N-CF to do. It fought Lloyd George's final Conscription Act which sought to apply compulsion for the first time to Ireland, and which raised enlistment age to fifty-one. It continued its unavailing pressure for the release of conscience prisoners, and publicised continuing brutalities. It collected tens of thousands of signatures for the peace ballots and memorials organised by other peace organisations. And it continued to give aid and comfort both to newly conscripted objectors and to their families, as well as to those who, under the 'cat and mouse' rule, were starting their third, fourth, fifth or sixth successive sentence.

At the same time the need grew to counter renewed pressure for retention of some form of conscription after the war. Labour in Asquith's coalition had acquiesced in the first Military Service Act when assured that it was a temporary expedient which would have no industrial parallel and would lapse when the war was over. Now, with Henderson out of Lloyd George's Cabinet, Labour, despite its continuing nominal representation in the Coalition, was behaving more and more like an all-out opposition party. More and more voices were heard suggesting that the assurances given in 1915 and

1916 could safely be ignored. In particular, there were widespread demands for a post-war scheme of compulsory military training, and for compulsory cadet service in schools.

Lloyd George's own pronouncements had an ominous ambiguity. As early as January 1918 he was declaring: 'It is not a question of whether you are going to stop conscription in this country, you must stop it in other countries, otherwise you cannot stop it here.' As the N-CF pointed out, this seemed to mean that 'conscription is to go on here until every nation has been induced to abolish it', including those continental nations on both sides of the struggle with long historic attachments to one form of conscription or another.

As the long-awaited armistice began to loom in the autumn, *The Tribunal* anxiously noted the renewed propagandising of the conscriptionists.

> Whoever reads the columns of our daily press cannot fail to realise that, as the prospect of peace comes nearer, the militarists are preparing for the greatest struggle of the war. We do not refer to the endeavour made by our yellow press to flood the country with so fierce a lust for revenge and desire for gain that the terrible calamity 'peace' may be postponed as long as possible, but that other aim, more deeply if more silently cherished, to see permanently established in this country that foundation on which the whole structure of a militarist state must rest, compulsory military service. Militarism and liberty cannot exist together, for militarism is the denial of liberty. Conscription is the foundation stone of militarism. We must work unceasingly for the abolition of this menace to freedom.[1]

On 11 November, Armistice Day was celebrated with a wild abandon which gave vent to the pent-up repressions of four terrible years. The German and Austrian armies were broken. Britain and her allies were victorious. The war was over—and won. Ten days later the Government promoted a Bill, passed as the Termination of the Present War (Definition) Act, 1918, empowering the Crown by Order in Council to fix a date to be treated as the official end of the war. Since both volunteers and conscripts had enlisted, or had been deemed to have enlisted 'for the period of the war', some such action was necessary to avoid the chaos of overnight demobilisation or mass desertion. But, of course, the Act also had the effect of continuing conscription into what was in effect, if not in law, peace time. Soon the farcical situation arose in which, even while general demobilisation began to get under way, conscripts were newly enlisted, more conscientious objectors were sent to prison, and the 'cat and mouse' rules were enforced with a continuing mechanical efficiency.

Lloyd George lost no time in capitalising upon his immense prestige as 'the man who won the war'. Parliament was dissolved on 25 November and a General Election called for 14 December. The N-CF drew up a questionnaire and asked its local branches to put the questions to both Coalitionist and anti-Coalitionist candidates, all of whom were urged to give the abolition of conscription a prominent place in their election address. For a time it seemed that the Fellowship was pushing at an open door. War weariness, and a general desire to forget the tribulations of the last four years and get on with the job of reconstruction, contributed to raising a considerable public pressure for abolition. Throughout the election campaign, Lloyd George found himself pushed by the public mood closer and closer to an outright promise to end conscription. Thus in his own constituency of Caernarvon Burghs, election posters proclaimed: 'Vote for the Prime Minister and No Conscription.' Half-way through the campaign he told a Bristol audience: 'The Military Service Act was passed in order to meet a great emergency. When the emergency is passed, when the need is passed, the Act will lapse and there is no intention to renew it.' Two days before polling day he described as 'a calculated and characteristic falsehood' a newspaper statement that a vote for the Coalition was a vote for conscription. And on polling day itself a message from Lloyd George declared: 'I wish to make it clear beyond all doubt that I stand for the abolition of conscript armies in all countries.²'

The anti-Coalition parties were more outspoken still, with a commitment which, unlike Lloyd George's, was uncompromisingly unilateralist. For the Asquith Liberals, Sir John Simon asked:

How can the country be asked at this moment to give its support to schemes of after-war policy which have never been defined? I hold that the supreme need of the country when liberty has been vindicated abroad is to re-establish it at home. Regulations endured during the last four years become intolerable restrictions on civic freedom when war is over . . . I am opposed to it (conscription) in any and every form. Its continuance would be nothing less than surrender to the very doctrines which our soldiers have given their lives to overthrow.[3]

And the Labour Party's manifesto, *Labour's Call to the People*, issued by the National Executive and signed by, among others, Ramsay MacDonald, Arthur Henderson, Sidney Webb and James Maxton, went even further by linking the demand for an end to conscription with a call for release of conscientious objectors:

> The Labour Party stands for the destruction of all war-time measures in restraint of civil or industrial liberty, the repeal of the Defence of the Realm Act, the complete abolition of conscription and the release of all political prisoners.

The 1918 election is remembered as the first in which women had the vote. It was also the first in which conscientious objectors had their vote taken away from them. On 20 November 1917 the Commons had carried a sub-clause to the Representation of the People Bill stating that:

> Any person who has been exempted from military service on the ground of conscientious objection, or who, having joined the Forces, has been sentenced by court-martial for refusal to obey orders, and who alleged conscientious objection to military service as a reason for such refusal, shall be disqualified from being registered or voting as a Parliamentary or Local Government elector.

This disenfranchisement was made to extend over the five years following the end of the war. Since the Order in Council officially ending the war did not come into effect until 31 August 1921, disenfranchisement, had it been rigorously implemented, would have penalised COs until the later summer of 1926. They would thus have been voteless not only in the 1918 General Election but also in those of 1922 and 1924, not to mention the annual local elections. In fact, this mean and petty clause became virtually a dead letter. In the post-war period there were more important matters to attend to than witch hunts of this nature. In any case, in one of his finest and most memorable speeches, during the passage of the Bill through the Lords, Lord Hugh Cecil effectively killed off the disenfranchisement clause by pointing out forcefully that 'there are a great many other people who have been court-martialled besides conscientious objectors'. There were 'the insubordinate, and deserters, and all those who have been sentenced for various military crimes and for crimes not merely military but civil, those guilty of criminal vice of the worst and most atrocious kind'. There were 'pickpockets, robbers, all those concerned in fraud, acts of violence, and those animated by the most odious lusts, the names of whose offences must not pass honest lips'. All these, declared Lord Hugh Cecil, would have the vote—criminals, sodomists, even women, but not conscientious objectors! It was a 'scandalous absurdity . . . to draw a distinction by which you admit all the worst people in the world, and only exclude the conscientious objectors.[4]'

The abolition of conscription was certainly an election issue in the sense that all parties were forced to declare a position on it in 1918, but the one issue that dominated the polls was the personal prestige of Lloyd George. He had led the nation to victory, had promised a land fit for heroes, and as the head of the Coalition Government had the support of the entire Conservative Party and the greater part of the Liberal Party. The Coalition won a landslide victory. Of Tory and Liberal candidates holding Lloyd George's 'coupon' of approval, 484 were returned. Fewer than a hundred Asquithian Liberals held their seats, and Asquith himself was defeated. The Labour Party's strength rose from thirty-six to fifty-nine, but both Henderson and MacDonald lost their seats. Ireland returned seventy-three Sinn Feiners.

It quickly became clear that Lloyd George was in no hurry to redeem his election pledge to end conscription. The King's Speech to the new Parliament on 11 February 1919 declared ominously that 'in order to reap the full fruits of victory and to safeguard the peace of the world an adequate army must be maintained in the field, and proposals which will be necessary to secure the forces required will be submitted to you in due course'.

William Adamson, the new Labour Leader, backed by J. R. Clynes, Sir Donald Maclean and Sydney Arnold, all pressed for an assurance from the Premier that this didn't mean the continuance of conscription. Lloyd George did not answer. Pressed again on 24 February, Winston Churchill, Secretary of State for War, replying for the Prime Minister, promised an early statement. The promise was kept. On 6 March a Naval, Military and Air Force

Service Bill was moved as a stop-gap measure to hold back demobilisation and freeze the services in their present form. Conscription would continue.

The Labour Party fought back with a united militancy it had not shown for five years. Adamson lost no opportunity to remind Lloyd George of his election pledge—and of the posters in Caernarvon Burgh. J. H. Thomas moved an amendment attacking the Bill as 'contrary to the oft-repeated pledges given by Ministers during the passage of previous Military Service Bills, and which is not in conformity with the declared policy of the Government at the General Election'. Churchill fell back on Lloyd George's multilateralism: Britain would abolish conscription if and when a general no-conscription agreement were secured at the Paris peace conference. As to election pledges, the Second World War Premier seemed to rebuke the First World War Premier for promising too much, too soon. It would have been better, he agreed, if the Coalition had foreseen the course of events and told the electors plainly that a further instalment of conscription was likely.

The Labour leaders were backed by a widespread public agitation against the new Bill. The National Council for Civil Liberties organised a 'No-Conscription Sunday' on 2 March, the third anniversary of the introduction of conscription, as a result of which demonstrations were held all over the country and resolutions passed by several hundred social, political and religious organisations. The Society of Friends' executive 'Meeting for Sufferings' on 7 March addressed to the Government a memorial professing its 'profound regret that we are once more, even since the Armistice has been declared, faced with a Government Bill providing for a renewed term of compulsory military service'. Two months later, in May, the Society's Yearly Meeting, one of the most significant forums of national Nonconformist opinion, addressed to all MPs a statement elaborating that of its executive:

> We appreciate the fact that conscription has been recognised as an evil by the signatories to the League of Nations Covenant, and we desire that abolition of conscription in Germany may be followed immediately by its complete abolition in other countries.
>
> Now that fighting has largely ceased we can see more clearly some of the immediate evils associated with compulsory military service;

men retained in the Army for purposes other than those for which they were enlisted; hundreds of conscripts in prison for offences known only to military law; many men still in prison who have proved their conscientious objection to all war.

Our objection to conscription includes an uncompromising opposition to compulsory military training; we view with grave apprehension the persistent attempts to introduce this into our schools. The developing mind and spirit of the child must be kept free from military control, and the idea of mutual service must be substituted for that of national domination.

Preparation for war is incompatible with the spirit of brotherhood.

But Quaker pacifism was incompatible with the spirit of the Lloyd George Coalition. The Naval, Military and Air Force Service Bill was carried on second reading in the Commons by 304 to 71, and after its third reading passed through the Lords to receive the Royal Assent on 16 April. Labour's amendment was, of course, rejected, along with back-bench amendments seeking to qualify the terms of the Bill.

During this time much of Lloyd George's energy had been absorbed in the quarrels at the Paris peace conference, where the merits of maintaining continuing conscript armies in Europe provoked heated clashes among the former allies. Marshal Foch argued that Germany should be allowed, indeed encouraged, to rebuild a conscript army. Lloyd George pressed that all kinds of conscription be forbidden to Germany until voluntary recruiting had been shown to have failed to produce whatever numbers were allowed in the peace treaties, at which point resort might be had to the ballot. The allied military committee backed Foch against Lloyd George.

The French motivation for what seems a puzzling policy was two-fold. The French Government undoubtedly feared a Soviet-type revolution on its own borders, with good reason since large parts of Germany were in a state of revolutionary ferment. Continuing conscription, it was thought, would restore order and discipline. But more important was the domestic military argument. Foch had spent his life building France's conscript army. If Germany abandoned conscription, the *raison d'être* of compulsion in France would be gone.

Domestic considerations were no less important to Lloyd George. He was faced with powerful pressures at home to end conscription, and was committed to a multilateral solution. If Germany were permitted to maintain a conscript army and Britain's continental allies followed suit, the Coalition Government would be faced with intensive demands, backed by Churchill at the War Office, for the permanent establishment of conscription in Britain. The resultant storm would certainly rock and perhaps wreck the Government.

For several weeks there was deadlock. Then the British delegation split the French camp by winning over Clemenceau to revised proposals for a voluntary German army. Foch capitulated, and on 21 July Lloyd George was able to ask Parliament for ratification of peace treaties which expressly forbade conscription in Germany. As Labour members were not slow to point out, there was now no valid obstacle to the final abolition of conscription in Britain, and Lloyd George promised that this was his intention.

> The greatest military power in the world is without an army [he boasted in a debate on finance on 30 October]. The navy that menaced us is at the bottom of the sea . . . Conscription has gone in the country that really drove other countries into conscription. The initiative in that movement was taken by Great Britain. Here let me say to those who criticise us as men who are doing nothing, that we have arranged that by the end of this financial year there will not be a conscript in this country.

The financial year ended in April 1920, when the Naval, Military and Air Force Service Act—the interim conscription measure—was also due to expire. On 20 May 1920, Winston Churchill told the Commons it was unnecessary to introduce a Bill to repeal the Military Service Acts as orders had been issued for all conscripts to be released. The Acts would automatically lapse on the official termination of the war. Thus conscription was left to fade away. When, at length, in August 1921, the Order in Council was issued declaring that the war would end officially on 31 August, the conscription laws quietly disappeared off the statute book—for eighteen years.

★ ★ ★

But at the signing of the Armistice in November 1918, some 1,500 conscientious objectors were still in prison. Work and hunger strikes had become common. So had deaths and medical releases. An N-CF petition for an amnesty was signed by nearly a thousand writers and academics of national reputation, bishops and clergy of all denominations, Labour leaders, and even a brigadier-general. In January 1919 it was presented to the Prime Minister by the Rev E. W. Barnes, Master of the Temple, Colonel John Buchan, Professor Gilbert Murray and Lord Parmoor. Another petition organised in Manchester carried the names of half the clergy and ministers appealed to, plus thirty-six magistrates and fifty county magistrates in Lancashire and Cheshire. The appeals were widely backed in the liberal press. The Government ignored them.

Not until April 1919 did the Government begin to act, and then its administration of releases proved to be as ill thought out and as bumbling as had been its administration of incarceration. The release plan started, sensibly enough, with the 'two-year' men—all kinds of prisoners under the Army Act, including COs, who had served a two-year sentence. Confusion arose, however, as to whether this category was restricted to men who had actually spent two years in jail, or whether it covered men whose two-year sentences had been whittled down to twenty months or more by good conduct remission. For a time it was left to individual prison governors to interpret the release order as they saw fit, but in the middle of April the Home Office clarified the situation by specifically including on the release list the men who had won remission. Even then confusion continued. On 22 April the Friends Service Committee gave the Home Office the names of twenty-month prisoners who were still awaiting release. The Home Office admitted that the matter 'had been overlooked', but promised that instructions would be sent to prison officers forthwith. When the FSC checked with Pentonville and Wandsworth prisons the following day, no instructions had been received. A telephone call to the Home Office produced the information that 'it was believed' the instructions were on their way. The following morning it was ascertained that the instructions had indeed arrived, and twenty-four men were released immediately from the two prisons.

The releases were staggered over several weeks and organised in small batches. With good reason, the War Office and Home Office feared the reactions of the press which was for the most part bitterly and noisily hostile to the release of any conscientious objectors before Army demobilisation had been completed. As it was, angry prejudice was aroused by continual complaints that COs were being set free to take the best jobs before the nation's heroes were out of khaki. The newspapers which set out to inflame their readers with a sense of injustice on this score failed to point out the extreme difficulties encountered by ex-prisoners in obtaining employment, or the fact that, as Winston Churchill emphasised, the release of 'prisoners under the Army Act' had been delayed until demobilisation was well into its stride.

By the end of May virtually all the two-year men, including of course those whose death sentences in France had been commuted to ten years, were free. Only a handful remained, those being men who had served their time in military rather than civil custody and who thus had to endure a more cumbersome and prolonged process of release.

Even during these releases, the Army continued to court-martial COs. At least four sentences of two years hard labour were pronounced in May 1919; and in the same month Morgan Jones, a former member of the N-CF National Committee who was soon to have the distinction of being the first CO elected to Parliament, was handed over to the army after seventeen months furlough on health grounds which had followed two successive terms of hard labour.

By the beginning of May, 650 COs were still in prison, and further attempts were made to get them out. Even Lord Salisbury, chairman of the Central Tribunal which had examined the COs in prison and pronounced on their genuineness, voiced the opinion that enough was enough. At the same time the larger battalions of the Triple Alliance of miners, railwaymen and transport workers threatened direct action if the release programme were not speeded up.

Those left now were the youngest and the oldest—those who had recently reached eighteen and had been in prison less than twenty months, and those conscripted after the raising of the enlistment age from forty-one to fifty-one. The War Office proceeded on the following extraordinary plan. All first sentences were reduced to 112 days, second sentences to six months, and third sentences to nine months. Thus those who had already endured most were made to

wait longest for release. But by this time the Government was
showing signs of being heartily sick of the CO problem. Liberal
remissions began to be granted, and in August 1919 the last batch of
objectors were released from prison. A few weeks earlier the Home
Office Scheme had been disbanded. After nearly three and a half
years, all conscientious objectors—those who had lived through the
experience—were again free men.

On release they were sent a terse note from the War Office advising them that they had been dishonourably discharged from the
Army, and warning that they would become liable to two years hard
labour if they ever tried to enlist again!

There were no pensions for these ex-servicemen. Many COs and
their families were literally destitute. In June 1919 several independent relief bodies merged to form a Joint Board for Assistance of
Conscientious Objectors and their Dependants, under the chairmanship of Dr Alfred Salter. Edward Grubb and Ramsay
MacDonald were joint honorary treasurers and Ernest E. Hunter
honorary secretary. Between 1 June 1919 and 30 April 1920 the
board raised and spent £7,185 in direct relief. In addition, the
Fellowship of Reconciliation organised a holiday scheme for men
released from prison as physical wrecks, and 149 such holidays were
provided, many of them at Fairby Grange convalescent home in
Kent, organised by Dr Salter. Nine hundred articles of clothing
were collected and distributed to released COs. In the meantime,
the Friends Service Committee and the N-CF organised vocational
and educational training classes, and ran an employment exchange.
As has already been noted, COs, with the double disgrace of a prison
record and a dishonourable discharge from the Army, often found it
hard to get work. Until well into the 'twenties several branches of the
Civil Service and public administration, including the Post Office
and the teaching profession, resolutely closed their doors to COs.
Needless to add, many private employers were no more liberal.

During the period of rising public concern which both provoked
and accompanied the releases, the civil administration and the Army
seemed at times to be vying with each other in their anxiety to
acquit themselves of any blame for what was increasingly being
recognised as the scandal of the war-time treatment of conscientious
objectors. While the nation was at war the War Office defended and
indeed demanded rigorous treatment for COs, parading the death

sentence as a deterrent to conscience and often closing its eyes (to put it generously) to systematic bullying and brutality. With its prestige and power cut back to size in the post-war months, this same War Office, under Winston Churchill, began to excuse its past conduct and indicate scapegoats. The organisation which had placed a military representative at every Tribunal hearing to oppose all exemptions now sought to blame the Tribunals for what had followed. The department which had gone to the brink in its trial of strength with Asquith now claimed that it had never wanted COs in the army and had always wished itself empowered to discharge them. This confession appeared in the course of a public statement published by the War Office in April 1919, which read—

> As a matter of fact the Army authorities themselves recognise that the lot of the conscientious objector is a hard one. They recognise that he has been the victim of ineptitude. Their view is that many hundreds of these men have been thrust into the Army whom the House of Commons never intended should become soldiers. The Tribunals, they consider, rejected the applications of hundreds of these men whose consciences were sincere, and to protect whom the conscience clause was expressly framed by the House of Commons. The Army did not want these men, and would have discharged them if it could. But the legal view taken was that having been made soldiers by Act of Parliament they could only be unmade by a similar measure, and the Government was unwilling to take that necessary step.

This, with the exception of the sentences totally absolving the Army from blame, was as neat a precis as could be hoped for of what the N-CF had been shouting into deaf ears since 1916. The wolf wasn't yet lying down with the lamb, but he had begun to borrow the lamb's vocabulary.

★   ★   ★

It was natural and inevitable that, with the war over and the armistice signed, as broadly based a movement as the No-Conscription Fellowship should begin to fall victim to internal dissensions. The requirements of active resistance had cemented a unity between religious pacifists and red revolutionaries, but when that resistance was over the cement crumbled to sand.

During the summer of 1919 there was fierce controversy within the movement about its future. Pacifists wanted an uncompromisingly pacifist organisation: Socialists wanted a revolutionary vanguard. Some wanted a caretaker committee which would hold a watching brief against any reintroduction of conscription and fight current proposals for compulsory military training in schools. Again, regional conferences were called to thrash out the differences, and the National Committee organised a small representative national conference at the Quaker centre of Jordans. As a result of these deliberations and soul searchings, Clifford Allen and Fenner Brockway came to the conclusion that the N-CF should be closed down and replaced by a series of specialist committees each pursuing independently the Fellowship's wide range of interests. Their view was expressed by John Graham thus: 'To have continued the N-CF in its then existing form would have been to allow it to become a cockpit for heated altercation on social ideals, and when one side or the other had won, they would have been in possession of an organisation which had no relation to its past, and was of very little use to the present; or it would have consisted of a few people with divided loyalties, and gradually would have petered out—like many another useful society which struggled on after its specific work was done.[5]'

After initial difficulty Allen and Brockway won the support of the rest of the National Committee and a national convention was organised for 29 and 30 November at Devonshire House. Four hundred delegates attended from local groups. The great majority were ex-prisoners. Ramsay MacDonald, George Lansbury and G. D. H. Cole were among the speakers, and Fenner Brockway moved the National Committee's resolution:

That this convention declares its belief that all systems of conscription can only be sustained by the denial of liberty of conscience, and that it is not within the rightful jurisdiction of a State to deny any man the right of free judgment in offering his life or to compel him to inflict death on others.

It further appoints a Committee to initiate a new organisation to oppose conscription no matter by what kind of Government it be imposed, or for what purpose, which will associate all those who will resist conscription, and shall get into touch with appropriate people in other countries with a view to the establishment of an international organisation.

That this convention appoint a Committee to take steps (*a*) to establish a new Society whose object shall be the spread of the pacifist doctrine of life and resistance to all forms of Militarism, and (*b*) to get into touch with people of like belief in this and other countries with a view to the establishment of an international organisation of which it shall function as the British section.

The resolution sought to accommodate several viewpoints. The reference to 'a new organisation . . . which shall associate all those who will resist conscription' was designed to meet the objections of those who had criticised the Fellowship's apparent exclusiveness in extending membership only to those who could affirm belief in an ultimately religious concept, the sanctity of human life. The 'new society' for propagating pacifism was to be a different body altogether, meeting a demand from different quarters. The internationalist references recognised the recent emergence of pacifist bodies in Germany, the United States, Holland and Denmark. Thus the resolution was designed to make a wide appeal and avoid identification of the National Committee with any single faction. But most important of all, its references to the formation of new organisations carried a clear implication that the N-CF's usefulness was over, an implication which Brockway made explicit in moving the resolution.

It was fiercely contested. In an organisation which had aroused such passionate loyalties there were naturally many opponents of voluntary liquidation. An amendment was moved advocating the continuance of the N-CF. It was defeated. By 244 votes to 171 the Fellowship voted itself out of existence.

On the Saturday night a great reunion of COs was held in the Central Hall, when 1,500 sat down to supper. At the central table sat six Labour mayors of London boroughs, including a quietly spoken army major, Clement Attlee, whose brother Tom had been a CO. But the high point of the convention, as of those others which had punctuated the Fellowship's five year history, was the presidential address by Clifford Allen. The frail, emaciated figure, looking much more than his thirty years, had barely begun to recover

from the three successive hard labour sentences, totalling fourteen
months, which had left him with tuberculosis and a permanently
weakened constitution. But those who were present at the concluding convention say, at half a century's distance, that they never
heard him in finer voice.

He began by recalling the Fellowship's special convention of
1916—

Three years ago there assembled in this hall a very notable
gathering. It represented men who held every variety of religious and
political opinion. We were on the eve of a memorable experience.
We were setting out on a voyage of discovery; discovery not only
of the working of conscription, which was new to us and to the
British people, but a discovery of our own ideas. We stood here
in silence and made a pledge. That pledge was to resist conscription
and the military power. Today we reassemble. We have survived
the test, and I suggest to you that that fact is in itself of very great
significance.

The test had involved great suffering—but others had suffered
more.

It seems to me that every one of us must be only too conscious of
how terrible is the comparison between the anguish of those who
have died and been mutilated in the war and the test to which we
have been subjected. Although it is an established fact that prison
has greater terrors for the soldier than the trenches, not one of us
would dare to compare our suffering with that of the men who were
actually engaged in warfare. Many of them are dead, but we still have
the opportunities of life before us. Our lives are now forfeit.

He recalled the mood of 1916.

The human race was in the grip of contrary instincts. On the one
hand were bitterness, hatred and terror, so that men were afraid to be
isolated from the life of the nation. On the other hand you had from
countless individuals what I suppose is really the most wonderful
exhibition of self-sacrifice and unselfish heroism of which history has
record. Above all things, men were held by a world spell, and that
was the spell of the military machine. Fearless men, keen-minded
men, gentle men, believed it their duty to bow before that machine.

Others held it to be infallible and irresistible. We, like others of our generation, were called upon to become part of this world adventure; we were challenged by the community to bow before the military power; we were expected to engage in war and acquiesce in conscription.

It is not possible for any man or woman to estimate the mental and spiritual struggle of facing that challenge unless they have in fact been potential conscripts. I know that often we expressed ourselves with arrogance, but I beg our friends to realise that situated as we were—cut off as a minority from the community, brought before Tribunals where we were placed always on the defensive, always on the look-out for traps set for us and our creed—we were forced to become self-conscious, so that it became difficult to say what we wished to say in a really convincing and genuine fashion.

Allen looked briefly at the varieties of objection which had arisen. In the thick of the struggle he had opposed every deviation from absolutism, but now—

It matters not whether we were in the Non-Combatant Corps refusing to bear arms, whether we took alternative service, whether we became part of the Home Office Scheme, or whether we were absolutist and remained in prison—all of us shattered the infallibility of militarism. That, to me, is a mighty achievement, and I am not willing to allow any false sense of humility to prevent my glorying in it.

We are proud to have broken the power of the military authority. We have witnessed its brutalities. We have seen the cruel degrading of human personality upon which its discipline depends . . . We have seen how it deprives its victims of that most sacred right, free judgment in right and wrong, how the system makes men hate each other, bully each other, despise each other, till they become so dehumanised that they can be made even to kill their fellow working men at home. We have defeated it; we will defeat it again if conscription should be continued.

All sections of the Fellowship were united in 'a belief that no international policies and no political or religious creeds can ever achieve happiness for the world which do not recognise the dignity and value of human personality.'

We in our prison cells have therefore expressed consciously or unconsciously that vision of the future of the world which inspires the new Labour movement. And thus, strange though it may appear, we are linked by our negative action with the most vital ideas motivating men's actions today.

Allen wanted to turn his listeners' eyes away from prison and towards the world outside, away from the past and into the future. So he identified the cause in which they had suffered with the cause of reconstruction.

In the old days social reform was concerned with material readjustments in the economic system; it did not challenge the relationship of master and man, it kept the incentive of profit-making which causes men to exploit each other. It was therefore prepared to tolerate poverty. And all because no recognition was given to the value of human personality or the importance of respect between human beings. Today the most vital social forces in the world stand for a contrary opinion. It is true they are still concerned with wages and hours, but those demands are playing only a small part in their programmes. The cry of the working classes today is for responsibility, for a new status, for the opportunity to be free servants of the community, for the chance of carrying into the era of peace the spirit of National Service they learnt in time of war. The responsibility of man to man is the keynote of the new social outlook, and that is precisely the ideal for which we have stood.

If this be a true description of the views that have inspired our resistance, I think it is clear to all of us how definitely our negative action has taken the form of positive and constructive social service. And yet these ideas may be admirably conceived and our achievement memorable, but if now that men are willing to listen we fail to live out our lives in service, the world will become once more disillusioned. It did not heed what we said when it was suffering. It is prepared to listen now. We have declared that hate destroys and that love is creative. But men are in a cynical frame of mind and need convincing of this. They are rejecting many of their old political myths; they are amused by religion. It is true that they need new political programmes, but they need far more a new motive which will inspire their lives, and we have a chance now to take no small part in rebuilding constructive hope in the world.

I cannot see how we could avoid the charge of disloyalty to our nation, but I would now plead that we may be considered genuine in our citizenship, believing, as we did, that if we remained faithful, we might help in preserving those very ideas of liberty for which the nations had gone to war . . . We had a chance of giving some evidence of personal sincerity and willingness to suffer for our ideas. It seemed to us to be the highest contribution we could make. Perhaps we did it clumsily, perhaps we did it in much the same spirit of pride in which the militarists of each nation waged war. But we did believe that our stand was a genuine expression of citizenship.

Allen concluded:

There have been times when I wondered if the struggle was worth while. But the certainty of hope for me lies in this. It was not some outworn isolated creed that we cherished. We have discovered in our prison cells that very notion which is today challenging the old world order—the notion that men will only feel obliged to serve the community, of which they are a part, when they have come to respect each other's liberty.

We were in prison—today we are free. But the world is still in prison. It can be released by the spirit of unconquerable love. 'Ye that have escaped the sword, stand not still.'

The applause that followed gave vent to three years of pent-up emotion. When eventually it subsided, Allen moved the Fellowship's final resolution, which the meeting adopted by standing in silence:

Throughout the war we have stood for the brotherhood of man, and in the name of that ideal have resisted conscription. We now reaffirm our unity of aim with those in all countries who have given their lives that they might serve the cause of freedom, but declare our belief that it is not by bloodshed that freedom can be won or militarism destroyed.

We acclaim the new hope of human liberty now challenging ancient tryannies in industry within the State and between the nations, and dedicate the liberty we have regained to such service as shall contribute to the healing of the wounds inflicted by war, and to the building of a world rooted in freedom and enriched by labour that is shared by all.

It is in this spirit that we go forth to meet new tasks, confident that through its long and bitter suffering mankind must yet come into the way of love.

It was left to Bertrand Russell, speaking at the Fellowship's final public meeting on the Sunday night of 30 November, to pronounce the N-CF's epitaph. He told the 2,000-strong audience—

The N-CF has been completely victorious in its stand for freedom not to kill or to take part in killing. The whole power of the State has not been able to compel the members of the N-CF to kill or help in killing. In winning this victory you have won an even greater victory; you have won a victory for the sense of human worth, for the realisation of the value of each individual soul. It is that, above all, that we must assert and put before the world, that sense that each human soul, each individual growing and living, has within him something sacred, something that must not be warped and destroyed by the imposition of outside forces.[6]

Before it dispersed, the convention, in pursuance of the National Committee's resolution, appointed three caretaker committees to carry on the Fellowship's work. An Anti-Conscription Committee was commissioned to act as a watchdog against the reintroduction of conscription. Appointed to it were Clifford Allen, Fenner Brockway, Will Chamberlain, Guy Aldred, Catherine Marshall, H. Runham Brown, Ernest E. Hunter and Charles Ammon. A Pacifist Union Committee was appointed to propagandise for pacifism, and it consisted of Allen, Brockway and Chamberlain, with Dr Alfred Salter, C. H. Norman, Edward Grubb, Joan Fry and J. Rowntree Gillett. Finally, the convention appointed a Committee to Oppose Military Training in Schools, consisting of Joan Beauchamp, Will Chamberlain, J. P. Fletcher, John Langdon-Davies, Theodora Wilson Wilson, John W. Graham, Stanley James and James Maxton.

So the historic No-Conscription Fellowship, vanguard of non-violent revolution, shock troops of pacifism, gently subsided in a proliferation of committees.

REFERENCES

1 *The Tribunal*, 24 October 1918
2 Quoted by Denis Hayes, *op cit*
3 Quoted by Denis Hayes, *op cit*
4 Parliamentary Report (Hansard), Lords, 16 January 1918
5 John W. Graham, *op cit*
6 *N-CF Souvenir*, 1919

Chapter XII

Postscript

OF THE three principal leaders of the N-CF, two are today (1967) active, unrepentant and notorious peacemakers. The third died in 1939.

On his release from prison, Clifford Allen plunged himself into political activity. In 1920 he visited the Soviet Union as one of a Labour delegation which also included Bertrand Russell. The two friends quarrelled bitterly over what they saw of communism in action. Russell was disillusioned, but Allen was optimistic, finding Lenin 'a profoundly astute but academic man'[1]. Reporting his impressions on his return, however, he showed himself to be already aware of the danger that 'Russian communism, with its principles of common service and social equality, may be swept away and a great centralised bureaucracy substituted, driving a disciplined nation to vast production and perhaps to a new and menacing form of imperialism'.[2]

While in Russia his health again broke down. His weight, only eight stone when he left prison, dropped to six. He was sent to an Estonian nursing home and thence to a Swiss sanatorium, but he so loathed the other patients, mostly elderly and rich, that he walked out as soon as he felt strong enough, and made his way home in a leisurely sun-seeking journey through Europe, during which he met his future wife, Marjorie Gill.

Home again in 1921, he was offered a safe Labour seat in the Gorbals division of Glasgow, but to his intense disappointment his doctors ruled that his health would not stand the strain of electioneering. But continuing illness did not prevent him from becoming treasurer of the ILP in the same year, and in 1922 he helped launch a new ILP newspaper, the *New Leader*, which soon outsold both the *New Statesman* and the *Spectator* at nearly fifty thousand copies a week. He rejoiced in the election of Ramsay MacDonald, now back in the Commons after his 1918 defeat, to the leadership of the Labour Party, but the timidity of the first Labour Government, which held office briefly in 1924, disappointed him. In April 1924 he became chairman of the ILP, from which position he pressed upon MacDonald the famous series of legislative measures which the ILP and much of the rest of the democratic Left believed would bring 'Socialism in our Time'. MacDonald, dependent for power on Liberal support, which he soon lost, showed little interest.

Allen's programme was far to the Left of that of the Labour Party, but it wasn't thorough-going enough for many ILP militants. In 1925 a breach developed between Allen and James Maxton over the question of compensation for nationalisation. Maxton repudiated Allen's moderate view that cash compensation for disappropriation was political wisdom if not a moral obligation. In the struggle, both ideological and personal, that followed, Maxton succeeded his old comrade-against-arms as ILP chairman, and Allen, bitterly hurt and disillusioned, for a time turned his back on politics altogether. He voiced his fear that Socialism was being sacrificed to the 'scramble for political power and position'. Ramsay MacDonald wrote to sympathise: 'Somehow or other,' he lamented, 'there has grown up inside the ILP, especially among those who are in most prominent positions, a petty small-mindedness on personal matters and a cheap melodramatic appetite in propaganda. You must have had a very sickening time.'

Allen went into the wilderness for nearly six years and did not re-emerge until the 1931 crisis when MacDonald, again Prime Minister, sought to solve the country's economic problems by paring down unemployment benefit, in pursuance of which measure he broke with his own Labour Cabinet and formed a predominantly Conservative but nominally 'National' Government. The ageing Snowden stayed with him as Chancellor. Almost the entire Labour movement condemned MacDonald's action as treachery; but to the bewilderment of his old friends on the Left, Clifford Allen emerged from obscurity to defend MacDonald and Snowden. On 22 October 1931 he wrote in the first of two letters to *The Times*:

> The consequences of [the Labour Party's] mood and action [in refusing to accept MacDonald's measures and join in the National Government] has been that a programme of evolutionary Socialism,

which under Mr. MacDonald's leadership was claiming a respectful
hearing, has now come to seem to be a revolutionary threat—a danger
instead of a help . . . I believe the present National Government—
even with Conservative predominance—is a more effective instrument for sheltering the workers from further suffering than government by my own party alone.

On the eve of the General Election of October 1931, which
overwhelmingly endorsed the National Government and routed
Labour, Allen wrote to MacDonald: 'We can never—as a Labour
Movement or as a Nation—be grateful enough to you for what you
have done.' MacDonald replied five weeks later, in a letter headed
VERY SECRET: 'My Dear Allen, Would you like to be a Lord? Please
let me know at once.' By return of post Allen replied 'Yes.' In the
New Year's Honours List for 1932 he was created Lord Allen of
Hurtwood.

Commented the *Morning Post* on New Year's Day:

> Even the most seasoned observer of events may excusably be be-
> trayed into at least a lifted eyebrow of surprise in encountering
> among the new Peers Mr Clifford Allen, best known to fame as chair-
> man and treasurer of the Independent Labour Party and, during the
> War, of the No-Conscription Fellowship. The cause for exclamation
> is not to be found in the nature of Mr Allen's political activities
> which, now rewarded with a Peerage, were formerly requited with
> imprisonment, but in the incongruous conclusion to such a career.
> Those who have known Mr Clifford Allen may have forseen varying
> destinies for him, but no one had the extravagance of imagination to
> see him as a Peer of the Realm.

The London *Evening Standard* made its comment in verse on
19 January:

> *We've read of Barons bold who, fighting, die:*
> *But noble Hurtwood would not hurt a Fly,*
> *Battles he frowns upon as social Crimes*
> *And with his Sword writes letters to the* Times.
> *Today his Efforts all the World applauds*
> *To make Men equal (from the House of Lords).*
> *We, too, would serve behind a Prison Wall*
> *Did Conscience but make Barons of us All.*

Most hurtful of all, however, was a verse headed 'Honour' in the paper he had helped found for the ILP, the *New Leader*, now edited by Fenner Brockway (whose own peerage was still thirty-three years away). After commenting bitterly that 'One past chairman of the ILP is a Viscount (Snowden) and another a Baron (Allen) while a third is Prime Minister of a "National" Government', the anonymous poet continued:

> *The years in passing witness many things,*
> *The rise of peoples and the fall of kings;*
> *Brave sacrifices borne in freedom's cause,*
> *And noble struggles 'gainst oppressive laws.*
> *How often, too, they see a trust misplaced,*
> *A life of service in an hour laid waste!*
> *Men will betray the cause that made them great,*
> *And turn the love of millions into hate.*
> *Our time a melancholy sight affords—*
> *A drear procession to the House of Lords*
> *Of men who once were urgent in the fight,*
> *And led in battle for the people's right,*
> *And now condemn their young and better selves*
> *To be forgotten on the gilded shelves.*
> *We know by almost cynical volte-face*
> *The Viscount Snowden earned his noble place,*
> *But why does Allen such an 'honour' reap?*
> *Has then apostasy become so cheap*
> *That one with ease towards a peerage climbs*
> *By writing two short letters to the* Times?

Lord Allen's political activities continued, first on the executive of the tiny 'National Labour Party'—the group which, expelled from the Labour Party, followed MacDonald—and then in the all-party 'Next Five Years' group, where he worked closely with Harold Macmillan. But his breach with the Socialist movement did not affect his concern for practical peace-making. Throughout the 'thirties he was keenly aware of the growing dangers of a second world war, and the menace of continental Nazism and Fascism. In 1933 he organised a campaign for collective security through the League of Nations, and began to criticise MacDonald's National

Government for lukewarmness towards the League. He still described himself as a pacifist, but now gave the term a breadth of meaning his younger self would never have allowed. He had no time for the 'no-force pacifists' of the War Resisters International and the Peace Pledge Union. He told the 1933 convention of the National Peace Council in Oxford:

I claim that Pacifism must be either constructive or meaningless. To be constructive it must be concerned less with how to get rid of force and more about how to stimulate and use reason. It will not place the emphasis upon the fact that the world would be saved if once force were got rid of; it will say the world would be saved if once reason were given a chance. Let us therefore turn our backs on all doctrinal controversy about whether you should or should not abstain from the use of force and if so under what circumstances. Let us go on to considering how at last in the twentieth century reason can be given its full opportunity. I am not interested in the discussion of logical dilemmas, like the early Christians described by Gibbon. I am only interested in constructive proposals.

I submit to you that Pacifism is not and never can be a political method if it is chiefly concerned with abstaining from the use of force. It is useless our making perorations to each other to prove that war would stop if only people would cease fighting; that is equivalent to saying that the world would be happier if everyone were good. Both propositions are obvious and both are meaningless.

You can of course define Pacifism by a reference to force, but you cannot thereby save the world from the use of force. Let us be frank with ourselves. No person in this room can claim to be called a no-force pacifist if he is prepared to restrain by physical force a little child from throwing himself into the fire. If you refuse to withdraw your child from the fire or decline to employ a policeman to save a little child from being raped, then and then only may you consider yourself a no-force pacifist. But in that case you must honourably face a definite political consequence. You must cease taking part in practical political affairs and go instead into the wilderness as an educator of opinion or as a religious propagandist. You have no right to take part in the government of a world that believes in working through force towards the reign of law and order. Either therefore insist on believing in Pacifism as something measured by the use of force and go out of politics, or define pacifism as something emphasising the power of reason and stay in politics.[3]

Politics and 'the power of reason' led Lord Allen to advocate the formation of an International Air Force to provide a 'world police-man'. But the Government argued that internationalisation would destroy the profits of national civil aviation. In 1935 the League of Nations was irreparably weakened by its failure to apply effective sanctions against Italy over the invasion of Abyssinia. Allen vigor-ously supported sanctions and criticised the British Government's inaction. If England allowed 'the spirit of defeatism to come into our hearts about the League', he warned, 'we would all go down to destruction'.

Contrary to the view of those who too easily bracket Lord Allen with the Right-wing appeasers of Hitler, he had few illusions about the menace, both domestic and international, of Nazism. But as in 1914 he had seemed to be befriending Germany by opposing the view that she alone was to blame for the war, so now he seemed to some to be taking her side again because he continued to press for the revision of the Versailles Treaty and declared Nazism to be the inevitable product of the post-war allied policy of 'squeezing Ger-many till the pips squeak'. He made several journeys to Germany, and met Hitler twice, in 1935 and 1937. He did not plead for peace. He used both meetings to press the case for the freeing of Germany's political prisoners and to protest at the treatment being accorded the Jews, details of which were just beginning to penetrate beyond Germany's border. By 1938 he had become convinced that the Jewish persecution alone would, if continued, lead to war, arising from 'our discovery . . . that there is a disparity of outlook between our two countries, so far as humanity and cruelty are concerned'.

But despite Germany's domestic policies Lord Allen was sym-pathetic to Hitler's claim for a revision of German boundaries which would give them back the lost territories of Czechoslovakia. He believed this was the wish of the majority of German-speaking Czechs. In August 1938 he flew to Berlin and to Prague and sug-gested to German and Czech leaders that the dispute be settled by a Four-Power Conference of Britain, France, Germany and Italy. The formula was agreed, and led to Munich.

'It is lovely', wrote Lord Allen to Mrs Corder Catchpool on

7 October, 'to think that the actual formula for the Four-Power
Conference, which we worked out and put to Ribbentrop when we
were in Berlin, should have been the instrument which saved the
peace of the world.' And the following day he wrote to his old
fellow-CO Hubert Peet:

> It was a highly controversial technique, but it had the supreme
> advantage of preventing the actual invasion of Czechoslovakia, stop-
> ping a world war and perhaps bringing Germany back into inter-
> national consultation.[4]

Five months later Hitler marched into Prague. But Lord Allen
never experienced the disillusionment that would surely have
crushed him. Twelve days before the German invasion, on 3 March
Clifford Allen died in his sleep while recuperating in Switzerland
from yet another racking bout of illness.

Among the messages of sympathy received by Lady Allen was
one from Joachim von Ribbentrop, Hitler's Foreign Minister. 'With
the greatest sympathy', the message ran, 'I deplore the death of Lord
Allen of Hurtwood, whose selflessness I have esteemed so highly,
and whose death I regret as the loss of an understanding full of
friendship.' Another message was from Fenner Brockway: 'Despite
the political difference of later years, my memory of him remains as
one of the happiest political companionships of my life.'[5]

Disillusionment with his old ILP colleagues clearly played a
large part in Allen's development, as it did with Ramsay Mac-
Donald. He never recovered from the hurt of being manoeuvred by
Maxton out of the ILP leadership. But Allen's transition from dog-
matist to pragmatist, though it failed to come to the surface until
ten years after the war, was already complete by the time the war
ended. As early as 5 August 1918, the man who had led the absolutists confided to his diary:

> I shudder at the sight of individuals or organisations or parties
> presuming to discover either from the lips of the Deity or the
> columns of the Bible—or indeed from anywhere—principles which
> are the final touchstone for all time. To accept this means either that
> you reject new experiences or phenomena which don't fit your
> principles or you condemn as moral backsliders anyone who having
> once shared your principles now abandons them. Should not a

principle be simply a standard of values which must only be abandoned on first rate evidence but which experience and new phenomena as much as the need for stability and care can change? If you take the absolute view of principles won't you be in danger of finding society stick to a principle and say it believes in it whilst in fact never regarding it?[6]

★ ★ ★

Three causes dominated the public life of Fenner Brockway on his release from prison. He organised the No More War movement and helped found the War Resisters International; he campaigned for Indian independence as secretary of the British Committee of the Indian National Congress, a foretaste of his later specialisation in the cause of colonial freedom; and with Stephen Hobhouse he became joint secretary of an influential Prison System Enquiry Committee which included Sydney and Beatrice Webb, Bernard Shaw, Margery Fry and Sir Sydney Oliver, ex-governor of Jamaica.

This latter concern exercised many objectors who had been given a taste of prison life. They felt a responsibility, as an unusually articulate class of ex-convict, to publicise the defects of the system. In 1918, on 14 November, *The Tribunal* had commented:

> Members of the N-CF are not necessarily agreed about prisons in themselves; most of us would like to see them abolished, while a few perhaps would retain them. But on one point we are unanimous: the prison system of today must go. It is brutalising. The purpose of a prison should not be punishment: society should seek peace by negotiation with its 'criminal classes'. The prison system that we know savours not of reclamation: it stands for the knock-out blow ... Every CO should make it his business to have our prison system altered—the silence rule, the useless, soul-destroying monotony of the never-ending heap of mail-bags, the degrading clothes of the convict must give way to a better regime, where an attempt will be made to instil a sense of responsibility and personal dignity into those who have sinned against the community—or against whom the community has sinned. A reform, a revolution in our prison system, then, is one task before the returning CO.

The Committee's report, which was a shade less utopian than *The Tribunal*, led to a number of reforms, the most important being abolition of the notorious silence rule. Thus Brockway achieved through committee work what he had failed to achieve by organised mutiny at Liverpool jail.

The Committee's activities had their light side. Brockway was rash enough to invite Shaw to contribute a preface to the published report. GBS assented, and came up with an essay which, while underwriting most of the report's recommendations, added one of its own: that incurable criminals be dealt with by way of the gas chamber. Hobhouse's Quaker susceptibilities were outraged, but Shaw refused either to amend his preface or let Hobhouse publish a disclaimer. 'I will not be disowned!' he told the embarrassed Brockway. In the end, the report and Shaw's preface appeared under separate covers.

In the meantime there was politics. Brockway stood as Labour candidate for Lancaster in 1922 and was defeated. In March 1924, during the brief life-span of the first Labour Government, he was adopted by Labour to contest a by-election in the Abbey division of Westminster—a traditionally safe Tory seat. He was opposed not only by an official Conservative but also by Winston Churchill, who had lost his seat in 1922 and was now standing as 'an Independent Liberal who supports the Conservatives'. To complicate the matter further, the Liberals adopted Scott Duckers, one of the most militant of the war-time absolutists, to contest the seat. Brockway fought on an election address written for him by Clifford Allen. It's keynote was an attack on Churchill:

> Of all politicians Mr Churchill has shown himself most unfit for the responsibility of government. His *forte* is to be a disturber of the peace, whether at home or abroad. He is a political adventurer, with a genius for acts of mischievous irresponsibility. He is a militant to the finger-tips . . . His use of troops during the railway dispute of 1911 and his wicked and wasteful expenditure of one hundred millions of British money in futile military attacks on Russia, prove how fatal it would be to place him in a position of influence at a time when the shattered world left by the war needs a healing hand of reconciliation . . . Mr Churchill's record shows him to be a public danger and a menace to the peace of the world.[7]

Churchill was defeated by the narrow margin of forty-three, the Tory scraping home with 8,187 votes to Churchill's 8,144. But the sensation of the by-election was Brockway's 6,156 votes for Labour. Scott Duckers polled 291.

For a time Brockway continued to divide his energies equally between the peace movement and the ILP. Pacifism was sprouting many offshoots. In 1926, after the collapse of the general strike, Arthur Ponsonby of the UDC organised his Peace Letter Campaign in the course of which many thousands of signatures were obtained for a declaration addressed to the Prime Minister whereby the signatories, 'convinced that all disputes between nations were capable of settlement either by diplomatic negotiations or by some form of International Arbitration', solemnly declared that they refused to support or render war service to any Government resorting to arms. At the climax of the campaign, on 5 December, nine thousand people gathered in the Royal Albert Hall, London, where one of the speakers, an ex-CO named Herbert Morrison, told them, 'I ask you to dedicate yourselves anew to the great cause of international peace. It is for you to let the Government know, and others know, that so far as you are concerned you are finished with war, and that you will take no part in it, either collectively or individually.'[8] The Peace Letter Campaign was an early version of the Peace Pledge Union, founded eight years later by the Rev. Dick Sheppard, with the support of George Lansbury, Aldous Huxley and Vera Brittain. In its first year the PPU collected 80,000 signatories to the pledge 'We renounce war and never again directly or indirectly will we support or sanction another'. Its pre-war membership rose at one point to 140,000 and with its weekly newspaper, *Peace News*, it came to dominate the pacifist field.

But by this time Fenner Brockway had moved away from what Lord Allen was dismissing as 'no-force pacifism', the pacifism that was personal rather than political. He edited the ILP's *New Leader*, which campaigned for collective security within the League of Nations, and for multilateral disarmament. But the ILP's primary preoccupations in the late 'twenties were domestic, centred on mounting unemployment and the deepening crisis of world capitalism. By 1929, when Labour again came to power and Brockway was elected to Parliament for the first time, relations between the ILP and the Labour Party were worse than they had been at any time since the war. In 1932, after MacDonald's defection and the consequent routing of Labour at the polls, the ILP voted to secede.

Brockway, who had lost his seat in the general rout, was the principal architect of the split.

The ILP walked out of the Labour Party and into the wilderness. And from the wilderness it watched the rise of Nazism in Germany, the consolidation of Fascism in Italy, the violent establishment of Right-wing totalitarianism in Spain and the collapse of the League of Nations. Hunting around for new allies, it flirted for a time with the Communist Party and made abortive approaches to the Communist International. Brockway's own sympathies with the Communists, which had prompted him to work for reunion between the Socialist and Communist Internationals, were shattered by the Spanish civil war. He went to Spain 'to help save Socialists from Communist hands'[6].

Many who had refused to bear arms in the imperialist war of 1914 were eager to shoulder arms against Spanish Fascism. Many more at home were advocating rearmament against German Nazism. Herbert Morrison was one of the sponsors of the 1938 National Service Campaign, which sought to speed up army recruitment, though on voluntary lines.

Renewed pressures for conscription led to the foundation in 1938 of a No-Conscription League organised on lines similar to those of the N-CF. Fenner Brockway was one of its sponsors, and other N-CF veterans associated with the League included James Hindle Hudson and Alfred Salter. It published a manifesto which began: 'The Net of Conscription is ready. It awaits only the most favourable moment to throw it over the People, who are not ready for it.' The League never recaptured the vigour of its parent, and only branches in Glasgow and Bristol survived the first years of war. A revived *Tribunal* died quickly, and peace propaganda was left to the Peace Pledge Union's *Peace News*.

Maxton, still leader of the ILP, opposed the war against Hitler. Brockway supported it, but continued to oppose conscription, on libertarian rather than pacifist lines. When Chamberlain introduced conscription in April 1939 he was prudent enough to avoid measures which would lead to a repetition of the scandals of 1916. Tribunals were better briefed, and the new Military Service Acts were administered more liberally. In any case, there was nothing comparable to the resistance of 1916. There were fewer 'revolutionary' COs: most were religious rather than political. Their interests were watched

over by a Central Board for Conscientious Objectors (CBCO), a
federation of fifteen pacifist and libertarian societies, of which
Brockway became chairman.

When Churchill's Coalition Government replaced that of Neville
Chamberlain, Brockway negotiated an agreement with the Minister
of Labour, Ernest Bevin, whose life-long opposition to pacifism in
the Labour movement had culminated in the attack which forced
George Lansbury's resignation from the party leadership. But
Bevin impressed Brockway with his understanding of the objectors'
position. The two men arrived at an agreement whereby Bevin
promised that the Ministry of Labour would exempt all conscientious objectors on condition that they contributed to a socially useful
organisation the difference between their incomes and the pay of a
private soldier. But no sooner was this concession won by Brockway
than it was rejected by the CBCO, which declared that sacrifice must
be voluntary and not forced by conscription Acts. The younger
Fenner Brockway, who had denounced alternativism as slavery,
would have warmly approved the Board's absolutism.

Twice Brockway stood as an ILP candidate in war-time by-elections. 'Maxton was disappointed that I did not come out for "Stop
the War" in my election addresses and speeches", he records in
Outside the Right, adding:

> Let me admit this. I felt painfully frustrated during the war. My
> mind was pulled in two directions. If I had been unreservedly anti-
> war I would have had a clear purpose as I had in the First World
> War, but I was too conscious of the evil of Nazism and Fascism to be
> completely pacifist. Yet I could not be pro-war. It would have been
> utterly against my nature and philosophy. I was in the dilemma of
> seeing everyone around me supremely engaged, and I could neither
> join in nor actively oppose.

He stayed with the ILP throughout the war, finding its isolation
increasingly intolerable. When in the 1945 Labour landslide the
ILP retained only its four war-time seats, fighting only five constitu-
encies altogether, Fenner Brockway knew that its independence was
no longer of significant value. He had attended the Blackpool conference of the Labour Party which had decided to break the Coalition and precipitate an election. 'The minds of the thousand delegates who packed the floor was on the Britain and the world which

the war had left. I had an extraordinary sense of unity with them and their demonstrative determination to build something better. If dynamism for change is revolutionary, then the revolution was here in the making. As I looked down on the cheering faces, I had no doubt that the ILP should be within the Labour Party and I knew then that I could not stay outside.'[10]

But the old wounds were beyond healing. The ILP was not disposed to seek reunification with the Labour Party and the Labour Party did not need the ILP. Fenner Brockway had to make his own way across the divide. In January 1947 he joined the Labour Party, and in 1950 returned to the House of Commons as MP for Eton and Slough.

Four years later, with Anthony Greenwood, Anthony Wedgwood Benn, the Rev. Dr Donald Soper and Sydney Silverman, a fellow-veteran of the N-CF, he was organising an Anti-H-Bomb Committee. There followed in 1958 the first Aldermaston march and the Campaign for Nuclear Disarmament.

Brockway became a vice-president of CND. He also lost his seat in the Commons in the 1964 election. Harold Wilson offered him a peerage, and when he accepted no one wrote outraged verse. The House of Lords had changed more than he had. His first public engagement following the announcement of his new title was at an 'old lags' reunion' organised by the Peace Pledge Union for COs of the two wars. A few months later Lord Brockway was organising the British Council for Peace in Vietnam in protest at the Labour Government's support of America's war.

* * *

The rise of 'nuclear pacifism' also served to bring another 'old lag' back into the front line of the peace movement. When CND was founded in February 1958 Lord Russell (he had succeeded to the title on his brother's death) accepted the honorary Presidency of the movement. Like the N-CF, CND was a coalition of Left-wing Socialists and traditional pacifists; and again like the N-CF CND indulged at least as great a taste for internal argument as for external propaganda. In 1960 Russell broke with the CND executive to form the Committee of 100, committed to mass civil disobedience leading to the kind of non-violent revolution of which the N-CF had dreamt. And when Lord Brockway formed the British Council for Peace in

Vietnam, Lord Russell followed with his more militant Vietnam Solidarity Campaign.

Peace organisations come and peace organisations go, but the peace movement goes on for ever, raising again for each generation the questions first raised in an acute form by the pioneers of the No-Conscription Fellowship. The reasonable man, the respectable liberal, admires its romantic past but keeps his distance from its disquieting present. 'The reasonable man,' Shaw observed in *Maxims for Revolutionists*, 'adapts himself to the world: the unreasonable one persists in adapting the world to himself. Therefore all progress depends on the unreasonable man.'

REFERENCES

1 Quoted by Martin Gilbert in *Plough My Own Furrow: the Story of Lord Allen of Hurtwood*, 1965
2 Quoted by Martin Gilbert, *op cit*
3 Quoted by Martin Gilbert, *op cit*
4 Quoted by Martin Gilbert, *op cit*
5 Quoted by Martin Gilbert, *op cit*
6 Quoted by Martin Gilbert, *op cit*
7 Quoted by Martin Gilbert, *op cit*
8 Denis Hayes, *op cit*
9 Fenner Brockway, *Outside the Right*, 1963
10 Fenner Brockway, *op cit*

SOURCES AND ACKNOWLEDGEMENTS

The father of this book is Richard Clements, editor of the Socialist weekly *Tribune*. He happened in 1964 to come across the verbatim account of a First World War conscientious objector's statement to his Tribunal, and was impressed by the solidity and sophistication of its argument—'much more convincing than the statements made in court by modern CND-ers'. He suggested I do some feature articles on the N-CF for *Tribune*, and perhaps go on to build them into a book. In the event, the book has come first, and *Tribune* is still waiting for the features.

Bertrand Russell and Fenner Brockway kindly gave me their public support and appealed to veteran COs and their families to let me see relevant diaries, letters and other documents. Their appeal was published, by kind permission of the respective editors, in *The Observer*, *The Guardian*, the *New Statesman*, *Tribune*, *Peace News*, the *Socialist Leader* and several provincial and overseas papers. The response was astonishing. For several weeks, every post brought quantities of documents. Some 600 COs, or families and friends of COs, got in touch with me. Almost all sent documents of value, and some sent what amounted to whole libraries. Rashly, I had told Russell and Brockway I would return all documents sent to me immediately they were copied. It was a promise which failed to anticipate an avalanche, and which was therefore broken. Some documents were kept for many months, packed tight twixt floor and ceiling of my tiny London flat. These became the raw material for *Objection Overruled*. I gratefully record my thanks to those who thus kept me supplied with material, and showed so much patience. In a book of this size I have been able to mention only a small fraction of the cases brought to my attention, but I know my correspondents will appreciate my problem. Every letter, every fragment that was sent me, whether or not it has been specifically quoted in my final text, has been a part of a jigsaw puzzle helping me toward a complete picture. I gratefully salute all my correspondents as co-workers with me in this book. If there were fewer than 600 I would gladly list them all.

Unpublished letters and diaries have been one principal source for *Objection Overruled*. War Office and other Government papers have been another. I have also made extensive use of relevant published material, much of which has long been out of print. John W. Graham's *Conscription and Conscience*, published in 1921, quoted a wealth of source material which has since disappeared, and I gladly acknowledge my debt to this standard work. Denis Hayes' *Conscription Conflict* (1949) was my principal source for the section on the National Service League. *I Appeal Unto Caesar* (1917), by Mrs Henry Hobhouse, and *Made Free in Prison* (1918), by E. Williamson Mason, both give graphic contemporary insights into prison life. Other published records of first-hand experience are acknowledged in footnotes to the text. It remains for me to stress my obvious indebtedness to contemporary newspapers and journals, in particular *The Tribunal*, the *Labour Leader*, *The Friend*, *The Herald* and *Forward*.

I wish finally to offer special thanks to C. W. Daniels, the publishers, for lending me invaluable file copies of a series of contemporary publications; the librarians and staffs of Friends House Library and the Marx Memorial Library, which complemented each other magnificently and matched each other in courtesy and helpfulness; and Rea Nicolaides, who did the bulk of the typing and retyping, and would take only an occasional glass of bitter lemon in return.

INDEX

Bone, Walter, 255, 266
Bottomley, Horatio, 35
Bowerman, C. W., 64, 98
Bowden, F., 266
Brace, William, 42, 76, 98, 185, 194, 198, 216
Brailsford, H. N., 21, 29, 43, 46
Brentnall, A. G., 266
Bridle, O. S., 266
Brightman, H., 266
Brightmore, James, 10–11, 149–52, 157
Briscoe, Major George, 217
British Council for Peace in Vietnam, 305
British Labour and the Russian Revolution, 241
British Prussianism, 136
British Socialist Party, 20, 30, 32, 40, 49, 101, 102, 109, 234
Briton's First Duty, The, 66–7, 86
Brittain, Vera, 302
Brocklesby, J. H., 170, 173
Brockway, Fenner, 30, 51, 65, 107–8, 110–1, 113, 120–1, 132, 180–1, 189–90, 197, 199, 207–8, 210, 223, 226–30, 258, 285–6, 291, 296, 299–306
Brockway, Lilla, 107–8, 227
Brook, Lt.-Col. R., 153
Brown, V. J., 217
Buchan, Col. John, 281
Burns, John, 49–50, 93
Burns, W. E., 253, 266
Butler, Arthur, 253–4, 266
Byles, Sir W. P., 93

Cainey, Thomas, 266

Campaign for Nuclear Disarmament, 305
Campbell, Alexander, 256–7
Campbell, N. A., 266
Campbell, P., 266
Campbell-Bannerman, Sir Henry 50, 81
Canterbury Clinker, 228
Carson, Sir Edward, 76
Carter, William, 240
Case Against Conscription, A, 9, 99
Casement, Roger, 50
Catchpool, Corder, 54–6, 65, 200, 298
Catherall, A., 175
Cave, Sir George, 166
Cecil, Lord Hugh, 276–7
Cecil, William Gascoyne, 216
Central Board for Conscientious Objectors, 304
Challenge to Militarism, A, 58
Chamberlain, Neville, 303–4
Chamberlain, William, 108, 135, 147, 180–1, 223, 228–9, 271, 291
Chancellor, H. G., 93
Christadelphians, 109
Christianity: A Danger to the State, 207
Churchill, Winston, 68, 71, 76, 277, 278, 280, 282, 284, 301, 304
Clarion, The, 70
Clough, W., 93
Clyde Workers' Committee, 102–3
Clydesiders, The, 104, 121
Clynes, J. R., 37, 48, 98, 277
Cobb, C. J., 257, 266